BOSTON
in the
GREAT WAR

Your Towns & Cities in the Great War

BOSTON in the GREAT WAR

Mark Green

Pen & Sword
MILITARY

First published in Great Britain in 2018 by
PEN & SWORD MILITARY
An imprint of
Pen & Sword Books Ltd
47 Church Street
Barnsley
South Yorkshire S70 2AS

Copyright © Mark Green 2018

ISBN 978 1 47389 081 7

The right of Mark Green to be identified as Author of this work has been asserted by him in accordance with the Copyright, Designs and Patents Act 1988.

A CIP catalogue record for this book is available from the British Library.

All rights reserved. No part of this book may be reproduced or transmitted in any form or by any means, electronic or mechanical including photocopying, recording or by any information storage and retrieval system, without permission from the Publisher in writing.

Printed and bound in England
by CPI Group (UK) Ltd, Croydon, CR0 4YY

Typeset in Times New Roman by SRJ Info Jnana System Pvt Ltd.

Pen & Sword Books Limited incorporates the Imprints of
Atlas, Archaeology, Aviation, Discovery, Family History, Fiction, History, Maritime, Military, Military Classics, Politics, Select, Transport, True Crime, Air World, Frontline Publishing, Leo Cooper, Remember When, Seaforth Publishing, The Praetorian Press, Wharncliffe Local History, Wharncliffe Transport, Wharncliffe True Crime and White Owl.

For a complete list of Pen & Sword titles please contact
PEN & SWORD BOOKS LIMITED
47 Church Street, Barnsley, South Yorkshire, S70 2AS, England
E-mail: enquiries@pen-and-sword.co.uk
Website: www.pen-and-sword.co.uk

Contents

Acknowledgements		vi
Introduction		vii
Chapter 1	The War at Sea	1
Chapter 2	Boston's Baptism of Fire	65
Chapter 3	Fighting on the Home Front	85
Chapter 4	Fighting on the Land	115
Endnotes		231
Appendix: Location of Boston's War Casualties		233
Bibliography and Sources		263
Index		267

Acknowledgements

You might want to skip past the acknowledgments in this book and dig into the good stuff. But don't forget there have been some amazing people who have helped and encouraged me along the way.

The editor, Pamela Covey; Roni Wilkinson at Pen & Sword for his patience, loan of his book collection and photographs; Don Jenkins from the Boston Great War Commemoration Society for the use of his personal collection; Georgia Burrows from the local Boston newspaper; Dr William Hunt for saving me copious amounts of time in letting me use his research to identify the men who had fallen; Gordon Leith, curator at the RAF museum; John C. Revell for inviting me to his home to share with me his memories and the use of his personal photographs; Dr Katherine Storr of www.modern-history.info and her guidance; the helpful history buffs on www.rootschat.com; Marcus Bateman, who supplied photographs; Sue Robinson for her personal memories; Helen Shinn, author of *Boston Through Time*, editor of *The Boston Old Times* and owner of *Railway Times* and the helpful staff at the Boston Library for their arduous trips into the basement for those heavy, bound newspapers.

I would especially like to thank my long suffering wife, Emma, for the quiet times she spent alone whilst I researched then wrote this book, and to my children, Charlie and Daisy, who endured countless recitals of the many stories.

Introduction

By 1914, Boston had long since devolved from the status of a town that enjoyed considerable power in the fourteenth century. Valuable exports leaving the town en route to Hanseatic ports to supply Nordic countries, Germany and the Holy Roman Empire primarily with wool, exporting 3 million fleeces per year, and cloth introduced the town to huge monetary income. Boston's international fair, which was one of the largest in England from 1150 until the end of the fourteenth century, enticed merchants from all over Europe. Historic architecture such as the religiously-inspired Guild Hall built in the 1390s by the Guild of St. Mary's remains as a witness to that time of grandeur when Boston's exporting power was second only to that of London. St. Botoloph's church, a striking example of medieval opulence that graces the town's skyline with its famous tower, known affectionately as 'The Stump', was built in a relatively short period of time; a timeless testament to the wealth of the town, thus ensuring an eloquent architectural masterpiece.

The end of the 1400s saw a decline of the local guilds and a move towards domestic weaving of English wool which in part was a consequence of the Hundred Years War as Flemish weavers fleeing both the horrors of war and French rule were encouraged to set up home in England, with many settling in Norfolk and Suffolk. Others moved to the West Country, the Cotswolds, the Yorkshire Dales and Cumberland where weaving began to flourish in the villages, making the town's foreign trade almost redundant. The silting of the Haven, the river on which Boston resides, only furthered the town's decline. Furthermore, sixteenth-century England witnessed radical changes to the constitution when Henry VIII succeeded his father Henry VII on 21 April 1509. The landscape of the town changed politically during the English reformation with Henry's closure of the Boston friaries built during the affluent thirteenth and fourteenth centuries.

VIII BOSTON IN THE GREAT WAR

Most notably, the old seaport gained the notoriety of imprisoning the Pilgrim Fathers following their first attempt to gain religious freedom in America in the early 1600s.

Fortunes did change in the latter part of the nineteenth century with the scouring of the Haven and with it a new port to help support the town financially, then with the coming of the railways further optimism arose as the new century dawned. Boston continued as a working port, exporting grain and fertilizer and importing timber, although much of the fishing trade was moved out in the interwar period. The first cinema opened in 1910 and in 1913 a new town bridge was constructed.

However, calm waters flowing up the Wash towards the Port of Boston before 1914 were a prelude to the figurative, destructive storm that was to flood the souls of the small, historic Lincolnshire town with grief and emotion that would send far-reaching ripples into the future.

CHAPTER ONE

The War at Sea

From the late 1890s, Germany began to create a naval battle fleet, forcing a shipbuilding arms race that shaped Anglo-German resentment. The German navy steadily built up momentum, particularly with its submarine programme. It was supported by the Kaiser, enthusiastically driven on and carefully managed by Alfred von Tirpitz, Secretary of State of the German Imperial Naval Office. This and the assassination of the Austrian Archduke Franz Ferdinand in Sarajevo in June 1914 and subsequent events including the German declaration of war on France and Belgium culminated in Great Britain declaring war on Germany, effective from 11.00 pm on 4 August 1914.

Epic sea battles such as Jutland or the Falklands are the 'glory battles' that have occupied mainstream media, creating heroes out of ordinary men from Boston. However, Bostonians should also be proud of the sacrifice their fishermen made for the town during the Great War; sadly, outside of Boston little is known about this intriguing chapter in the history of the East Lincolnshire town.

Sunday, 26 July 1914

Signalling the Boston fishermen's fate, the German protagonist Admiral von Ingenohl explained to the flag officers of the German fleet the political situation and the necessity for preparing for the outbreak of war; interestingly, with information to hand such as a report that King George of England had aligned himself, in the sense of neutrality, to Prince Henry of Prussia.[1] The High Seas Fleet divided itself, with Squadron 1 steaming to Wilhelmshaven in Lower Saxony under the command of Vice Admiral von Lans

'Ghost of the pilot.' Forcing the resignation of Bismarck was the perceived catalyst for the Kaiser's obsession with war in Europe and the unification of Germany. Perhaps the diplomatic genius of the former Foreign Minister was haunting Kaiser Wilhelm II.

and Squadrons 2 and 3 with the fleet flagship returning to Kiel in the German state of Schleswig-Holstein. This tactical placement was manifest proof that the German commander saw a real danger lying to the east in a naval threat from France and Russia and from Britain to the west.

Meanwhile in Boston, dressed in black oilskins, pairs of deck boots and heavy woollen sweaters, the crews of nine Boston trawlers prepared themselves for another few weeks away from home by loading up their trawlers with ice to keep the fish in good condition for the public market and loading stores for the trip. The weather-beaten boats would head down the Haven to the Wash, out to sea and through the Boston Deeps into the North Sea, then out to the fishing grounds. These trawlers

Gustav Heinrich Ernst Friedrich von Ingenohl, commander of the German High Seas Fleet at the beginning of the First World War.

Boston fishermen returning with their catch.

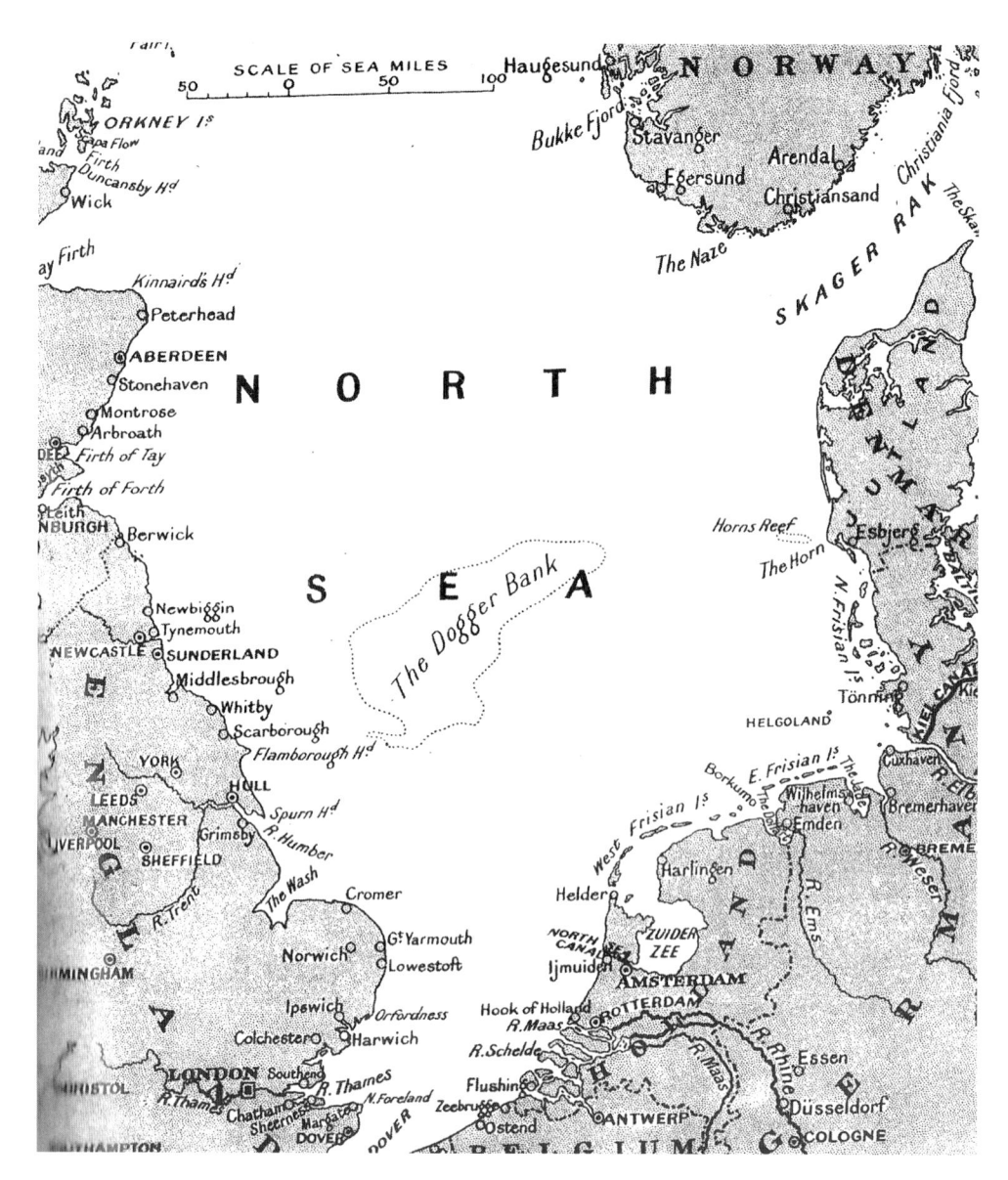

The North Sea, an unexpected battleground for the Boston fishermen (Leyland, 1917).

would have travelled in ones and twos subject to the tides for up to seven to ten days, contingent on how good the catch would have been. Years of experience revealed knowledge to the lead captain of the Heligoland and neighbouring waters, instinctively telling the turn and the run of a tide. The lives of continental fishermen had been romanticized for hundreds of years, as in the case of the Venetian fishermen, in stark contrast to life in the small, dirty holes where the Lincolnshire men would eat, drink and sleep during their fishing trips.

Fully dressed, tired and reeking of coal, oil and fish, they would climb into the closed black box they called a bunk, draw the shutter and sleep until a deep voice bellowed from above 'Haul up your trawl, boys, haul.' With cold, cracked, bleeding hands the men would bring the trawl up and the hard work of cleaning and packing the catch would be done. Dangers lurked everywhere, from the slippery, oily deck to the immense coils of steel wire where warping was frequent and a sudden tautening might cause anyone in the way to lose a limb or even be slashed in half.

Postcard of Boston fishermen.

A typical steam trawler, built in 1916, was 117ft long. Bunker capacity was about 125 tons, with triple expansion engines, a nominal 75hp boiler with a working pressure of 150lb and a large double-barrelled winch of 1,000 fathoms capacity. There were also trawlers larger than this and very many much smaller, but these dimensions will afford an understanding of the size of the temporary homes for the trawlermen.

Timeline

1 August 1914: Squadron 2 docked in Kiel receives orders to mobilize to the North Sea as Anglo-German relations deteriorate.

4 August 1914: The German High Seas Fleet receives a message at 7.45 pm: 'Prepare for war against England.' An order was also given to the cruiser *Kronprinz Wilhelm*, beginning the introduction of guerilla operations on the English coast.

12 August 1914: Light cruisers *Koln* (flagship of the first flag officer of the destroyer flotillas, Rear Admiral Maass) and the SMS *Hamburg* go to sea with Flotilla VI.

The Boston trawler Skirbeck.

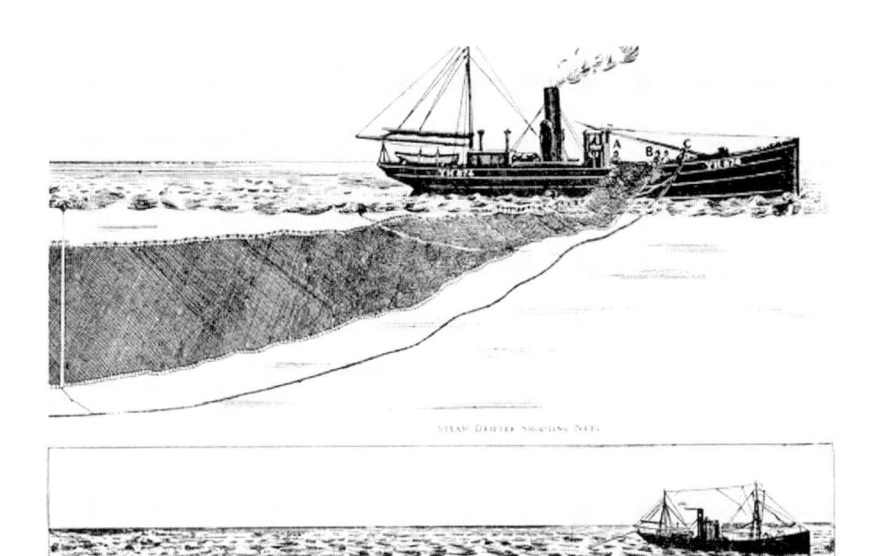

A Steam Trawler at work. The diagram shows the trawl-warps and the method of dragging the great net on the bottom of the sea. By permission of Smith's Dock Company, Ltd.

21 August 1914: Flotilla VI makes a sweep of Dogger Bank with a view to searching the fishing grounds for English fishing smacks. This cruise catches out six fishing steamers that were found, well separated, in a circle round Heligoland and were destroyed on the assumption that they were working with English submarines.

25 August 1914: These cruises confirm that the Germans could not expect to find considerable numbers of enemy ships in the southern part of the North Sea. Two mine-laying cruisers, the *Albatross* (Commander West) and the *Nautilus* (Commander Wilhelm Schultz) receive orders to lay a minefield at the mouths of the Humber and Tyne. On their way back six Boston fishing steamers are sunk.

27 August 1914: The crews of the *Lindsey*, *Walrus*, *Wigtoft*, *Skirbeck*, *Flavian*, *Indian*, *Porpoise*, *Julian*, the *Kesteven* that belonged to the Deep Sea Fishing Company, and the *Marnay* belonging to Messrs Parkes, Stringer and Pesterfield land at Wilhelmshaven naval base and are taken as PoWs.

8   BOSTON IN THE GREAT WAR

Floating mine.

Daniel Rushton (left) of Church Street, Boston and Charles Walkerly of Marks Terrace, who were captured on board the Indian *and* Julian, *respectively.*

A first-hand account related by Henry Peter Neilson, who was third hand on the first boat to be attacked, the *Marnay*, describes his experience. Neilson, who lived at 11 Glebe Terrace, Skirbeck, explained that the crew and fish were taken off the *Marnay* and put on board the cruiser and then three bombs were placed on his trawler, fired upon, then subsequently exploded, sinking the vessel. In the case of the other boats fishing in the vicinity, these were relieved of their crews and fish and then fired upon. Neilson recollects seeing four shots pouring into the *Skirbeck* and three into the *Julian*.

The men lost all their personal possessions and were taken ashore to Wilhelmshaven, some without hats and boots. Their arrival at Wilhelmshaven was greeted with abuse as a 2-mile walk through crowded streets was littered with men, women and children jeering the prisoners, shouting 'you bad dogs' and other 'epithets of opprobrium'.[2]

Once at the prison, the Boston fishermen were placed in different cells. Some had the luxury of just sharing with one other, while others had to share with four, five or six other men. Neilson goes on to explain that the guards would treat them 'harshly' and feed them 'bread and water for breakfast and tea and thickened soup for dinner'. Fortunately Neilson was repatriated relatively quickly owing to his Norwegian nationality; Norway was neutral, and he was therefore sent home. Neilson made his way back to Boston.

Recollections of harsh treatment endured before arriving in Wilhelmshaven were shared by two trawlermen, Arthur Higgins and R.W. Kemp on the boat *Lobelia*. The 1918 book *Fishermen in Wartime* by Walter Wood records the account of R.W. Kemp. Although this was a Grimsby trawler, it is worth noting that many Boston men worked in that rival port and suffered equally distressing adventures.

The book explains graphically the conditions endured by the men once captured by the Germans:

> I had started from home to earn my livelihood a fortnight before Christmas in 1913, and I worked away up to August, 1914, when the war broke out.
>
> We had come into port, Grimsby, not knowing what was going to happen, and lay there for ten days before the insurance people would permit us to go to sea. When we sailed it was on condition that we fished within a certain limit.
>
> We sailed on August 20, and the day before a friend and myself went for a bit of pleasure to a little country place a few miles from Grimsby.
>
> We went to sea, and he was blown up by a mine and I was taken prisoner by the Germans, and after sixteen months of shameful treatment was sent home a broken man.
>
> The *Lobelia* was in the nor'-west corner of the Dogger, what we call the Nor'-West Rough, and there were other steam trawlers about. It was fine, calm summer weather, and we were in good spirits, for we had 160 boxes of fish in the fish-room, the result of five days' fishing. We were making another haul and then we were going home.

It was three o'clock in the afternoon, and we were hauling. We had got our otter-boards up to the gallows and should soon have had the cod-end of the net unlashed when we saw, all at once, ten torpedo-boats and three cruisers, and as soon as they hove in sight we knew that they were Germans.

One torpedo-boat rushed up – she was like an eel, and must have done forty knots. She came right alongside and made her bow rope fast to our bow; then, while the German sailors covered us with revolvers, the commander shouted to me and ordered me to produce the ship's papers. That was all he wanted – he bullied and scurried us about, and would not let us stop to get any of our belongings.

There was nothing for it but to obey, and so we jumped on board the torpedo-boat, and immediately Germans were sent on board the *Lobelia* and put bombs in her engine-room, then the torpedo-boat cast off and steamed some distance away, and we saw the *Lobelia* blown to pieces.

All this had happened so swiftly that I could hardly realise it, then I saw that there were another two fishing crews on board the torpedo-boat, and that these craft were scurrying round destroying all the British fishing vessels that they came across. These fishing vessels were absolutely helpless, and had not the slightest chance of escaping or defending themselves.

It was only ten minutes after we left the *Lobelia* that she blew to pieces, carrying with her every stick and stone that I possessed – and it was the same with the rest of the crew; and in addition to that our 160 boxes of fish and the fish that was in the net – all that we had worked so hard for – went to the bottom. The Germans were in a hurry and wanted to get the job over, and they made no attempt to do anything but get the ship's papers.

Having done this to the *Lobelia*, the torpedo-boat commander went to another steam trawler – I forget her name, but she was a Grimsby boat – and did the same thing as he had done to us; so we had another fishing crew on board with us, making about forty fishermen in all. We were kept on deck, under an armed guard, but we were allowed to talk amongst ourselves. I must say that while we were prisoners at sea we were treated fairly well under the circumstances, but once we stepped ashore and got under the military we copped old boots.

We were on board the torpedo-boat for about six hours, until nine o'clock in the evening. I could never find out her number or any marks on her, and I believe she had none; but, as I say, she was like an eel. Her commander was a young man of about thirty-five years, and he spoke very good English, as so many of these Germans do. He began at once to try and find out things, but we told him nothing.

He said, 'You have got no men; but we have got the men and we have got the food.' I remember those words.

The commander asked us a lot of questions about the British Fleet and said he wanted to know the reason why we went to war with Germany, but we could say nothing.

The sailors gave us something to eat and drink, and we could talk, and were pretty free on board the torpedo-boat – she was not a destroyer; but soon we were to be more strictly treated, and that was when we were transferred to a cruiser. I suppose we were put on board the cruiser because the torpedo-boat was not big enough to house us.

The cruiser was a tidy size; she had three funnels, but one of them was false.

We were put down in the forehold of the ship, and armed guards were posted over us. There were portholes in the sides, but the dead-lights had been fastened down, so that the only light we had was from lamps. We could not, of course, see anything, but we were kept pretty well informed as to what was going on, and in a curious way, for the pilot came down to see us from time to time and told us what was happening. We knew, because we had seen then that the cruiser carried a lot of mines on her after deck, and the pilot told us that she was going off the English coast to lay them. We afterwards heard that she had thrown them overboard five miles off Blyth and off Flamborough Head; then the cruiser steamed away for Wilhelmshaven, with other ships. But the Germans were about as much afraid of their own mines as they were of ours, for we heard the cable rattle, and the pilot told us that we had brought up under Heligoland, where I had been ashore many a time in the old days of the sailing fleets, when the island was ours. I would have liked a peep at it again, but the Germans took good care that we should see nothing, and we were not allowed on deck.

There we were, crowded below in the forehold of that cruiser, for two days and nights, with nothing but artificial light, constantly expecting to strike some horrible mine and be blown to pieces. But we were even more afraid of going athwart one of our own warships, for that would have put us down the locker. We should not have had the slightest chance of escape, so we were glad when we knew that we had reached the Wilhelmshaven that the Germans are so proud of. What it is really like I don't know – all I saw of it was some tall houses and a lot of shouting women and children, who jeered at us and threw dirt and stones at us – two hundred helpless fishermen, who were marched four deep through the street; for the gallant German Navy had sunk about a score of fishing vessels – ten Grimsby and ten Boston – that could not defend themselves, and had made prisoners of the unarmed crews. Some of these craft had been blown up, as the *Lobelia* had been; others had been sunk with shot. On board the cruiser one of the officers – I do not know his rank – had tried to get something out of us about the British Navy, but he learned no more than the commander of the torpedo-boat had done.

We soon learned that the 200 fishermen prisoners had been captured by the ten torpedo-boats and three cruisers. They had done the business of sinking the ships, but we did not see all of it, because the trawlers were working over a big area, and most of them were out of sight of the *Lobelia*.

With German soldiers on each side of us, and the women and boys and girls shouting at us and running after us and pelting us, we were marched through the streets of Wilhelmshaven to a prison, a real prison, and an awful hole at that, and when we got to the lock-up we were thrust into little cells. Each cell was about 8ft. by 5ft., just big enough to cage one man, yet four of us were put in one of the black holes. In my cell there was nothing but a bit of planking on the floor as a bed, but with no bedding of any sort, and a tiny wooden bench. This cell was like the rest. There were bare stone walls, with no window, and there was no light of any sort, neither lamp nor candle.

I had never seen the inside of a cell in all my puff, and when I got in there it fairly knocked me on one side altogether. With four of us in such a place there was not room to move. We could not lie on the plank bed and we could not sit on the tiny bench, so we just had to be cramped together, talking and sleeping.

For four terrible days and nights we were prisoners in these awful cells, our only change being for one hour a day, when we were allowed to go out on to a green or garden – and a blessed change it was to get out into open air and the sunshine and stretch our aching legs. The sentries brought us our meals, which we ate in the corridor outside the cells. If we wanted to get out for a wash or anything we had to ask leave of the sentries. At the end of those four days we had a cruel disappointment. We were only fishermen, who had been captured by German warships and made prisoners. We had nothing whatever to do with the war or fighting – many of the poor chaps had lost everything they had in the world – and we did not see how we could be kept in Germany. We fancied we should be sent home, and, as a matter of fact, we were told that we were going to be sent back. Our very souls sank when the cruel tidings came that, instead of going home, we were to be sent to Sennelager as prisoners of war; and to Sennelager we were taken.

Sunday, 30 August 1914

Trawlers *Brotherton* and *Sutterton* returned to Boston on 30 August and the skipper of the *Brotherton* reported picking up lifebuoys marked *Lindsey* and *Boston* and other wreckage from fishing vessels, fuelling speculation that all was not well.

Saturday, 5 September 1914

Back home in Boston, worried relatives had still not heard anything from their fishermen. A small piece in the *Boston Guardian and Lincolnshire Independent* confirms this in an article:

> Overdue Boston Trawlers.
>
> On inquiry this (Friday) morning we are informed that no news has been received concerning the overdue Boston trawlers.

Saturday, 12 September 1914

Erroneous reports filtering back after an enquiry into the lost boats caused some distress to the families; however, it wasn't until a week later that an official communication confirmed the fears of some and the relief of others that at least their loved ones were still alive. The *Boston Guardian and Lincolnshire Independent* of Saturday, 12 September 1914 describes the Admiralty announcement and the fate of the missing crew members:

> The Admiralty announced on Saturday that a German squadron consisting of two cruisers and four destroyers had sunk fifteen British trawlers in the North Sea. A quantity of fish was captured, and the crews taken to Wilhelmshaven as prisoners of war.

Although there is no confirmation, it is believed that the ten Boston boats were amongst the number, and that their crews are held as prisoners of war. Mr. Walker, the manager of the Deep Sea Fishing Co., has been in communication with the Admiralty, and the War Insurance, and other authorities, but beyond the announcement made on Saturday, there is no further information to be obtained.

The *Derby Daily Telegraph* similarly reported:

GERMAN SQUADRON IN THE NORTH SEA – 15 BRITISH FISHING BOATS SUNK – BOSTON TRAWLERS INCLUDED.

The following message from the Admiralty appeared in most of our late final edition on Saturday night:-

'The Admiralty announce that a German Squadron, consisting of two cruisers and four destroyers, have succeeded in sinking 15 British fishing boats in the North Sea. A quantity of fish was captured, and the crews of the fisherman taken to Wilhelmshaven as prisoners of war.'

This message is believed in Boston to explain the mysterious disappearance of the ten local trawlers, the *MARNEY* [*MARNAY*], owned by Messrs. Parkes, Stringer and Pesterfield, and the *LINDSEY*, *WALRUS*, *WIGTOFT*, *SKIRBECK*, *FLAVIAN*, *INDIAN*, *PORPOISE*, *JULIAN* and *KESTEVEN*, belonging to the Boston Deep Sea Fishing Company. The crews of the ten trawlers number 91 men and boys. Most of the men are married, and some have large families, who are being cared for by the fishing company and others in the town.

The trawlers are each worth from £2,000 to £4,000, and were fishing about 30 to 50 miles east of Spurn Point. It is understood that the Admiralty have arranged for more adequate protection of the fishing fleet on the North Sea grounds. This will, of course, lessen or altogether remove the chance of any further raids on trawlers.

> The boats sunk are covered by war insurance, and it is expected that the Boston boats now in dock will resume operations almost immediately. This course is rendered possible by knowledge of the fact that the loss of the other 10 vessels was not due to the presence of mines.

Although the announcement allayed some doubts, the information coming out of Admiralty House was sketchy to say the least. What had happened to the crews of the overdue boats? What fate had befallen the *Lindsey, Walrus, Wigtoft, Skirbeck, Flavian, Indian, Porpoise, Julian* and the *Kesteven* that belonged to the Deep Sea Fishing Company and the *Marnay* belonging to Messrs Parkes, Stringer and Pesterfield? How were the ninety-one men and boys, most of whom were married with families, coping in a strange, foreign land?

Other newspaper reports tell us that the men eventually dispersed to various places in Germany including Hamburg, then passed on to PoW camps including the notorious Sennelager and Ruhleben which were on the outskirts of Berlin.

Evidently, and by their own admission, some of the men had been treated well, particularly the ones interned temporarily in Hamburg and Cuxhaven. In the book *Boston, Its Fishermen and the First World War*, the authors Paul Meyer and John C. Revell include revealing letters from some of the more 'fortunate' prisoners.

Later reports illustrate the conditions that the men actually endured. However, note the soft tone of the letters trying to reassure their families at home.

Mrs Rudd of Duke Street received a typical letter of encouragement from her husband, who had been on the *Kesteven*:

> Dear Wife,
>
> I am in this port a prisoner of war. I am well, and am being cared for. Plenty of food and clothing. I cannot say when we shall be sent home, but hope to meet you soon.
>
> Your loving husband
>
> W. Rudd
>
> Cuxhaven, Sept. 15th

A bird's eye view of the intimidating Cuxhaven Harbour on the River Elbe.

With a sense of naivety the following letter was sent to Mr Brightey of the Fishing Apprentices' Home by a fishing apprentice, William Henry Harris who, with others, was a prisoner at Cuxhaven:

> Dear Mr Brightey and all the boys,
>
> I suppose you missed us when we did not come home. I am pleased to say that both the crews and all the apprentices are safe and well in Germany as prisoners. We are being treated with every respect, and with the greatest of civility. We have plenty to eat, and tobacco allowed us. There is Stearns, Cornford, Gobo, Titch, Graham, Bronco and 'Lizzie' all in one room. We have the crews of the *Lindsey*, *Kesteven*, *Porpoise* and a Grimsby trawler here in Cuxhaven. They have taken to Bronco as one of their own.
>
> Each night the boys entertain the others by singing songs until about 9 o'clock. We have football in the morning and in the afternoon for one hour so you can see that we are getting treated well. All the boys wish Jennie many happy returns of the day and hope she will live to see another twenty-four years, and we all hope her son is doing well. Tell mother not to trouble about us as we are faring well. Please write back, and remember us all to mother, Jennie, Mrs. Horlich, G. Armstrong, Murrey, Moon, and all the other boys. With very best regards from your boys, Albert Stearns, John Willmot, Robert Forster, Thomas Cornford, Charlie Smith, John Graham and 'Lizzie' Harris.
>
> We are seven jolly fishing apprentices captured at sea.

Sennelager: 'The Black Hole of Germany'

Wilhelmshaven and Cuxhaven could be described as holiday camps compared to the PoW camp Sennelager, also known as Senne Camp. Senne was a large camp near Paderborn, Westphalia, 50 miles south-west of Hannover. It was situated on open sandy country made up of heather, pine and bog and was used as a summer training camp prior to the war.

Upon arriving at Sennelager by rail one prisoner reported how he was 'unceremoniously bundled out of the train. The sun poured down unmercifully, and after twelve hours' confinement in the stuffy railway carriages.'[3] Sennelager camp lay upon a plateau overlooking the railway and it was approached by a winding road. He continues his account, after leaving the train, 'the activity although somewhat steep is not long, but we, famished and worn from hunger, thirst and lack of sleep, found the struggle with the sand into which our feet sank over our ankles, almost insuperable.'

Once inside the camp the situation deteriorated, as R.W. Kemp, captain of the *Lobelia* said:

> Things had been bad enough at Wilhelmshaven, in the dark holes of the lock-up, but they were nothing compared with what we had to go through at Sennelager. As soon as we got there we were thrown into the fields, and for three weeks we slept on the grass or the bare ground, for in some places there was no grass. We had no covering, nothing whatever.
>
> It was during the daytime that we lay on the ground and slept, because then it was warm and dry, sun out, and at night, when there were heavy dews, we walked about and tried to keep warm.
>
> At the end of the three weeks the rainy season came on, and we got tufts of grass and built little huts, about as big as dog-kennels, and crawled into them for shelter.
>
> The Germans stripped us of everything we had. They would not allow you even a lead pencil or a bit of paper or money; if you had any money they took it from you.

British prisoners at Sennelager; note the clogs the men had to wear.

But they were not content with that – they disfigured us by cutting one half of the hair of our heads off and one half of the moustache, cropping close and leaving the other half on, making you as ugly as they could. They took the hair off from the centre of the neck right down to the centre of the forehead, so that those who had long hair looked frightful. This was done out of spitefulness – the Germans don't do it now. It was a nasty thing to do; but we made the best of it, and laughed at one another.

They fed us very badly. For breakfast they gave us coffee, made out of rice, no sugar or milk and for dinner we had cabbage-water, the cabbage cut up into little bits. Sometimes a little bit of greasy fat pork was put into the water, but it was only by chance that you got one of these bits, about as big as the bowl of your pipe. At teatime you had 'coffee' again, and then you got the black bread, which had to last you twenty-four hours, and that was a piece only as big as your fist. When we were taken out of the fields we were put into big canvas tents, holding about 600 men, and there we were packed like sardines in a box. We were forced to lie on the ground, and all sorts of men were crowded together, foreigners and British – far different from the way prisoners of war are treated in England.

Our being at Sennelager was a great time for the inhabitants, especially on the Sundays, when they would come – Boy Scouts amongst them – and push up to the barbed wire fences and tease and torment us and do all manner of things.

As time went on we got so that we had no clothing, and no soap, and no means of washing our underclothing. Some of the men washed their shirts by scrubbing them with sand. I tried one day when it was bitterly cold weather, to scrub my shirt by rubbing it on a bit of a wooden platform we had in the grounds, and it froze so hard to the woodwork that I could not get it off.

For the first five or six months we had a cat-and-dog life. The Germans used to hustle us about, kick us, give us a crack with the butt-end of a gun or a prod with a bayonet, and when they were tired of that they would set a big savage dog on to us, a German brute, to hurry us up. The dog used to help the guard when we were hustled along the roadway to the canteen, about half a mile away, to get our dinners. The dog was a sort of man-hunter, and would go for anything. The brute was on a chain, which was held by a soldier, who let him out a certain length; but at times the soldier would slip the chain, so that the dog could fly at a helpless man.

I saw one of our fishermen cruelly torn in the legs by this savage monster, which had a craze for rushing at poor chaps from behind. And you dared not touch the beast or complain or do anything, if you did you suffered for it.

The poor fellow that the brute bit complained to the head commander, and there was an inquiry on the job. And what happened? The man got lashed to a tree for two hours in the morning and two hours in the afternoon for

The War at Sea 21

Men in the hands of the Germans at Sennelager including the chief engineer of the Lindsey and Fred Parker of the Wigtoft.

complaining and that was in the wintertime. He is now at home, but he still suffers a great deal with it, and was in hospital in Germany a lot because of the bites and the lashing to the tree.

Can you wonder that as the result of such brutal and inhuman treatment men died through sheer exhaustion?

They did. Several of our poor fishermen died, and they are buried in Germany – all through privation.

In the winter we used to go about with our knees through our trousers, and we had no jackets to wear. I never had a pair of stockings or socks for the whole time I was there. My feet were wrapped up in rags, with old wooden Dutchman's shoes.

The Germans provided us with bar-racks, but we still had to lie on the ground. We lay on the ground for the whole of the sixteen months I was in Germany. We just had straw – we had nothing to cover ourselves with, no blankets or anything. The only way to keep warm was to keep as close together as sardines. They used to place us like this – one Englishman, one German, one Russian and one Frenchman, to keep you by yourself, so that you should not have your own countryman to talk to.

Some of the prisoners used to have to go to work trench digging, pulling roots of trees out of the ground, and so on. I did the root-pulling, but I got nothing whatever for it. We used to drip in the warm weather. All our food was drink, drink, drink. There was no stayable food all the time I was there, and if it had not been for the help from good friends in England we should certainly have starved altogether.

We used to have to form up in the morning, and if you did not keep exactly straight in line you got punished. They would make us run round a pole with half a dozen bricks on your back, or dig the ground with a shovel, with the same burden. And they used to go through a form of inspection with you, forcing you to be stark naked, no matter what the weather was like.

We were driven about like sheep, and for the first five months of our imprisonment we were not allowed to write or receive letters, and when at last we were given liberty to write home the Germans either destroyed the letters or would not let them go. This meant that your people at home were in an agony of doubt all the time as to what had happened to you, and did not know whether you were alive or dead.

After a whole year of this sort of suffering at Sennelager I was transferred, with other fishermen, to Ruhleben, which was an exchange depot. This was the first time the Germans had allowed seafaring men to be exchanged, and we were only allowed to go as the result of a visit to Sennelager which the American Ambassador had made. Men over fifty-five and lads under seventeen were in the exchange.

I learned in time that there were eighty-five of us fishermen prisoners to be allowed to come home in exchange, and that the ages ranged from sixty years to fourteen – yes, there were mere boys as prisoners. One came home when I did. He was just under seventeen; but there were younger lads as prisoners, and they were treated exactly like the men. I am glad to say that we had not a boy on board the *Lobelia*. Fancy treating little chaps like that!

Some of our chaps were a bit obstinate, and they got the worst punishment. The Germans were all push and drive, and if you didn't show yourself willing to do just as you were told, and turned sulky, well, shoot them – that was the order. I saw two or three Belgians and Frenchmen shot just for this offence, turning sulky and refusing to obey orders. There was a sort of court-martial or trial about it; they were shot where they stood.

A very common punishment was to lash the men to trees and make them work with the load of bricks on their backs, as I have described – the Germans were rare boys for that sort of business. At Sennelager there were only 200 British fishermen prisoners of war, but there were 2,300 Russian, Belgian, and French prisoners, all civilians, some of them burgomasters and so on. And they were rough-uns, too, some of them; but that was no excuse for the terrible punishments which the Germans carried out.

All the time we were in the camps we were never allowed any information or newspapers, except about German victories. They had a pole, and when they had a bit of a victory they flew all the flags they could put on it – and they put a birchbroom on the top of the pole, after the style of Old Tromp when he boasted that he had swept the English from the seas. The Germans hadn't done that, but they used to make a rare to do if they got a little advantage at all.

For twelve months out of the sixteen during which I was a prisoner we never saw a knife, fork, or spoon. We had to walk about half a mile for our dinner, such as it was, and stand in a crowd, like a mob, to get it. When we had had the stuff served out we used to scoop it up the best way we could, with an oyster shell or a bit of tin, or anything else that we were lucky enough to pick up from the ground.

I got back to my home on Christmas Day, after an absence of more than two years. Had I had enough of it? Yes, so far as imprisonment goes; but if I had not been too old I should have done as a lot of my old friends have done – gone mine-sweeping. Instead of being able to do that I had to take a shore job inland, so I am still away from my home, and likely to be. Winter is coming on again; it takes me an hour to walk to my work and an hour to walk back, and as the result of my sufferings as a prisoner of war in Germany I have bad rheumatism. However, I am still here – which is more than I can say for my poor friend who went out with me for a bit of pleasure and was soon blown up by a mine. And there are still six of the *Lobelia*'s crew prisoners in Germany, only four of us having been exchanged and allowed to come home. When I went away to fish I had everything, I came home a wreck. And that is what the war has done for me.

Ruhleben

Other fishermen had been transported to Ruhleben, considered by most to be the main camp for civilian prisoners including merchant seamen.

The War at Sea 25

The shop at Ruhleben.

Count Scherwin, commandant of Ruhleben, said in 1916 to an American visitor 'you mustn't suppose that the camp was always like this. When the men were first brought here, the place wasn't fit to keep pigs in. All that you have admired in the camp they have themselves created.'

Before Count Scherwin uttered those words, Ruhleben was formerly a racecourse a few miles from Berlin. The book *The History of Ruhleben* by Powell and Gribble describes the camp in detail. The principal buildings were three grandstands, a little restaurant known as the 'tea house', a club house called the Casino, residential quarters and offices for various functionaries and eleven stables. It was these well-built stables that served as barracks

'Camouflage', the barbed-wire fence hidden by shrubs and creepers.

26 BOSTON IN THE GREAT WAR

Parcels arriving at Ruhleben.

Journalism at Ruhleben: some inmates produced magazine covers.

for the fishermen and they were housed in the horse box and the lofts that were used for storing fodder. When the prisoners arrived, some of those horse boxes were filled with horse dung.

Bedtime would have been very uncomfortable with dirty straw used as bedding. Straw was thrown into sacks to improvise as mattresses. Crammed into each horsebox 11ft square, six men had to sleep, eat and keep any possessions close by with dry washing on improvised clothes lines stretched from beam to beam.

Stable No. 10 had twenty-seven boxes containing

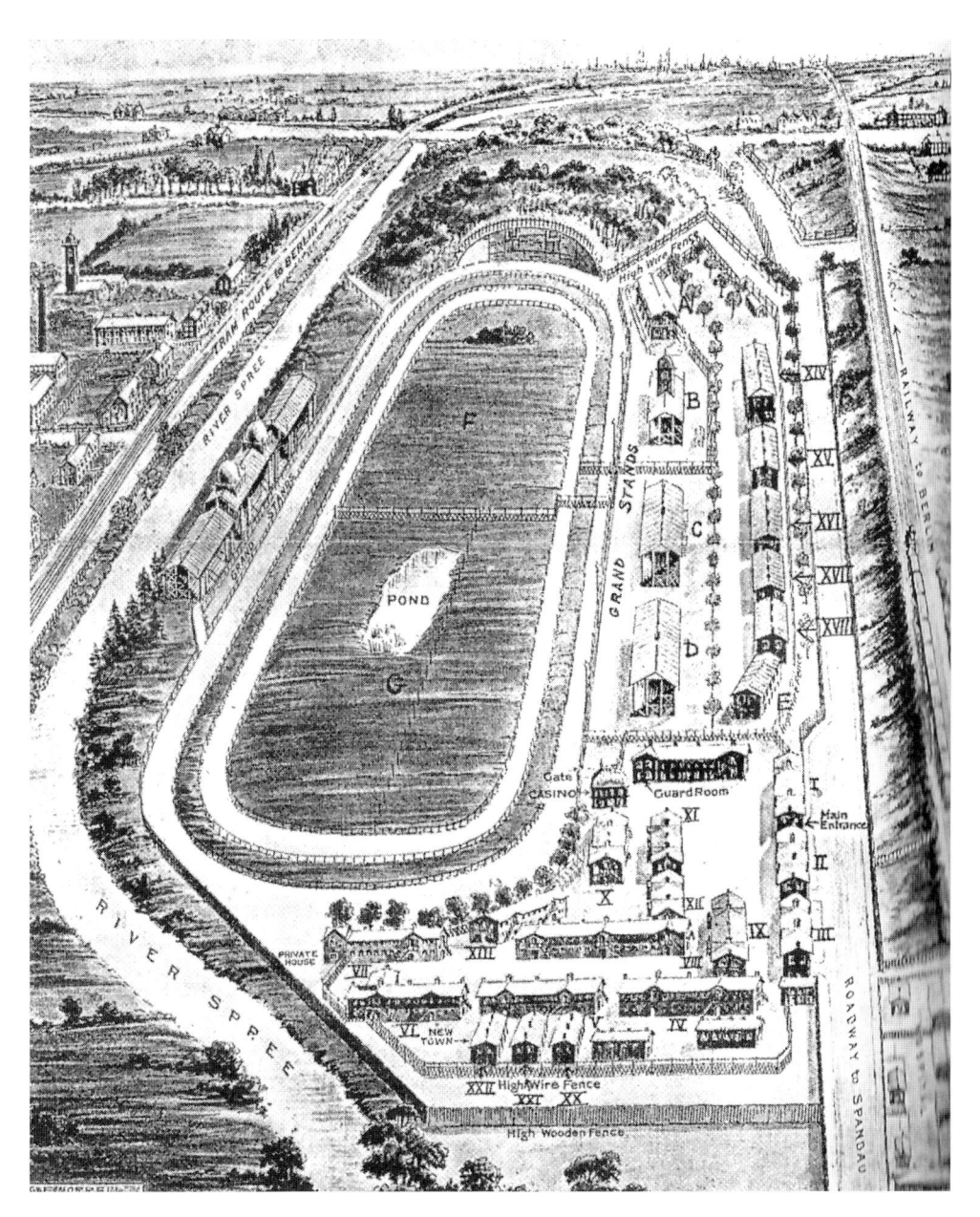

A bird's eye view of Ruhleben drawn by G.F. Morrell from Fishermen Against the Kaiser, Vol. 1, *Douglas d'Enno.*

The Captain of the Camp and the Camp Council: Names from left to right: J. Powell, Captain Woolner, Captain Thomson, H. Redmayne, F. Bell.

six iron field bedsteads for the men to sleep in, three fitted on top of each other. This stable, designed to accommodate 27 horses, housed 365 men. No arrangements had been made for heating and the lighting was 'grossly inadequate'. Observing the order for sick men not to be interned was ignored, 'sufferers from tuberculosis, bronchitis, cancer, rheumatism were pitilessly mixed with the rest.'

How did the Boston fishermen respond to having to carry out tasks such as clearing out manure, scrubbing floors without shovels or brooms and sleeping in cold, damp conditions?

Answering that question with the quintessential British stiff upper lip were the prisoners themselves in a selection of letters published in the *Boston Guardian and Lincolnshire Independent*.

Mr T. Goodacre of Liquorpond Street received a postcard from John Bourne, a prisoner at Ruhleben, who says:

'Trafalgar Square' at Ruhleben. Prisoners named streets such as this in order to feel more at home.

'Bond Street' at Ruhleben.

Winter view of Ruhleben with Spandau in the distance.

A hand-drawn postcard of Ruhleben Camp from 1914–15.

Prisoners boxing at Ruhleben, helping to ease their natural frustration.

Just a few lines to let you know I am quite well at present. Was very pleased to receive your card on 29th. Shall have something to thank you all for telling me the children were given a treat at Christmas, I should like you to thank the editors of the Boston papers for their generous parcel, which was the envy of the seamen; they said, 'Good old Boston.' We are having very cold weather, but have received some warm clothes. Give my love to all the boys at the Loco.

J. Fletcher wrote to his mum: 'My dear mother, thanks for the Christmas card you sent me…please tell Edith that I am getting on well…please write back. From your loving son, with best love to all.'

Back Home

Socially and economically Boston suffered greatly in the First World War. In retrospect the fishermen of Boston, for all their exploits including fishing and minesweeping, should have been given an honoured place in Boston public life. During the early part of the war, the people left at home and the men in the camps would view that form of romanticism as incomprehensible. In reality the impact on everyday life would be paralyzing for the families left behind.

What comfort, if any, was afforded the wives and children who depended on the Boston fishing trade for their family income?

In May 1915 an Interned Boston Fishermen's Fund was organized for men at Ruhleben and Sennelager by Mr Walter Royal of the Loggerheads Hotel and brother of Fred who was the second hand on the trawler *Lindsey*.[4] Mr Francis of Messrs Willer and Riley gave boxes and Mr F.M. Woodthorpe supervised the packing of herrings, ship's biscuits, loaves, plum loaves, café au lait, tea, tins of salmon, tins of tongue, tinned meat, Oxo cubes, tins of mustard, salt, pepper and so on. The *Boston Guardian* and the *Standard* both organized a relief Christmas fund in 1914 for the internees, and the Prince of Wales set up a fund for the families of interned men. Spalding's Shipwreck Society cared for the widows of deceased members and on 13 February 1915 at the annual dinner it was reported that there had been only one claim for loss in connection with the auxiliary branch of the Royal Navy: minesweeping. Mr Royce said that the sailors and fishermen had paid the sacrifice the country had asked of them, both cheerfully and courageously. They were bequeathing a legacy like none before. In early 1916, the position of dependants of fishermen who lost their life or liberty at sea through the hazards of war was placed on a more satisfactory basis by a scheme of the War Risks Association, approved by the Board of Trade. A special committee was formed at Grimsby to administer the scheme. It comprised an equal number of trawler-

Such was life at Ruhleben, the men eagerly awaited parcels from home, even the bare necessities.

Men receiving welcome parcels from England. Note the washing hanging in the foreground.

owners and labour representatives who had the power to award a widow £300 and an additional £26 annually for each child under 14. In cases where the man was a prisoner, £1 weekly might be allowed during his captivity.[5]

The *Boston Guardian* also reported an appeal for assistance that was printed in the *Boston (Massachusetts) Evening Transcript* for their readers to show 'practical sympathy' by assisting the wives and families of men who 'follow a dangerous and arduous calling'.

Seven Released from the German Prison Camp at Ruhleben

'But for Walter Royal's parcels three parts of us would have been dead and buried long ago.' Those were the words of one of the Boston fishermen who returned home in 1916. The men had endured tough treatment at Sennelager before moving to Ruhleben. At Sennelager, the Germans had pursued a policy of starvation in order to force England into feeding the prisoners through the post. From 25,000 to 30,000 parcels were said to have reached Ruhleben every month. John Graves, former engineer on

John Clark, Herbert Fox and Charles Smith.

the Boston trawler *Indian*, agreed when he told a *Standard* reporter: 'Only for the food parcels sent out to our men from Boston, they would be starving. They could not live on the German food served to them.'

All the men who returned described themselves as very lucky to have survived, thanking all the people of Boston for their support. The seven men returned home to Boston were Herbert Fox of the *Julian*, Harry Lawrence of the *Kesteven*, George Anderson of the *Wigtoft*, John Clarke of the *Lindsey*, Harry Bolton of the *Marnay*, Thomas Baines of the *Kesteven* and Charles Smith, aged 17, also of the *Lindsey*.

John Graves, engineer on board the Indian who was held at Ruhleben and was a grateful recipient of food parcels.

October 1914

Hostile feelings were whipped up following the sinking of the trawlers, including five German nationals being arrested in Boston and transferred to a 'concentration camp' in Wakefield. Further anti-German fever was directed at the Cantenwine family. The Red Lion Bowling Club was presided over by the German-born Mr G. Cantenwine, who was described by the chairman as a 'very able and a very good player'. Mr Cantenwine's family were also the proprietors of a pork butcher's shop on the High Street. The *Yorkshire Post and Leeds Intelligencer* reported on an incident that made the front page of the *Daily Mail*: 'A wild scene took place at Boston on Saturday night, when a mob attacked the premises of Messrs Frank and Co., pork butchers, High Street.'

The business was owned by Messrs Leonard and George Cantenwine, both German by birth but naturalized British citizens. It was alleged that Mr Leonard Cantenwine had 'spoken in terms derogatory to the British forces', an allegation that was 'stoutly denied'. At about 11 o'clock there was an alleged crowd of a couple of thousand people outside the shop. Someone threw a missile through one of the plate-glass windows, which was a signal for attack. Shop windows both upstairs and downstairs were smashed with shouts from the crowd such as 'Down with the Germans'. Fortunately the Cantenwine family escaped and were sheltered by friends but remarkably the shop was re-opened on the following Monday.

Leonard Cantenwine took the oath of allegiance in 1891 and his brother George a few months later. Both brothers married English 'ladies', owned a 160-acre farm at Wrangle and had been regarded as 'pillars of the community'. When war came in 1914, both brothers made a public announcement of loyalty to the king, the announcement reading: 'Furthermore, being British subjects, we are quite ready and willing to do everything in our power for the interests of the country of our adoption.' Despite that, the Cantenwines had been targeted by the prejudice of the day. After the trial, the brothers continued trading in Boston until May 1915 when the sinking of the *Lusitania* occurred; it incited further demonstrations at their premises. The witch-hunt of Leonard and George didn't stop there: George was accused of showing lights to a Zeppelin that was on a raid in eastern England. A summons was issued and George was honourably acquitted of every charge that it was attempted to bring against him.[6]

Another former German national, the 74-year-old Julius Ungar from Old Leake, was fined for travelling more than 5 miles away from his registered place of residence. Although he had been living in Boston for ten years, he was still a registered German citizen.

Progressive struggles encountered by the Boston people continued when fishing trawlers were requisitioned by the Admiralty. Historically, fishermen have been described as 'hard men' and 'schooled' in discomfort. Walter Wood in his book *Fishermen in Wartime* powerfully describes the life of a fisherman, saying that the

> engine room life was unmercifully wearing and tormenting, and only necessity enabled human beings to live it; but it was the very sternness of the existence which enabled the men trained in that school to bear and survive the hardships and dangers of the sweeping and patrolling which they subsequently undertook.

Admiralty House expected a response and with absolute bravery, before a gun was barely fired on the Western Front, the fishermen of Boston rallied to the country's aid. Who would have thought that anyone would owe this community or even supposed it essential to our naval efficiency? It was not the government wage that brought these men together; that was just a few shillings a day compared to the income from a good catch. Three of these crews belonged to the *Bostonian*, *Cambrian* and the *Etrurian* who entered naval service in October 1914. Other trawlers – the *Alsatian*, *Angerton*, *Fishtoft* and the *Hungarian* – were also being prepared for patrol service and it was likely that some of those crew members would be men from Boston.[7]

The converted trawler, the Imperial Queen.

One trawlerman said:

> Fifteen hours of drenching and buffeting were our portion that day. The vessel with the pull of the tackle and the drive of the engines keeping her like an half tide rock, never clear of sweeping seas. Thud, slap, crash and swish as they came over our bows and swirled along the deck, never ceasing. If there had been frozen feet in the trenches there have been frozen fingers on the sea.

Typically the crews enrolled for the duration of the war in the navy reserve and were paid 4s per day. The men usually worked for ten days, then took six days for rest and refitting. Despite the conditions experienced, no fewer than 1,455 trawlers, 1,372 steam drifters and 118 motor drifters were pressed into naval service.[8]

An armada of 250 ships from gunboats to converted trawlers patrolled the North Sea twice a day in all weathers. A path was swept clear of mines and those left on each side of the channel acted as protection against raids by German craft.

The Fightback

Enlisting in the Royal Navy came more naturally to some than enlisting in the army or air force owing to the close connection Bostonians had with the sea.

Newspapers of the time are littered with exploits of the men who followed that 'calling'; however, space limitations allow only a few to be related here.

22 September 1914

An ambush occurred on 22 September 1914 in which three obsolete royal cruisers, manned mainly by reservists, some of which hailed from Boston, were sunk by one German submarine commanded by *Kapitanleutnant* Otto Weddigen who took command of *U-9* on 1 August 1914.

Included on board the royal cruisers HMS *Aboukir* and HMS *Cressy* were three naval reserve men from Boston who were involved in the action: Charles Thomas Butler of 7 White Horse Lane on the *Aboukir*, Arthur Cousens, Skirbeck Quarter and

Royal Naval Division recruitment poster.

40 BOSTON IN THE GREAT WAR

Skirbeck Quarter Lieutenant Charles Sinclair Wood, RNR of the HMS Motagua (his brother is Lieutenant Basil Wood, see page 126).

Kapitänleutnant Otto Weddigen, commander of U-boat U-9.

Daniel Frederick Ladds, landlord of the Boat Inn, High Street, Boston on the *Cressy*. HMS *Aboukir* and the other two cruisers had been assigned to prevent German surface vessels from entering the eastern end of the English Channel. In command of the three ships was Captain J.E. Drummond of the *Aboukir*. The Boston

A trio of Boston men on ships sunk by U-9.

HMS Cressy.

men were 20 nautical miles north-west off the Hook of Holland when the submerged U-boat fired one torpedo from a range of 500 yards which struck the *Aboukir* on the starboard side, flooding the engine room and causing the ship to stop immediately. Drummond assumed that his ship had hit a mine as no submarines had been sighted, inadvertently drawing the other two cruisers to the killing zone by ordering them to help. Twenty-five minutes later the *Aboukir* capsized and sank after five minutes. Only one lifeboat could be launched due to the failure of the steam-powered winches needed to launch them. *U-9* rose to periscope depth to observe the two other cruisers rescuing men from the sinking ship. The start of the action was at 0620 hours and by 0720 the three ships had been sunk and 1,397 men and 62 officers – mostly part-time men from the Royal Naval Reserve – had been killed. A further 837 men were rescued by steamers and trawlers in the vicinity.

Boston coast guard Arthur James Lewis, seaman on board the Cressy.

Germany struck a savage blow to the morale of the British, shaking public opinion and the reputation of the Royal Navy worldwide. By contrast, Weddigen's name was on everyone's lips in Germany; in particular this victory released some of the frustration encountered by the German navy compared to the supposed heroic deeds of the army.

The *Birmingham Daily Post* of Saturday the 26th printed a list of nearly 235 names of men who survived the sinking of the *Aboukir*. Charles Thomas Butler – who left a wife and four children – Arthur Cousens, and Daniel Frederick Ladds – leaving a wife and three children – of Boston were not on this list. Arthur Cousens was single and resided with his parents.

Boston coastguard Arthur James Lewis, based at the Hobhole Station near the Scalp, was one of the seamen on HMS *Cressy*. Arthur's story is far more fortunate than that of his Boston comrades. In volunteering to save others, Arthur was lucky to escape the fate of hundreds of his fellow seamen.

Arthur's story starts in Chatham, Kent where he joined the *Cressy* lying in the dockyard there, remaining in the dock for a few days waiting for the ship to be fitted, that is 'clearing out all the superfluous things'. The *Cressy* was ready five days later, proceeded to sea, and then began patrolling the North Sea stopping at various ports for coal. Searching the seas, Arthur and the crew of the *Cressy* latched on to the rest of the fleet.

Hearing piping going on on the upper deck, Arthur had been told that the *Aboukir* had been struck by a German torpedo. Closing all the watertight compartments behind them, the men went below. Suddenly a mighty explosion from the *Aboukir* forced the men, on the captain's orders, to throw overboard every possible piece of woodwork and drop the lifeboats so that the seamen on the sinking vessel would get assistance. The *Cressy* closed in at the same time, creating a swimming distance between the two ships. Arthur bravely went on the *Aboukir* to help clear away all the

Artists' impressions of the loss of the three cruisers.

woodwork and throw that into the sea so that the men could cling to it. Apparently there was no panic on the ship, even though by this time she was going over.

After throwing the wood overboard, Arthur volunteered to go in a whaler with some others to pick up seamen from the *Aboukir* who were in the water. Those who could do so stood on the deck of the *Aboukir* and several of them jumped into the sea. As the ship listed more and more, they could no longer stand on the deck and had to jump into the sea. The whaler got close to portside while men were swimming towards Arthur's boat, then helping them in, they took as many on board as possible. Others were clinging to the side of the boat. Arthur described the scene as heartrending when he saw the hundreds of bodies in the water, some drowning and some floating just above the surface. Those who could clung to everything possible: tables, chairs and other woodwork, even hammocks, just to try to save themselves.

The Second Attack

Some twenty minutes later, the men in the whaler heard another explosion on HMS *Hogue*, blowing out iron and woodwork into the air. The explosion seemed to be more above deck; it transpired later that the torpedo had hit the powder magazine. Unfortunately the lifeboat was full, and with the sea rough it was difficult getting alongside the *Cressy*, making it challenging for the men to get on board to relative safety. There were lines at the side of the *Cressy*, making it easier for the men. The whaler was being constantly washed away from the side; however, they tried to get to the other side to get the boat to leeward. As they were getting round the stern, a torpedo struck the *Cressy*. A great wash from the screw brought the ship astern and then another from a long way astern. The ship had watertight compartments, so she bore the first attack; however, the second torpedo smashed into her, throwing the men into the sea. This finished her and she went over quickly.

The gunners of the *Cressy* sighted the German submarine and fired on it right up to the time she went down. After the *Cressy* went down, all the surviving men from the three ships clung to anything they could, and those who could not drowned.

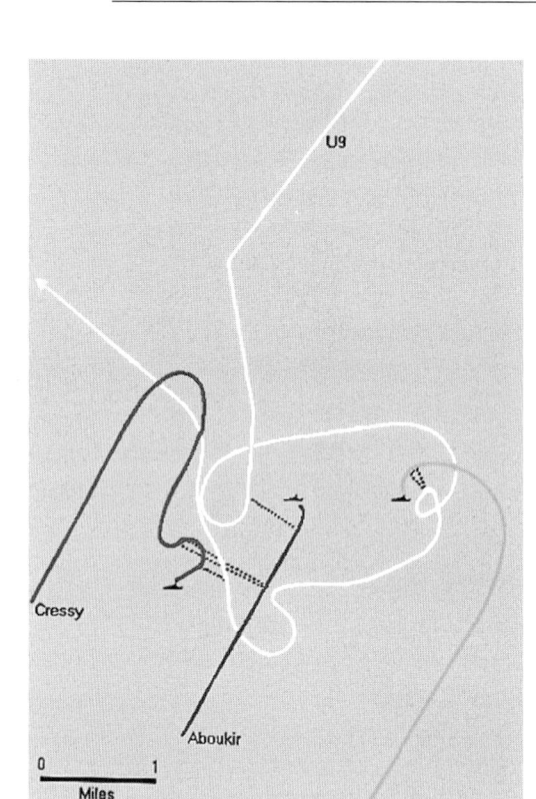

Naval manoeuvres showing the battle.

Arthur and the other 'lucky' survivors kept afloat until they were picked up by Lowestoft trawler 639. In the haste of leaving Chatham, some of the lifeboats had been left behind. During the time the last boat was sinking and in response to the wireless call, the flotilla soon came up, but this was some time after they had been aboard the trawler. The flotilla took in large numbers of men from the trawlers.

Poignantly, Arthur describes in his own words a most fearful sight:

> It was a most horrible sight to see hundreds of brave soldiers drowning before my eyes. We saw no German

The fate of the outdated British ships.

boats despite the submarines.... We were in a small boat, and we could not give any assistance and it was horrible to see men drowning who could not get into the boat... scores of bodies were floating about, but they would sink in time.

All the men died bravely – I saw my own messmates going down as the *Cressy* listed. The men were quite cheerful and when it was supposed the English had sunk a German submarine, even the men struggling in the water cheered heartily. Yes, and perhaps they drowned soon afterwards. It wrecked my nerves, but I am getting over it now. I am pleased I am saved. My luck must have been in.

The Fighting Sailors of the Royal Navy Division

Mr Edward H. Porcher of Carlton Road, Boston had volunteered for active service and joined the Royal Naval Brigade. Edward had what was described in the *Boston Guardian* as a 'baptism of fire'. Gallantly assisting in the defence of Antwerp with another 10,000 men, enduring incessant shot and shell, Edward came out 'without a scratch'.

Royal Navy Reserve marching towards Antwerp.

Edward H. Porcher.

Reporting for the *Boston Guardian*, a representative called to see Edward about three hours after his arrival on Wednesday morning and was told an interesting story of the defence of Antwerp.

After being mobilized he was, with others, placed on the *President*, a training ship on the Thames, for three weeks while training for active service on a battleship. Afterwards he was moved to Walmer near Deal in Kent to a naval brigade on land. It was here that Edward learned about skirmishes and ship movements. He was there for three weeks. On 4 October he marched from Deal to Dover and took a boat, *Mount Temple*, from Dover to Dunkirk. After arriving at 0700

Belgian soldiers welcoming the Royal Navy Reserve to 'the fight'.

hours on the Monday he entrained and went straight to Antwerp. It was a quiet ride, with time to relax and enjoy the scenery. Edward arrived in Antwerp on the Tuesday morning on a requisitioned London bus and was given tins of fish by the Belgians. Marching on to the market, the men were informed that they were going to

Soldiers digging trenches just outside Antwerp in 1914.

Lacking modern arms and equipment, the Belgian army retreated northwards to Antwerp.

'have a smack at the Germans' in order to relieve the Belgians as much as possible.

After the German invasion of Belgium in August 1914, the city of Antwerp was besieged to the south and east by German forces. Britain sent men of the Royal Naval Reserve to interrupt the German advance and support their Flemish allies who were rushing back to help their own countrymen.

In the Trenches

The brigade went into the trenches, which were about 5 miles south of the city. This would have been at dusk on the evening of Tuesday, 6 October. Describing the trenches as 'muddy and full of clay', Edward could clearly see the Belgians in the trenches in front

Royal Navy Reserve entrenched outside Antwerp.

of him and overhead the Antwerp forts were firing their heavy guns, passing German shells that were hurtling towards the city in the opposite direction. The Germans had not quite got their range and their shells fell beyond Edward's trench. Later, when the bombardment got a bit 'hot', the British men reluctantly retreated from their trench as they were 'dying to get a smack at them'. Now holed up in close trenches 3 miles from their original position near the Antwerp forts, the bombardment became more condensed, shells now smashing the city's defences.

On Wednesday night Edward saw the enemy for the first time; the Germans came out in a large phalanx from an adjoining wood. British bullets fired at the body of troops, which were in close formation, for twenty minutes, forcing them to retire. 'One or two troops were wounded in our trenches,' Edward told the reporter, 'but none were killed.'

On the morning of Thursday, 8 October at about 11 o'clock the German bombardment intensified, inflicting heavy damage confirmed by some naval brigade men from another detachment when they said 'Antwerp was in flames and our billet in the suburb had been burned down.' By Thursday evening the Belgian guns were silenced, forcing the Belgians to leave them. Edward and his comrades were stuck in between the advancing German army and the burning city of Antwerp. Shelling was so intense that the men were still in their trenches, unable to move because of the shellfire.

Dusk arrived with 'thousands of German troops' bursting out of the wood. A fusillade was set up but 'the more we knocked down, more came up.' The Maxim was firing about 300 rounds per minute and a 'hole' was made in their column, but it filled up as swiftly as the Germans were being knocked down. For twenty-five minutes the British subjected the Germans to this onslaught of hot metal, until finally the Germans had made it to within about 80 yards of their position. Edward received the order to retire, after 'knocking one down with a parting shot'. Retreating quietly and quickly towards Antwerp, the bombardment continued behind them. Walking towards a blazing city with thousands of refugees for company, the men saw Antwerp Cathedral almost 'like the Boston Stump – but was not ablaze or on fire.'

The War at Sea 51

'Big Bertha': Germany's devastating 42cm howitzer that destroyed the Belgian forts and confronted the Boston lads of the RNR.

The garrison leaving Antwerp alongside thousands of civilians.

A Forced March

After a while the men came across a pontoon bridge, the original bridge having been blown away. Straggling men who could not keep up with the company would not reach the temporary bridge before it was blown up. However, Edward made it across.

Marching upon a small village called St. Nicholas, the men were greeted with water and food given to them by local people. Mingling with the men were thousands of refugees that had also left the city, all seemingly unsure of where they were going. Belgian artillery was all along the road and, like the British, in full retreat. With Antwerp blazing behind them, back-dropped against the dark sky, the men marched for a period of thirty-two hours without rest and covered a distance of 32 miles. Edward picks up the account:

> Three men got lost, but we soon found another detachment and kept up with them. We marched on and came to a village called St. Gillis, where there was a railway station. We were very tired, I can assure you. There were thousands of refugees in the tremendously long train by which we travelled, and several of us rode on the roof of a carriage and got to our destination that way. We proceeded very slowly with this huge load. Once or twice we heard the Germans, but we were not attacked.

Arriving in Bruges on Friday evening the hungry, exhausted men stayed in the station with the refugees, having been fed by the Red Cross and allowed to shower under a water tank. Leaving Bruges, the men started their journey to Ostend before arriving on Saturday afternoon at about 2 o'clock. Startling news was shared with the men that 2,000 of their 'fellows' were missing. Sleeping on a boat that night the men were moved to the *Minnesota*, loading any ammunition they had left.

Shortly after setting sail, the *Minnesota* got stuck on a sandbank just off Dunkirk. Resigning themselves to having to wait for the next tide to release them, the Channel boat *Victory* came alongside and the men were transferred to her. Landing in Dover, tea, bread and bully beef were served to the hungry men. Later they entrained for Deal, walked to their camp in Walmer and re-erected some tents. Edward, along with the others, was given a week's leave and came home to Boston at about 7.40 am on Wednesday.

Events in Belgium did not dampen Edward's spirits, as he explained to the reporter: 'At the end of this time I go back to Walmer. I am ready to have another go at the Germans.' The commander of Walmer told the men that they had achieved their objectives in Antwerp and held the trenches for people to leave the city. Ruing the fact that the British did not have any 'big guns', Edward said they had 'no reply with our guns to their "Jack Johnsons"'.

Sydney William Grummitt: Child Sailor

On the night of 13 March 1915, the HMS *Amethyst* was badly damaged while attempting to clear a minefield laid by the Ottoman enemy in the Dardanelles. On board that ship that night was Sydney William Grummitt, who was described in a Sheffield newspaper as a 'First Class Boy'. Sydney was born in Boston on 25 April 1898, the oldest of three children of Robert Grummitt (a rope-maker) and his wife Catherine (Kate) Grummitt. Although his family had moved to Sheffield, Sydney still had strong family ties in Boston.

Prior to the war, Sydney was employed by J.H. Mudford and Sons (rope manufacturers) of Sheffield, following in the same trade as his father, Robert. He left to join the Royal Navy as a Boy 1st Class seaman.

The Dardanelles campaign began as a purely naval operation. Throughout the campaign, attempts were made by submarines to pass through the Dardanelles and disrupt the Ottoman Empire's shipping in the Sea of Marmara. HMS *Amethyst* penetrated at full speed through the mines as far as Negara and returned to anchor again. She was struck by shells while exchanging fire with some Turkish forts.

"FIRST CLASS BOY."

Sydney Grummitt, age 16, who worked for J. H. Mudford and Sons, of Sheffield, prior to joining the Navy, was killed on board the Amethyst in the Dardanelles.

Sydney Grummitt, who enlisted as a 'boy' sailor.

Twenty-eight of her crew were killed including Sydney and about thirty others wounded, some described as seriously.[9]

Boston Trawler Horror

'BOSTON TRAWLER HORROR' was the headline greeting the readers of the *Lincolnshire Standard* on 12 June 1915. Strong subheadings such as 'shelled without warning by German Submarine', 'four men murdered', 'pirates' cowardly attack in the North Sea' and 'survivors picked up after eleven hours' added angry sentiments to the shocked people of Boston.

Four crew members of the trawler *Arctic*, including the skipper, had been killed by shells fired into the vessel at short range and allegedly without any warning by a German submarine. The skipper and part-owner Ernest William Pesterfield was just making his last haul after what had been a prosperous trip when an explosion ripped the boat apart, instantly killing Ernest and his first hand Walter Mace. Both men were leaning over the port side watching for the fish boards to come up.

The Germans sighted the boat which was illuminated to assist the men in hauling up the trawl. Shellfire burst between them, blowing away part of Walter's face and throwing Ernest into the sea. Sensing blood, the Germans fired a deadly second shot, killing deck hands James Taylor and William Fuller. Blood and mutilated bodies lay on the now dark deck and confused men rushed up from below, slipping on the blood and oil, trying to stay upright as the boat listed to port.

Despite the darkness, the survivors managed to get the ship's boat overboard, for the first time catching sight of their hunter. The hull of the murderous craft was lying on the water at no great distance; however, mist and fog concealed the boat from the submarine which was scanning the killing zone with a searchlight, looking for its prey. Underhandedly, the Germans also resorted to using a siren and then answering it with a buzzer to make out that they were another trawler.

After standing by the sinking trawler for a time, hoping that the men left on board had just been stunned, the boat was allowed to drift away from the locality, using the rising sun to guide them back to England. Insufficiently clothed, tired, thirsty and hungry, the men were spotted after twelve hours by the Grimsby trawler *Jurassic* which took them on board.

There was a large crowd at the Great Northern passenger station to meet the survivors after entraining at Grimsby, including Councillor Fred Parkes and Alfred Stringer, partners in the *Arctic*, and a number of relieved friends and relatives. The returning men were all 'knocked up' after their dreadful ordeal, especially George Coleman who was suffering from the effects of gas inhaled from the exploded shells.

Interestingly, the customs officer at Grimsby referred to the incident as the 'worst case of deliberate murder on the high sea so far experienced by the fishing fleets during the war'.

The names of those killed were Ernest William Pesterfield (skipper), Walter Mace (second hand), James Taylor (deck hand) and William Fuller (deck hand).

Although Edward Todd of James Street and Fred Martin of National Terrace were survivors, this was the fourth time they had been involved in a shipwreck. Walter Mace had lost part of one arm a year earlier when it got caught in a winch. He was also part of the Boston Civil Guard.

Ironically, this would have been the last trip for James Taylor as the 23-year-old had found a job ashore, something that he and his new wife had been looking forward to. Ernest Pesterfield, a native of Boston, had just celebrated the birth of his daughter on his last birthday. Aaron Pesterfield, Ernest's son, was committed to avenging his father. In a report in the newspaper he is quoted as saying in a quiet but determined voice: 'I shall have my revenge, I shall go into the Navy.'

More Boston Men Blown Up

Thomas Strickland was the first Boston fisherman to fall victim to mine-sweeping in the North Sea, according to one contemporary report. Thomas was a ship's mate on board the trawler *Banyer* which hit a mine, buckled up and sank. After the explosion the skipper saw Tom with his hands clasped to his head and his face covered in blood. His home was Lion House, Skirbeck and he left a widow and a grown-up son and daughter.

Exploding in the North Sea after hitting a mine, the minesweeper *Lady Ismay* was lost with some of its casualties from Boston. Previously the ship was a large wheeled steamer that had been employed as a passenger ship running summer trips in the Channel and elsewhere. As a patrol boat, she carried a crew of more than forty hands. Robert Sharp, Thomas Baines, Henry Ainsworth and Percy Brocklesby, all from Boston, were casualties. Thomas Baines was now getting used to being blown up as this was his second time; he had only just returned from Ruhleben where he had been interned as a prisoner.

Another Boston minesweeper went down with his ship: Frederick Dixon, whose mother received a letter written on behalf of his wife conveying the unpleasant news. Enlisting in the minesweeping section of the Royal Navy when war broke out, he was sent to Grimsby and had been sailing out of that port up to the time of the accident.

Single 35-year-old Arthur Gosling joined the naval service on 13 August 1915 and was present when British warships were engaged off the Belgian coast in October 1914. His ship the *Brighton Queen* was mined by Herbert Pustkuchen and his U-boat *UC-5*.

Prisoners Return

The years passed by, distressing times punctuated by a surreal sense of living, ending with the welcome news in the *Lincolnshire Echo* of Monday, 7 January 1918:

> Exchanged Prisoners of War
>
> Arrival at Boston: Touching Scenes.
>
> This morning 632 repatriated men were landed at Boston on their return from Ruhleben Camp and other German internment camps. The number was made up of 379 civilians, 235 soldiers and 27 officers.
>
> Some of the men had been on board the vessels which were engaged for the voyage since Wednesday. Their arrival before Saturday afternoon was far advanced and the Home Office Officials, Government interpreters and other authorised personages were conveyed by tender to Boston Deeps, where the voyagers were remaining on board until the morning. Four Tenders were already standing by, ready to steam up to the dock side with the liberated men. Immediately, the necessary

The War at Sea 57

BOSTON MEN BLOWN UP.

Fate of a Large Patrol Boat in the North Sea

MR. R. SHARP.

MR. T. BAINES.

MR. H. AINSWORTH.

MR. P. BROCKLESBY.

How the crew of the Lady Ismay's *photographs appeared in the newspapers.*

Lady Ismay *at Cardiff before the war.*

Frederick William Dixon, a Boston minesweeper crew member killed at sea.

Arthur Gosling, who went down with the Brighton Queen.

The First World War minesweeper Brighton Queen, *the final resting place of Arthur Gosling.*

Former prisoners awaiting their turn to disembark at Boston.

arrangements for transferment could be completed and the Embarkation Officer, Col. Evans-Lombe, had everything in readiness for the work of transfer.

The Chief Magistrate, the Dock Management Committee and Naval and Military representatives received the first of the four tenders on its arrival at 10.15 am and half an hour later the first batch of civilians were moved from the pontoon to the Seaman's Institute to undergo a formal examination. As they walked down to the dock gate they carried their baggage and most of the men wore heavy winter clothing as much-needed protection from the intense cold. Seeing the crowd awaiting them, several of the travellers shouted out, 'A Happy New Year', which met with a reciprocal response from their compatriots before entering the portals of the Institute. One of the men told the Press Association representative that 'although the ships were comfortable, they had been too long aboard and there had been some shortness of rations.'

The *Earl Roberts* tender was speedily followed by the *Marple*, the *Humber* and the *Frenchman* tenders. On the way up from Boston Deeps the home-coming voyagers were greeted with cheers from groups of Lincolnshire folk at isolated farmsteads.

Stalwart Boston fishermen were greeted with the warmest enthusiasm by their fellow townsmen, and there were some scenes which evoked tears as well as jubilation.

One of the best known of the arrivals was William Henry Parker, skipper of the trawler *Wigtoft*. His grown-up daughter leading her little brother sprang forward at a first glimpse of her long-absent father and was folded in his arms to the delight of the much moved onlookers. Skipper Parker was taken prisoner in August 1914 and was the only one of nine belonging to the *Wigtoft* who has regained his liberty.

Charles Walkerley, master of the trawler *Julian* returned to his own family after an enforced absence of three years and five months. He came direct from Ruhleben

The War at Sea

The mayor of Boston welcoming the men home.

but he was fifteen months at Sennelager. When asked what he thought of the latter place he was silent but his face took on a 'look more eloquent than words'. Groups of relatives of the men roamed to and from the Seamen's Institute, where affecting meetings took place.

Boston Men Among the Prisoners

The Boston correspondent wrote:
Amid much excitement and scenes of great enthusiasm the repatriated prisoners arrived at the dock about ten o'clock this morning. With the exception of the naval and military men and the officials no one was permitted on the dock but the banks of the river were lined with people to watch the four tenders conveying the men from the three ships in the Deeps to the dock. There were cheers from the banks, re-echoed by the men on board the tenders. 'Are we down-hearted?' incited a most emphatic 'No!' There are

sixteen Boston men amongst the prisoners, as follows: E. Rear, W. Parker, H. Crowder, F. Gale, J. South, W. Chaffey, J. Bourne, J. Taylor, F. Pearce, C. Walkerley, W. Cole, L. Braime, A. Johnson, W. Ward, W.T. Bird and W. Woods. One man said 'Thank God, at last!' The majority of the men were looking fairly well. From the pontoon many of the men were marched or conveyed, with their luggage, in motor cars to the Seaman's Institute or the Workhouse. Mr. Walter Royal and Mr. F.M. Woodthorpe were at the dock gates to accord the Boston fishermen a hearty welcome. Wives and children and friends were present and there were joyous but pathetic scenes.

Standing in a puddle close to the river's edge and as near to the boats as they could get were two little old women in shawl and apron, mothers of two brave Boston fisher boys who had been imprisoned for three years. Wiping away tears with one hand and waving 'welcome home' flags with the other, the old women looked on anxiously, waiting for a glimpse of their loved ones.

The French tender *Balonwing* brought in to Hull the sick and mental ones, 'of the latter there are about 18'.

A touching poem was printed in the late edition of the *Lincolnshire Standard* in January 1918:

At last we felt the motion of the train,
As slowly it glided through the fog and rain.
I think a cheer escaped from every lip,
A long and loud 'hip-pip-hurray-hip-pip',
What mattered the pain, the stifled groan,
We were free – away from that horrible zone,
I think a prayer went up from every heart,
To God for the kindness he had wrought.

We sighted in the distance Boston Stump,
I think in every throat arose a lump,
What mattered that we were maimed and cold,
When soon in our arms our loved ones we'd hold,
We cheered, a welcome cheer back to us,
We thanked God for sending us safely back.
Another cheer, ''twas for the Union Jack'.

The War at Sea 63

Walter Royal and Mr Woodthorpe with the third batch of parcels destined for the interned fishermen.

Throughout the war the British fishermen had been of special interest to the German navy, from the early months of the 'gentlemen' engagements to the years after the changes to the rules of engagement where men had simply been left to die or were shot, cold-bloodedly, while clinging to broken pieces of wreckage. Allied and neutral fishermen had become victims of the ruthless methods that had been adopted by the German navy to destroy the fishing fleets.

The story that has been told shows what the fishermen did during the war, how they suffered for their country, how they worked for their families and how they fought for an ideal in which they believed.

Someone wrote 'it is a record, in so far as may be, of their patriotism and heroism, their unflinching loyalty to duty and their constant fight with death.'

64   BOSTON IN THE GREAT WAR

In memory of the fishermen, men of the Royal Naval Reserve, Royal Navy and the sailors of the Royal Naval Division of Boston: 'Lest we forget.'

Revelation 20:13: 'And the sea gave up the dead which were in it; and death… delivered up the dead which were in them…'

Boston steam trawler, Arctic BN30 – *model by John C. Revell.*

CHAPTER TWO

Boston's Baptism of Fire

Spurred on by propaganda, hatred towards Germans was rife among the towns dotted along the east coast, particularly after the raids on Scarborough, Hartlepool and Whitby resulting in 137 fatalities, many of whom were civilians including little John Ryalls whose mother was from Boston.

Previous wars had chiefly excluded civilian involvement but when Count von Zeppelin, as a retired German officer, developed his airships, it forced Britain into what historians call 'total war'. In retaliation against the French bombing of some German towns the Kaiser signed off use of the Zeppelins against British towns and cities, starting with the raids on Great Yarmouth and King's Lynn in January 1915; the first bomb, an early Christmas present, fell harmlessly on 24 December near Dover. Boston was in the front line of this threat from Zeppelins which generally arrived in Britain via the North Sea from their bases on the north-west German coast.

Initially Britain largely ignored the Zeppelin threat. Winston Churchill, in his book *The World Crisis*, remarked: 'I rated the Zeppelin much lower as a weapon of war than almost anyone else. I believed that this enormous bladder of combustible and explosive gas would prove to be easily destructible.'

Now known as the 'Hun baby-killers', the German menace had found a new way to literally rain down terror on another east coast town: Boston. During the air-raid of Saturday night, 2 September 1916, five bombs dropped on the town. Commanding L23 over England for the first time at about 3,000ft, *Kapitänleutnant* Wilhelm Ganzel approached the Norfolk coast over the Wash, releasing a number of incendiary bombs in the sea at 10.15 pm

HARTLEPOOL ⎫ Bombarded from 8.15 to 8.50 a.m
WEST HARTLEPOOL ⎬ by 2 Battle CRUISERS &
⎭ 1 Armoured CRUISER
Estimated about 500 Shells fired
91 Killed including 30 WOMEN & 15 CHILDREN
about 300 Wounded; Gasometer, Waterworks &
Towns much damaged

HELIGOLAND NAVAL BASE to HARTLEPOOL 330 Nautical Miles or a[bout]
14 HOURS PASSAGE for a FAST CRUISER SQUADRON at 22-25 Kn[ots]
their average spee[d]
journey can therefo[re]
done under cover o[f]

WHITBY to HARTLEPOOL 28 Miles

WHITBY Bombarded 9.15 to about 9.30 a.m.
by 2 Battle CRUISERS, about 30
shells fired; 2 Men killed, 2 Boys
wounded; Coastguard Sta. ABBEY,
Town & inland villages damaged

Trees Mouth
REDCAR
SALTBURN
[M]IDDLESBROUGH
St Hilda's Church
WHITBY
RUSWARP Shelled
The ABBEY Shelled
EAST CLIFF
River Esk
Fylingdale Moor

ROBIN HOOD'S BAY
RAVENSCAR
Petard Point

SCALBY

NORTH BAY
OLD CASTLE Shelled
St MARY'S CHURCH Hit →
SHOP Set on FIRE
EASTBOROUGH
OLD CAS[TLE] Dam[aged]
NEW HARBOUR
LIGH[T] Da[maged]
MANY HOUSES HIT this crowded quarte[r]
BALMORAL HOTEL Hit
HOUSES Hit
TOWN HALL
ROYAL HOTEL Hit
CAFE Struck
SOUTH BA[Y]
PROSPECT ROAD
HOUSES Hit
GLADSTONE ROAD
HANOVER ROAD
VICTORIA ROAD
BARWICK ST
[?]HOUSE Hit
CRESCENT
RAILWAY STA.
GRAND HOTEL Struck 3 times
FALSGRAVE ROAD
WESTBOROUGH
SCARBOROU[GH]
Bombarded from 8.5 to 8.[?]
by Battle CRUISER & Ar[moured]
CRUISER, estimated ab[out]
Shells fired; 17 KILLE[D] includ]ing 8 WOMEN & 4 CH[ILDREN]
about 100 Wound[ed]
RAMSDALE PARK
VALLEY ROAD
S⁺ MARTIN'S CH. Damaged
SOUTH CLIFF Shelled

Map of the horrific attack on the East Coast by the Zeppelin menace.

near Snettisham. He then crossed the Wash, appearing over Kirton Fen, south of Boston, where he dropped a high-explosive (HE) bomb. The exploding bomb broke windows and damaged a hen house, killing some unfortunate chickens.

Just prior to this at 10 o'clock, the Boston Town Guard received word to report to the Post Office for immediate duty with little indication that a Zeppelin was approaching the town, using 'the Stump' as a waypoint. Despite the time, the town was still alive with shoppers finding their way about the already dark streets. Cycles and vehicles were 'passing here and there' with their shaded lights on.

Kapitänleutnant Wilhelm Ganzel, the Boston killer from above.

Lights Out

Light rain could not mask the sound of the dull subdued hum resonating from the dark skies above, forcing the vigilant special constables to order every ray of light to be extinguished. The sound of the hum grew so intense there was little doubt that an aircraft of some sort was close to the town. An eye-witness describes the sound that night of a 'whirring' that 'gradually increased in volume until it exceeded many times the noise of a railway train'.

First World War public air-raid warning poster.

PUBLIC WARNING

The public are advised to familiarise themselves with the appearance of British and German Airships and Aeroplanes, so that they may not be alarmed by British aircraft, and may take shelter if German aircraft appear. **Should hostile aircraft be seen,** take shelter **immediately** in the nearest available house, preferably in the basement, and remain there until the aircraft have left the vicinity: do not stand about in crowds **and do not touch unexploded bombs.**

In the event of **HOSTILE** aircraft being seen in country districts, the nearest Naval, Military or Police Authorities should, if possible, be advised immediately by Telephone of the TIME OF APPEARANCE, the DIRECTION OF FLIGHT, and whether the aircraft is an Airship or an Aeroplane.

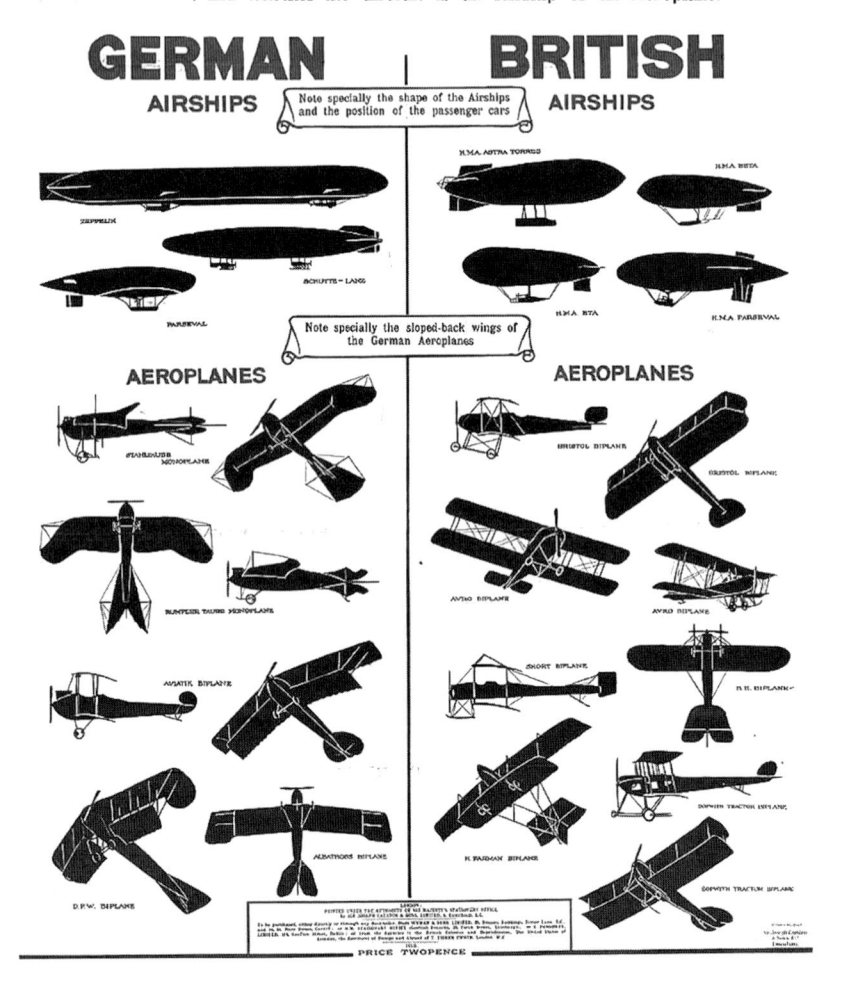

GERMAN | BRITISH

AIRSHIPS | AIRSHIPS

Note specially the shape of the Airships and the position of the passenger cars

Note specially the sloped-back wings of the German Aeroplanes

AEROPLANES | AEROPLANES

PRICE TWOPENCE

Suddenly, and before anyone knew what was happening, a flash of light from the cigar-shaped aircraft heralded the first bomb, accompanied by a shrill whistle. 'There was a vivid flash of light, a deep intonation, and Boston had received its baptism of fire.'

Horace Oughton, aged just 16 (17 in some accounts), was the first victim of this deplorable act. Horace's father was a member of the Town Guard and keeper of the Grand Sluice Bridge, and was just about to go on duty when he heard the roar of the Zeppelin. Seeing a flashlight, he ordered the owner 'Dinghy' Clark to put it out; Clark refused and an argument broke out. Alerted by the raised voices, Horace and his pregnant mother came outside to investigate when a whistling bomb struck the Grand Pier of the Sluice. His mother was injured by glass flying in her face and Horace had no chance to run into the house and was downed by the explosion. The medical examiner was called and found the boy lying, still alive, on the floor with a large hole on the right side of his back and half of his left side blown away. His removal to hospital was ordered, where he died from haemorrhage, shock and injuries caused by pieces of the bomb.

The jury returned a verdict in accordance with the medical testimony, and added a rider to the effect that had the 'light in a certain portion of the town been out no Zeppelin would have bombed the town'.

The consequence of this attack was more rigid enforcement of the blackout regulations; too little, too late for young Horace.

Almost immediately after the first bomb, the second hurtled down on innocent people from the 'dastardly Germans' who had 'transgressed all moral law and regulations of war by again dropping their death-dealing bombs on a defenceless town'. With the sky flashing, two more bombs dropped towards the spectators, tense with the uncertainty of what might happen next.

Unspectacularly and rather fortunately, a bomb fell into the garden of a naturalized British subject Mr H. Nagele near the Sluice Bridge. An unoccupied house on the site had its windows blown out and doors blown off their hinges.

Mr Sharpe's house further down on Fydell Street was the victim of the third bomb; however, fortune favoured the residents of Fydell Street when the bomb found its final resting place in the garden, making a hole some 5 or 6ft deep, blowing out the windows in the

Bombs similar to those dropped on Boston.

greenhouses and the nearby homes. The brickwork of the houses was pitted with fragments, demonstrating the wisdom of the householders in staying indoors, heeding the warnings posted in the town.

One miraculous escape was to be made by Mrs Belton of Carlton Road. Like the soil on Fydell Street, Carlton Road had soft clay making up the terra firma and happily the bomb fell on this, albeit stripping the trees of their fruit and foliage. Mrs Belton, who was 86 years old, was sitting with her friend Miss Brooksbank and another companion enjoying supper. Windows smashing close to where the ladies were seated brought immediate distress and confusion to the late diners. The back door and the door of a small conservatory were torn from their hinges, while the glass of the conservatory and a good deal of the framework was smashed.

Although the bombs caused death and damage, some people in the town still flouted the blackout laws. Brought before the bench in April 1917, Samuel B. Chamberlain (baker and confectioner of Market Place), Alfred Chester (foreman at a factory on Tawney Street) and Ebenezer Hugh Morgan (Wesleyan minister) were all fined for not screening their windows.

Interior view of a Zeppelin cabin.

The Zeppelin cabin at battle stations.

The Curious Tale of the *King Stephen*

Wreckage sighted on 5 February 1916 was thought to be that of the Zeppelin airship L19 that went down over the North Sea after straying into Dutch air space over Hollum. Intense rifle fire had reduced three of its four already troubled engines to lifeless metal scrap as it was guided slowly into the North Sea by its commander Lieutenant Captain Odo Loewe.

Just before daybreak on Wednesday morning, the Grimsby trawler the *King Stephen* with a Boston deck hand on board was passing slowly, attracted by lights flashing in the distance. On standby until daylight, the crew of the trawler found the wreckage of a German airship with the identification mark L19. Buoyancy was keeping a large portion of the Zeppelin afloat, while the cabins were well under water. On a raised platform on the top of the envelope were seven or eight members of the crew shouting in broken English, 'Save us, save us! We will give you 5 pounds.'

According to the trawler captain William Martin, the crew numbers swelled to about twenty-two when a number of other men came up a companion-way leading to the platform. Other men were heard banging from within, possibly effecting repairs in an

Illustration showing the King Stephen *and the trawler.*

attempt to stay afloat longer. Zeppelins of this type on a bombing run would normally have a crew of about sixteen to eighteen.

Zeppelin L19 had been involved in a raid over a few towns near Birmingham just two days earlier at a cost of sixty-one lives including women and children. A verdict of 'Wilful murder against the German Emperor and his son' was returned by one jury for the murderous destruction of the towns by the Zeppelins. Evidently the crew of the *King Stephen* had not been aware of the raids; however, William Martin decided that rescuing the Germans would then outnumber his crew of nine hands with twenty armed German men. Fearing a mutiny that might take him and his crew back to Germany, he left the men floating until he could get help. Loewe, who 'spoke like a gentleman', pleaded with Martin to rescue his men and took a dying oath that he 'would not interfere' with the crew of the *King Stephen*. Ignoring their pleas, Martin decided to make for port and communicate to the authorities in order for a better-armed and crewed rescue boat to take the Germans then on board back to Britain.

Two naval vessels that were sent to the scene of the disaster, having made a complete search of the area, returned to their base and reported that there was no sign of the airship. Archival research suggests that the *King Stephen* was operating in a zone in which fishing was prohibited and Martin may have been worried about his fishing business if he was found to be in illegal waters.

Worsening weather hastened the demise of the P-class airship of the *Kaiserliche Marine* (Imperial German Navy) as it remained afloat for a few hours longer. Desperately hoping that someone would find their final thoughts, the crew threw messages in bottles into the sea. Six months later a Swedish fisherman found such a bottle at Marstrand, the 'time capsule' encasing the last personal messages from the airmen to their families and Loewe's final report:

> With fifteen men on the top platform and backbone girder of the L19, floating without gondolas in approximately 3 degrees East longitude, I am attempting to send a last report. Engine trouble three times repeated, a light wind on the return journey delayed our return and, in the mist, carried us over Holland where I was received with heavy rifle fire; the ship became heavy and simultaneously

three engines broke down. 2nd February, towards one o'clock, will apparently be our last hour.

Polarizing public opinion, the incident encouraged Arthur Winnington-Ingram, Bishop of London, to applaud Martin for prioritizing the safety of his crew. In Germany, Martin was maligned by the press who used the incident as propaganda to fuel the notion that the British were a cruel nation with no regard for humanity.

L19 sank with no survivors and William Martin died of heart failure in Grimsby on 24 February 1917, just over a year after his altercation with the Zeppelin.

The Fight Back

The year 1916 witnessed something of a turning-point with the improvement of British aircraft design and performance. Hydrogen-filled aircraft needed to mix with oxygen to create an explosion; however, normal ball-type ammunition just pierced a hole in the fabric of the Zeppelin, releasing the hydrogen gas into the atmosphere. Aircraft by now had been fitted with explosive/incendiary machine-gun ammunition such as the Pomeroy or Brock versions. This lethal mix of explosive and incendiary rounds swung the odds in the British airmen's favour.

Newly-achieved British air superiority forced the Zeppelin designers to compromise regarding weight versus comfort. Although these new airships could climb to altitudes of 20,000ft, their compasses no longer worked, thermometers froze and the engines were starved of oxygen, the vital fuel. Still the Germans pushed on, even painting the undersides of the airships black to make them less visible to British searchlights. This new class of Zeppelin included models L35, L36, L39, L40, L41, L42 and L47, all of which could reach altitudes between 16,000 and 20,000ft.

The Zeppelins turned their attention to Boston once again on the night of 19 October 1917 when four naval Zeppelins, L44 (*Kapitänleutnant* Franz Stabbert), L47 (Kapitänleutnant Max von Freudenreich), L52 (*Oberleutnant zur See* Kurt Friemel) and L55 (Kapitänleutnant Hans Kurt Flemming) flew over. Bostonians had been spared that night by the deep cloud and fog obscuring the town. Heading down the Wash, L44 continued its journey up the Whitham

Boston's Baptism of Fire 75

Le Petit Journal

LE CHATIMENT DU PIRATE
Au retour d'un raid sur l'Angleterre
le Zeppelin " L-19 " sombre dans la mer du Nord

Le Petit Journal *newspaper showing the moment the Zeppelin sank.*

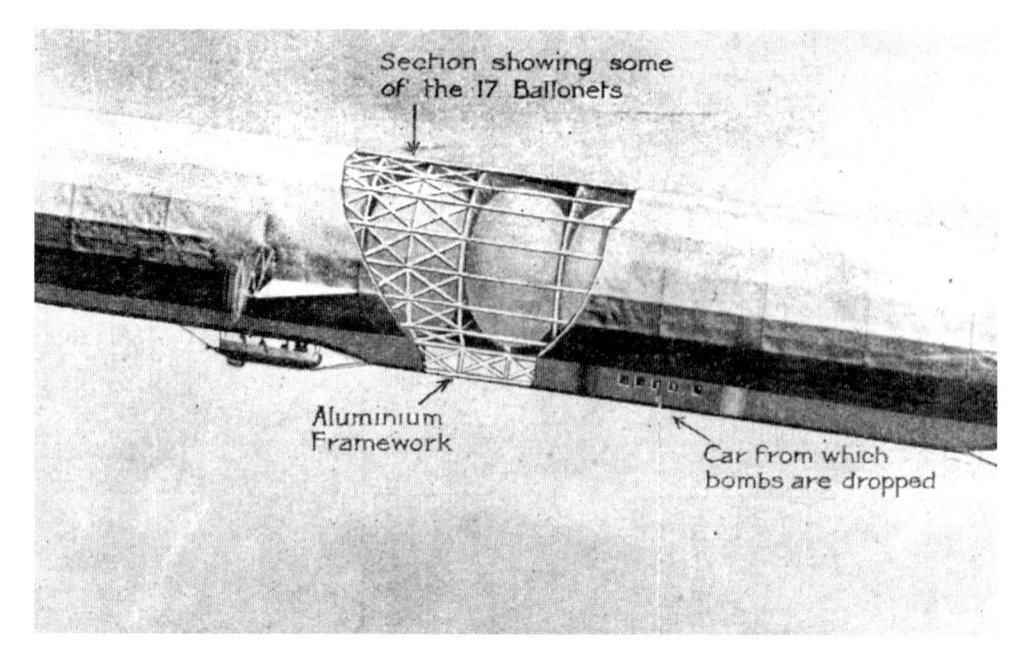

Dissected view of a Zeppelin.

Haven River before using the railway line as a guide to Peterborough, on its way to Bedford where bombs claimed more lives.

Zeppelins had carte blanche to inflict indiscriminate damage over the British Isles for lengthy periods of the war with the weather as their only enemy. Monday, 5 August 1918 saw six height-climber Zeppelins encounter light winds at 16,400ft as the Channel could be seen in the distance below the cabin. With the English coast in sight, three British planes flew seaward towards them. Major Egbert Cadbury (of the chocolate company fame) and Captain Robert Leckie as his rear observer in a two-seater DH4 opened fire with a single Lewis gun. One Zeppelin, the L70, was soon engulfed in flames and began to fall. Two other airships saw the fate of the L70 and then turned for home, narrowly escaping attack.

Not a single bomb was dropped on England that day by the three Zeppelins that got away. It was the Germans' last sortie over British soil. At last, the Zeppelin threat was over.

In total 115 Zeppelins had been built for the sole purpose of killing civilians and bringing misery and devastation to those left behind. Of those built, 25 had been lost to enemy air or ground attack over England and the continent; 19 were damaged and wrecked on landing; 26 were lost in accidents; 22 were scrapped in service; 7 were interned after being forced down; 9 were handed over to the allies at the end of the war; and 7 were scuttled at the end of the war.[10]

Below is a table showing the air-raid calls in Boston that heralded the coming of hostile German aircraft between the outbreak of war and the Armistice:

DATE	CALLED OUT	ALL CLEAR
13 October 1915	8.30 pm	11.15 pm
31 January 1916	6.45 pm	11.30 pm
5 March 1916	9.15 pm	11.30 pm
19 March 1916	9.55 pm	12.30 am (20 March)
31 March 1916	9.40 pm	3.45 am (1 April)
1 April 1916	10.35 pm	2.00 am (2 April)
3 April 1916	9.55 pm	3.40 am (4 April)
4 April 1916	9.00 pm	10.40 pm
5 April 1916	9.25 pm	1.30 am (6 April)
30 July 1916	12.55 am	4.00 am
31 July 1916	10.00 pm	3.40 am (1 August)
4 August 1916	2.00 am	4.15 am
10 August 1916	1.00 am	3.15 am
2 September 1916	10.35 pm	5.00 am (3 September)
23 September 1916	8.40 pm	4.10 am (24 September)
25 September 1916	8.30 pm	3.25 am (26 September)
1 October 1916	7.45 pm	4.50 am (2 October)
27 November 1916	9.15 pm	6.10 am (28 November)
16 June 1917	10.50 pm	12.00 midnight
21 August 1917	10.20 pm	3.20 am (22 August)
24 September 1917	11.00 pm	5.15 am (25 September)
19 October 1917	6.45 pm	1.45 am (20 October)
12 March 1918	8.35 pm	1.05 am (13 March)
21 May 1918	1.30 am	2.30 am
5 August 1918	9.30 pm	1.55 am (6 August)

Despite the air-raid warnings, the local constabulary were kept busy policing the district, bringing people to task who flouted the law. Court proceedings reported in the *Lincolnshire Echo* on 22 August 1917 highlight the problem. George Taylor of Butterwick and Thomas Mack were both summoned and then subsequently fined for the offence of 'failing to screen the house window' and were fined ten shillings each.

A Boston Aviator

'Our time has come. Be brave and die like a man. Good-bye.' These courageous and awful words were uttered by an officer of the Royal Flying Corps (RFC) to John Baker of Boston, who was in an aeroplane with him when the engine stopped at a height of 3,000ft over Boulogne.

John, who was a hairdresser in the RFC, wrote of his thrilling experiences to his parents in Threadneedle Street, Boston:

> Here I am in Regimental Hospital at Netheravon, Wilts and I am writing in pencil as I cannot hold a pen. My arms hurt me, especially my right one, and also my right leg. It is broke just below the knee. But don't worry. Doctor says he can have me walking about in a month. The officer I was with when the machine came down has got two doctors attending him, and he has told a lot that he so does like me and he comes to me every day sometimes twice. He sends me fruit, and everything I want. I am well looked after in every respect.
>
> Yes mother, it was unlucky for me as it would have been an honour for me to have gone to the front. But it was a big honour to fly over to France. How the accident happened I cannot tell, only I know we were flying over Boulogne, France, when the engine on the aeroplane stopped altogether. And a good job we were 3,000 feet up in the air, or I should have been killed outright.
>
> When the engine stopped the officer said to me 'Baker, our time has come. Be brave, and die like a man!' And he shook hands with me. And I shall always remember as

long as I live the ten minutes. Then the next I remembered I was in a barn in a field. I was removed to Boulogne, and afterwards to Netheravon, being conveyed from Southampton by motor ambulance.

Freiston Airbase Royal Naval Air Service (RNAS), Freiston Shores

In the borough of Boston, Freiston was chosen to accommodate the expansion of the nearby airbase at RAF Cranwell. Permanent buildings including hangars and a control tower were built. Initially the base housed the RNAS School of Aerial Fighting and Bomb-Dropping. A flight of Bristol Scout aircraft was also stationed at Freiston which were employed on anti-Zeppelin operations including the interception of Zeppelins in transit over Boston. BE2s flew from Freiston on the night of 19 October.

Shaded under a tree in a quiet corner of the historic grounds of St James's Church, Freiston, four Great War airmen rest peacefully.

Flight Sub-Lieutenant James Theodore Sims, RNAS was killed on 26 May aged 30 as the result of a flying accident. James was the elder son of Mr James Sims of Redruth, Cornwall. At the outbreak of war he enlisted in the Duke of Cornwall's Light Infantry, but obtaining a commission as

Freiston village.

80 BOSTON IN THE GREAT WAR

> Oxford for learning
> London for wit
> Paris for fashions
> But this place
> Not FIT.
>
> ↓ FREISTON AERODROME
> G. Powell

A Freiston serviceman's thoughts of the aerodrome.

A First World War Bristol Scout.

Boston's Baptism of Fire 81

Freiston hangar.

The officer commanding No.44 SoAF&G, Commander Harold Kerby DSC (left), stands in front of a Sopwith Camel at Freiston in 1918.

82 BOSTON IN THE GREAT WAR

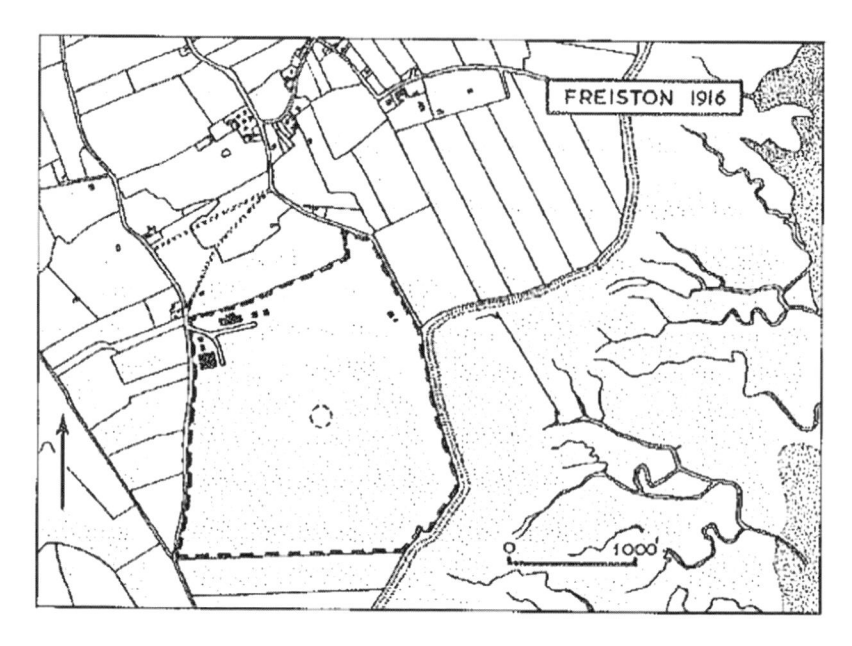

Map of Freiston Air Station, 1916.

a sub-lieutenant with the Royal Naval Volunteer Reserve (RNVR) he joined the RNAS as an observer. After training he was sent to Dunkirk and distinguished himself by the photographs he took in the air under heavy shellfire, receiving the Croix de Guerre (with Palm) and being presented to the king by his commanding officer. Just after coming to Freiston he died in an air accident flying from Cranwell in an Avro 504E.

Another who died over Boston was a pilot from Freiston: Sub-Lieutenant Owen Hewitt Bennett of Birmingham. An eye-witness described how Owen was flying 300 to 400ft above him and suddenly fell. The nose of the witness's machine jammed under the carriage of Owen's and they locked together, rolled and then banked for 300ft. The lucky witness managed to break his aeroplane free, while Owen crashed to the ground. The coroner recorded a verdict of accidental death.

On 1 April 1918 the RNAS Gunnery School was redesignated the SOAF&BD and finally as No. 4 FS on 29 May 1918, now only equipped with the 504J/k, Camel, Snipe and Pup. No. 4 FS was disbanded on 18 March 1920 and Freiston closed down

Official letter suggesting the training of pilots from Cranwell to Freiston from declassified documents. (Author's private collection)

St James's Church, Freiston, final resting place of four Great War airmen.

Reverend J.R. Trotter, vicar of Freiston and Butterwick.

shortly afterwards, but not before a serious storm had demolished the hangars and several wooden buildings.

From Zeppelin aircraft to propaganda leaflet drops, the role of aircraft played a significant part in the First World War, opening up a terrifying new theatre of war. Although the number of civilians killed by aerial machines remained small during the war, these air-raids nonetheless caused widespread terror to the residents of Boston.

CHAPTER THREE

Fighting on the Home Front

In developing a psychology that motivates a particular curiosity about fighting, men are able to translate this by engaging in warfare. Boys played with toy soldiers and girls played with dolls; a tradition that filled most homes on Christmas morning. So deciding to leave their families, jobs, friends and homes was, for some men, an easy decision to make; a patriotic call stronger than the call of domestic responsibility.

It seems that in Boston, as in many other towns, people had observed the war situation with calmness. Advice was given that 'a hard financial situation was to be met, and it is pleasing to note that we look like viewing it, as a community, sensibly and calmly.'[11]

Reporting from army recruiting offices, one article describes its pleasure in seeing 'numbers of young men who have been presenting themselves for the purpose of enlisting. It shows that the patriotic spirit is there and that it comes out when war clouds lower over the country.'

What about the people left behind? Total war meant that everyone was expected to support the war effort, regardless of any personal beliefs. It was regarded as socially unacceptable to be unpatriotic; however, women played the patriotic role to perfection. The First World War proved to be the catalyst awaited by women for improved equality between themselves and men.

When war broke out, women were encouraged to 'keep the home fires burning', i.e. to demonstrate their patriotism by 'continuing their domestic duties as wives and mothers.'[12] While coping with the lack of news about their husbands, women had to also demonstrate their resilience by coping with shortages of food and fuel; at the same time they would have been providing emotional support to other family members left behind by the menfolk.

Recruiting poster for the Land Army encouraging women to 'do their bit'.

Poster encouraging women to preserve already depleted resources.

Once men had begun to enlist at a steady rate, particularly from among the low-paid farming community, Boston suffered an agricultural manpower gap that required immediate attention. Faced with some people's attitude that a woman was incapable of doing a man's job, especially one as demanding as ploughing or handling livestock, what was the response?

The question of the shortage of agricultural labour was discussed in the House of Commons on Wednesday, 24 February 1915. Keir Hardy drew attention to the shortage of food and on behalf of the Board of Agriculture, Sir Harry Verney suggested several methods, including the employment of women, by which farmers might try to obtain the necessary labour before resorting to child labour which was advocated by some politicians in the same session.

Thoughts in other circles endorsed the views of Verney, with one person writing in the *Lincolnshire Echo*, 'no women work harder than the foremen on farms unless it be the wives of small farmers'[13] and their lives have 'no Sabbath day rest'. Differing opinions divided the farming community, with some thinking that a woman would only be useful for milking a cow and remarkably this opinion was printed in the county paper. With dated rhetoric they had been told that the 'places of men should be taken by women and children, but people who talked like that showed lamentable ignorance. If the land were to be cultivated…women and children were useless.'

Despite some negativity the recruitment drive began, and to entice the women the following terms of service were offered: board and lodging during instruction, plus one free outfit of high boots, breeches, overalls and a hat, and wages of 18 shillings per week or more if a district paid it. Experienced women selected by the War Agricultural Committee and Women's National Service Department would supervise the welfare of the girls. Even motor plough schools were opened.

The following letter was circulated to farmers in Boston by the prime minister:

> We have now reached a crisis in the war, when to ensure victory, the heroism of our armies at the front must be backed by the self-sacrifice and tireless labour of

Women's Land Army recruitment poster.

everyone at home. To this end the production of each quarter of wheat and oats, and of each bushel of potatoes is of vital importance. The work of the next few years must decide the harvest of the year; and in the nation's interest I urge you, at whatever personal sacrifice, to overcome all obstacles and to throw your fullest energies into the work.

Bucking the social trend, in 1915 Mr George Caudwell of St Lambert's Hall, Weston was employing more than sixty women and proposing to employ many more. By October 1916 George had 300 acres of onion crop and to help him harvest this he had in his service as many as 400 women (including 60 war widows) from the Boston and Spalding district. The women were housed at the Peacock and Royal Hotel which had been converted into a hostel. Miss Lyke of Spalding and Miss Halstead, for some time the sister at the VAD (Voluntary Aid Detachment) hospital Holden House, had been appointed matron. The women were transported in the morning and taken back in motors and horse-drawn vehicles. No doubt the women worked on different areas of Mr Caudwell's 3,000-acre farm.[14] The girls worked from 7.00 am to 5.00 pm and were guaranteed the minimum wage of 25s per week. Locals would have witnessed the unaccustomed sight of a huge motor bus entering

Women's Land Army handbook given to all women joining before they commenced training.

Women's Land Army with a single-furrow plough.

Ploughing the land on a field in Boston.

The return of women and girls by motor bus after their day's work on the farm.

the town by way of Town Bridge and High Street with cheery, chattering and healthy-looking women, up to sixty-three of them crammed into the same bus, looking forward to a well-earned rest.

How did the women fare? Mr H.P. Carter, a prominent farmer who represented the Board of Agriculture in Boston, said that farmers in the district were now employing women to do a good deal of their work. He employed around 100 women in the East Fen and many women on his other farms, and said they were 'doing splendidly everywhere'.

Liberation for women wasn't only found in the fields, as scores of Boston women answered the call in the *Lincolnshire Echo*[15] for women to work in the munitions factories where

> the first thing that strikes a visitor in a munitions factory is the splendid type of intelligent women who

Fighting on the Home Front 93

The Girl on the Tractor

can drive the machine just as well as a man, although it develops 24 h.p. The Overtime Farm Tractor is simple and cannot go wrong. At Winchester, in February, our operator jumped off the tractor (which was pulling a 4-furrow automatic self-lift plough) when machine and plough turned 4 perfect furrows the full length of the ½-mile field without human guidance!

| 24 h.p. | ## The Overtime Farm Tractor | 39 cwt. |

Investigate the work this Tractor is doing on average farms to-day. Call and see it at our showrooms, or write us for advice of demonstrations and nearest farmer using the machine, NOW!

Price
£285
Delivered

JAMES SMITH,
Motor Works, Grantham.

Women were used to advertise tractors in the Grantham Times.

When I went to stay with Jane

I TOOK a tin of Elect Cocoa in my bag. Of course I offered her some, but Jane is a bit old-fashioned. "I never drink cocoa," she said. She could see how much I was enjoying it, but she said nothing all that breakfast time. Next day she said, a little shyly, "I think I'd like to try just one cup of your Elect Cocoa." She tasted it, and I could see by her face how pleased she was. "I never knew," she said, "that cocoa could be so delicious." She was as brisk as could be at work that morning, and she never starts out on the van nowadays without having had her cup of Elect Cocoa.

a cup of Rowntree's Elect Cocoa makes a biscuit into a meal

have chosen to do their bit by munitioning…there are all grades of society…the university and public school girls, the titled lady, the secondary school girl, the dressmaker, milliner and the maid, all are working side by side.

Interestingly, Sunday labour had been adopted in the munitions factories on account of the heavy demand for output. Women and children were normally classed as protected workers; however, such work was legalized to meet the demand.

During the Great War Lincolnshire-based firms produced more aircraft for the RFC, RNAS and RAF than any other county. In 1916 the Boston women's chief duties would have been the testing of various small metal parts. The work did not require 'any special degree of intelligence'[16] but keen observance was important in detecting flaws. In the drawing office girls were employed as tracers, with a better salary due to the particular skills involved. If the women had shown sufficient proficiency in testing, they were promoted to the departments engaged in making the materials for the wings of the aeroplanes.

Land Army uniform.

Women: Supreme Work in the War

The statue of Florence Nightingale in Waterloo Place, London reminds tourists and passers-by of the supreme work carried out by women in wartime. The wounded who were brought back from the front line were cared for in unprecedented numbers, proving the truth of Cromwell's well-known phrase 'the crowning mercy'.

Behind the well-known Red Cross and Order of St. John of Jerusalem who sent out thousands of well-trained volunteers to

Working in an aircraft factory was a male preserve before the Great War.

staff hospitals in the war zone and elsewhere were the thousands of members of the VAD who looked after hundreds of hospitals scattered throughout the United Kingdom, including Boston.

The *Grantham Journal* of 15 August 1914 highlighted a warning issued by the Red Cross:

> The British Red Cross Society write to point out that they are threatened with the same confusion that so crippled Red Cross effort in the South African War with the same evils of overlapping, of uncoordinated and disunited work. Private houses are being turned into hospitals and convalescent homes without reference to any organising body, and without regard to any rational scheme.

The War Office showed sufficient concern for the lack of nursing in the event of another major war by organizing a territorial

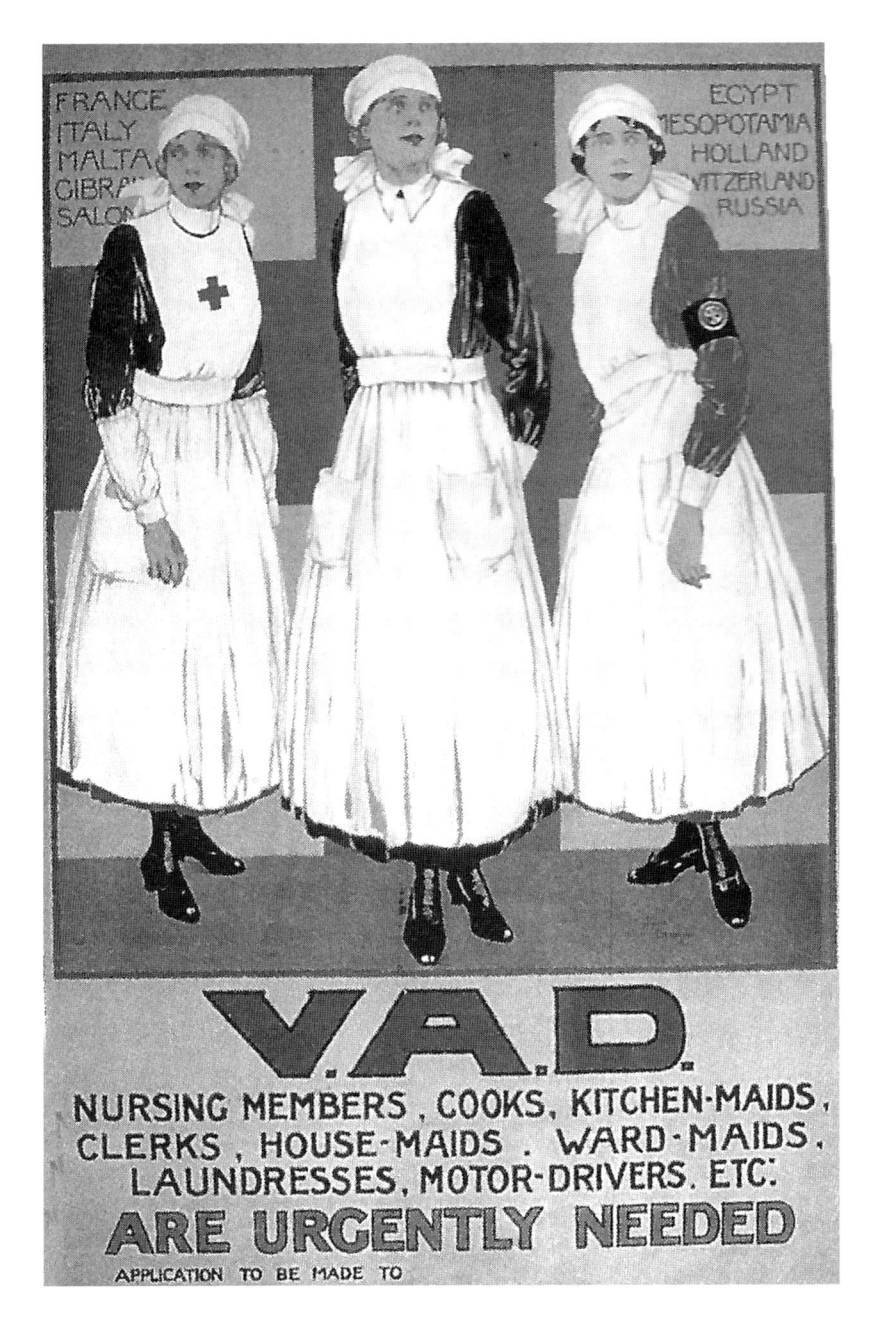

VAD recruitment poster.

nursing scheme. This provided a solution to the problem of finding experienced or trained nurses at very short notice. Further to this, on 16 August 1909 the War Office issued its scheme for the 'Organisation of Voluntary Aid in England and Wales', with a similar scheme for Scotland in December of the same year. By early 1914, 1,757 female detachments and 519 male detachments had been registered with the War Office.[17]

The female detachments varied in size according to local conditions, but for the most part consisted of a commandant, a medical officer, a quartermaster and twenty-two women, two of whom were to be trained nurses, and pre-war the detachments varied in how seriously they took their responsibilities. Some didn't take their responsibilities too seriously, while others were intent on being well-prepared for a role that they might never be called upon to fulfil. The detachments were intended for home service only, to staff auxiliary hospitals and rest stations and they received no payment or salary for these duties; all the women would have been in a position, at least initially, to give their services for free.

Detachments had to meet at least once a month, with many meeting as often as weekly, and women had to work towards gaining certificates in Home Nursing and First Aid within twelve months of joining, and they learned to bandage, to do simple dressings, and the basics of invalid cookery and hygiene. In some areas it was arranged for them to go into local hospitals for a few hours each week to gain an insight into ward work, and due to the low number of men being recruited in certain places, women could also gain experience in outdoor activities, stretcher duties, the transport of sick and wounded and improvisation with whatever came to hand.

When war came, the Red Cross and auxiliary hospitals sprang up rapidly in church halls, public buildings and private houses, accommodating anything from 10 patients to more than 100. The proportion of trained nurses in the units was small and much of the basic work was the responsibility of the VADs: they cleaned, scrubbed and dusted, set trays, cooked breakfasts; they lit fires and boiled up coppers full of washing. They also helped to dress, undress and wash the men, which was of course a big step for young women who may never have been alone and unchaperoned with a member of the opposite sex before, other than their brothers or other family members.

The perils of non-combatants.

During wartime the VAD organization was administered by the Joint War Committee of the British Red Cross Society and the Order of St John and run from Devonshire House in Piccadilly, loaned for the war by the Duke and Duchess of Devonshire. Many of the senior administrators were educated women who had been involved in the movement since its beginning and had a proven record of good organizational skills. There were about 50,000 women involved in the movement immediately before the war, and it is thought that in total somewhere between 70,000 and 100,000 women served as VADs at some time during the war; some for very short periods, others for up to five years.[18]

In August 1914 there were twenty-eight Red Cross detachments in Lincolnshire. The Boston Red Cross with Mrs C. Mawer in charge had the Park Council School ready for the wounded, but was later moved to Holden House. Allan House was also offered, and again Boston people furnished it. All the medical men and Red Cross ladies gave their services free. Holden House and Allan House had a combined total of forty-six beds.

Exceptional devotion was shown to the injured men coming back from the front line. On 21 October 1914 twenty wounded Belgians moved from Lincoln to Boston and were accommodated at Holden House, South Square. Holden House was donated through the

Nurses and patients outside Allen House, Boston.

The nurse in charge was Mrs Healey Johnson, assisted by nurses Stephenson, Smith, Gill, Tuxford, Trevitt and other helpers of the detachment.

kindness of Mrs Farrow. Most of the men had sustained minor injuries; however, some were severe medical cases. They were accompanied by Lieutenant Dickinson, RAMC and were met by local members of the St John Ambulance Brigade. An enthusiastic crowd greeted them at Boston Station.

Funds raised locally supported the hospitals; for example, a jumble sale at Kirton Town Hall raised £25 for Allan House Hospital and £25 for Holden House Hospital. The Kirton Red Cross Sale Committee invited fifty-eight wounded soldiers from Holden House and Allen House to VAD hospitals. Some 2 tons of potatoes were given by a Mr A. Graves for the sale which were quickly bought and given to the Holden and Allen House kitchens.

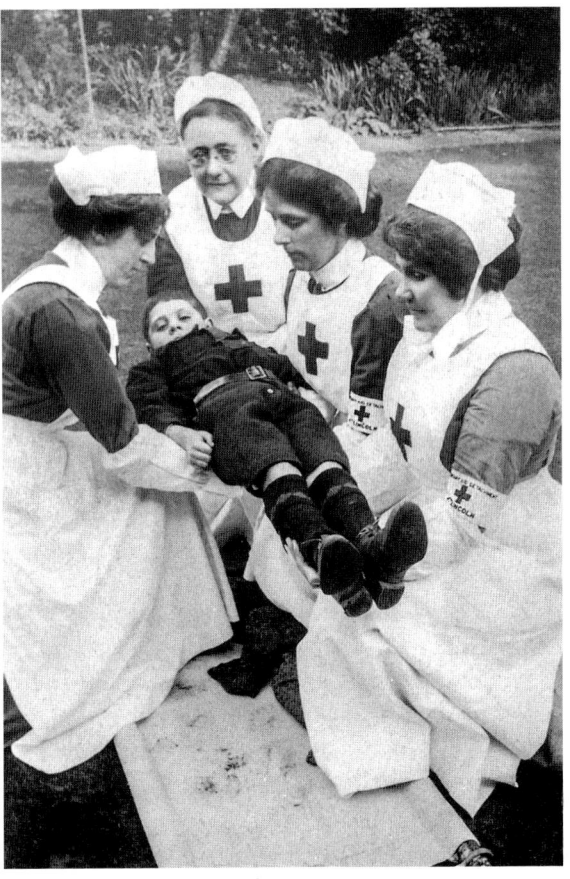

Local VAD nurses patching up a young 'victim'.

Grateful soldiers spent an afternoon at a farm owned by Mr and Mrs Frank Allen, Langrick Bridge, in the parish of Brothertoft. 'It was a right royal time we spent,' remarked one wounded soldier. The soldiers from Holden and Allen House chartered two charabancs and arrived in good time at the farm. An 'excellent' tea was provided, followed by a concert with a 'good' programme being submitted. Songs, recitations and sketches kept the atmosphere 'fun, fast and furious'. 'The party returned home in good time, and there was no mistaking the enjoyment they had experienced.'[19]

Even dogs are welcome in this home.

    More wounded but grateful men were entertained when Private Kilfour of the Cameron Highlanders Regiment, who was undergoing treatment at Holden House, headed a procession of wounded soldiers playing his bagpipes. Once at their destination, West Skirbeck House, a most welcome reception was the order of the day. Games including cricket, croquet and bowls had been thoughtfully arranged by their hosts. Tea was provided on the lawn.

    Kindness was certainly repaid to the people of Boston with this outstanding story of bravery by a wounded soldier from Holden House. Fred Walter Good was a 5-year-old boy who decided to take an unexpected dip in the River Haven at the back of the VAD

Women Unionists' garden party at Spalding.

hospital. Fred, whose parents lived on Spain Lane, Boston, had a narrow escape when he fell into the water while playing on the bank. Crying out, his distress was heard by Private Stone of the Leicestershire Regiment who went to ascertain the cause. Seeing the boy in the water, he at once got down the bank and, without divesting himself of any clothing, bravely plunged into the water and saved the boy, holding him up and eventually bringing him to the side. Meanwhile, an assistant at the market place informed the local duty policeman PC Batchelor, who quickly arrived on the scene. The men got the boy out and then took him home, apparently only a little the worse for his swim.

Recognition was received when the Secretary of State[20] for War issued a list of workers in connection with the Joint War Committees of the British Red Cross Society and the Order of St John of Jerusalem in England who had rendered valuable nursing services in connection with the war. Recipients included Nurse Miss A. Staffurth, VAD Holden House, Boston. Other Lincolnshire nurses mentioned in dispatches, as listed in the *Grimsby Daily Telegraph* of 22 March 1918, were as follows:

LINCOLNSHIRE NURSES MENTIONED IN DISPATCHES

Miss E.A. Bell, Grantham Auxiliary Hospital

Nurse Miss A. Bond, Rutland and General Infirmary, Stamford

Nurse Miss M. Carter, Red Cross Auxiliary Hospital, Holden House, Boston

Nurse Miss M. Currington, Johnson Auxiliary Hospital, Spalding

Sister Miss M.G. Dawson, Stamford Rutland and General Infirmary

Quartermaster Miss R.E. Dawson, Red Cross Auxiliary Hospital, Holden House, Boston

Quartermaster Mrs F. Heath, Sleaford Auxiliary Hospital

Assistant Quartermaster Miss A. Ingoldby, Sleaford Auxiliary Hospital

Assistant Quartermaster Miss G. Mann, Horbling

Auxiliary Hospital, Folkingham
Mrs A. Picker, Sleaford Auxiliary Hospital
Nurse Miss E. Pool, Bourne Auxiliary Hospital
Sister Miss G. Praeger, Stamford Rutland and General Infirmary
Lady Superintendent and Nurse Mrs E.H. Pretty, Grantham VAD Hospital, Grantham Barracks
Matron Miss E. Pugh, Easton Hall, Grantham
Senior Quartermaster Miss L. Staffurth, Red Cross Auxiliary Hospital, Holden House, Boston
Quartermaster Mrs E.F. Thompson, Grantham Auxiliary Hospital
Miss D. (late Commandant VAD) Welby, Easton Hall Auxiliary Hospital, Grantham

Another nurse mentioned in dispatches was Nurse Ruck from Eastville. Nurse Ruck trained as a nurse at the Leeds General Infirmary where she was enrolled as a Territorial and was mobilized shortly after the outbreak of war. She commenced her military duties at the Fishmongers' Hall, London, later at the City of London Military Hospital and Beckett's Park, Leeds and was drafted to France in January 1915.

The most high-profile death of a Red Cross volunteer was that of Mrs Frances Staniland. Earlier in the war, Frances, the mother of four sons, had lost her brother-in-law Geoffrey and more tragically her husband, Captain Meaburn Staniland, late town clerk of Boston and captain of the 1/4th Lincolnshires. The illness that killed Frances was of only five days' duration and was a double infection of scarlet fever and German measles. Dr Walker of Peterborough was called in; however, Mrs Staniland passed away at 5.30 pm at the age

Nurse Ruck, who was mentioned in dispatches.

Mrs Staniland and her four children.

of 32. Frances was vice-president of the local VAD of Red Cross nurses and had already devoted much time and work to Boston.

Women also paid the ultimate sacrifice by giving their lives in the service of others. During the war 128 nursing members, 11 general service members and 6 Joint War Committee hospital members were killed. More than 100 other VAD members not directly working for the Red Cross were also killed. The Roll of Honour contains records of the deaths of 498 Joint War Committee members. Although the cause is not clear, most of the deaths recorded were probably due to health problems associated with old age. Examples of disease included cerebrospinal meningitis, tuberculosis and septic poisoning due to contact with infected wounds. It was tuberculosis that claimed the life of 34-year-old Mabel Sargisson who died on 1 January 1918. Mabel, a keen sports player who worked as a VAD at Allen House, was diagnosed with TB in November 1917.

We do know that eight VADs died in the sinking of SS *Osmanieh* on 31 December 1917. Contracted as hired transport by the Royal Navy, the boat struck a mine laid by the German U-boat *UC-34* and quickly sank, killing 199 people including 8 VAD nurses. They are commemorated at the Alexandria (Hadra) war memorial cemetery.[21]

The most commonly-stated cause of death was pneumonia as a complication of the so-called 'Spanish flu' pandemic of 1918.

Dr William M. Hunt's labour of love *A Town Remembers* poignantly recalls the sacrifice of two women who lived in Boston:

> Frances Merchant was a civilian nurse who died on October 22nd, 1914. She was married to Captain John Victor Merchant of Tower Road, Boston. She was 49 years of age when she died.
> Frances, known as 'Fanny', was born in Nottingham on July 26th 1865, the daughter of a baker and confectioner... Fanny married Sergeant Victor Merchant of the Lincolnshire Regiment at Lenton Church, Nottingham in 1885...they came to live in Boston in 1902 and she was appointed a district nurse.
> Frances died as a consequence of performing her nursing duties. There had been a number of cases of typhoid

(3).   COPY.   ii

FORM OF DECLARATION OF LOYALTY

TO BE SIGNED BY V.A.D. MEMBERS APPOINTED BY THE
JOINT V.A.D. SELECTION BOARD TO HOSPITALS AND
FORMATIONS OTHER THAN THOSE UNDER THE MILITARY
AUTHORITIES OR JOINT WAR COMMITTEE.

J.W. 7.   DEVONSHIRE HOUSE,
                                                  LONDON.

TO THE JOINT V.A.D. SELECTION BOARD.

I, ...

      of..

hereby agree to serve as a........................

    1)   I declare that I am a British Subject and am loyal to His Majesty King George.

    2)   I am fully aware that while serving I am under the Officers of the Unit to which I am appointed and that I am subject to Discipline.

    3)   During the period of my Service I will devote my whole time and skill to the good of the Sick and Wounded, and will obey all orders given me by the Officers of the Unit to which I am appointed.

    4)   I engage to do all in my power to uphold the good name of the V.A.D. Organisation and to do nothing which might in any way bring discredit upon my uniform.

    5)   In the event of my death or injury by accident or otherwise neither I nor my relations or others shall have any claim whatsoever against the British Red Cross Society or the Order of St. John in respect to my decease or injury or otherwise.

    6)   I undertake to inform the Joint V.A.D. Selection Board at once if for any reason I leave the Unit to which I have been appointed by them.

Dated this............day of..............191

Signature.

Address.   Member of

Witness to Signature.

Address.

N.S.V.W.14.

Terms of Service with the Voluntary Aid Detachments of the British Red Cross Society and the Order of St. John.

MILITARY HOSPITALS—NURSING MEMBERS.

Terms of Service.—One month's probation, and if considered suitable, contract for six months' service in the same hospital.

Pay for first seven months at rate of £20 per annum.

    (a) Members who enter immediately on a second or subsequent term of six month's employment are to be paid at the rate of £22 10s. per annum, instead of £20 per annum from the first day of the further time of employment.

    (b) Members who agree to serve for so long as required will be eligible for further increments of £2 10s. each half-year until they reach a maximum rate of £30 per annum. The first increment takes effect six months after the date on which they become entitled to £22 10s. per annum.

Uniform Allowance.—£2 10s. every six months after first month's probation. This is paid on signing or renewing contract.

Other Allowances.—Quarters, food, washing, travelling.

Age Limit.—23 to 42 for Foreign Service.
    21 to 48 for Home Service.

Service under the Joint Committee of the British Red Cross Society and Order of St. John Abroad.

Terms of Service.—Members considered suitable after one month's probation, and who wish to remain, are required to sign a declaration to serve six months, including the month's probation.

Allowances.—There is no salary and no uniform allowance, but all expenses such as Travelling, Board, Lodging and Washing are paid from the date the member leaves home.

Age Limit.—19 to 50.

Note.—Women must write legibly when filling in the form, and give their address in full, stating the county in which they reside.

Women who have already volunteered, and have not been accepted, should not apply again.

V.A.D. Officers and members must not answer this appeal, but must send up their names in the usual way, through their officers.

All who have worked for the sick and wounded at any time during the War, and have since taken up other work, are asked to consider whether they would not serve their Country best by again devoting to the service of our soldiers at this critical moment the knowledge and experience they have already gained as V.A.D.'s.

The Director-General particularly requests women who are already in employment, and who answer this appeal, not to give up their work until called upon by the Authorities. For full particulars and forms of application, write to the Director, Women's Section, National Service Department.

(13600) 8736.437. 1000. 5/17. M. & S.

Terms of service for a Voluntary Aid Detachment.

WOMEN'S LAND ARMY.

CONDITIONS AND TERMS.

There are three Sections of the Women's Land Army:
- (1). AGRICULTURE.
- (2). TIMBER CUTTING.
- (3). FORAGE.

If you sign on for A YEAR and are prepared to go wherever you are sent, you can join which Section you like.

THE PROMISE—
- To serve in the Land Army for ONE YEAR.
- To come to a Selection Board when summoned.
- To be medically examined, free of cost.
- To be trained if PASSED by the Selection Board and take up work after due notice.
- TO BE WILLING TO GO TO WHATEVER PART OF THE COUNTRY YOU ARE SENT.

THE GOVERNMENT PROMISES—
1. AN INITIAL WAGE to workers of 20/- a week. After they have passed an efficiency test the wages given are 22/- a week and upwards.
2. A short course of FREE INSTRUCTION if necessary.
3. FREE UNIFORM.
4. FREE MAINTENANCE in a Depot for a term not exceeding 4 weeks if the worker is OUT OF EMPLOYMENT through no fault of her own.
5. FREE RAILWAY travelling, when taking up or changing Employment.

——— OR, ———

If you sign on for only six months, you can join the Agricultural and Timber Cutting Sections, but not the Forage.

THE PROMISE—
- To serve in the Land Army for 6 MONTHS.
- To come to a Selection Board when summoned.
- To be medically examined, free of cost.
- To be trained if PASSED by the Selection Board and take up work after due notice.
- TO BE WILLING TO GO TO ANY PART OF THE COUNTRY YOU ARE SENT.

THE GOVERNMENT PROMISES—
1. AN INITIAL WAGE of 20/- per week.
2. UNIFORM FREE.
3. FREE MAINTENANCE in a Depot for a term not exceeding 2 weeks, if the worker is out of employment through no fault of her own.
4. FREE RAILWAY travelling when taking up or changing employment.

No training is given, therefore the initial wage is only 20/-. Should the worker be able to pass an efficiency test, it will be raised to 22/-. Two weeks' maintenance in a depot only is allowed.

Terms of service for the Women's Land Army.

Nurses tending to the wounded on board a sinking ship.

fever in the town that she had been attending and she contracted the disease. She was bed-ridden with the illness for three weeks but then pneumonia developed and she died on the evening of Thursday, October 22nd, 1914.

A very large crowd attended her funeral on Sunday, October 25th, including some 30-40 Red Cross nurses... One tribute was from the Belgian Soldiers of Holden House which was a brass shield, mounted on oak. On the shield was engraved: 'A Souvenir des Blesses Belges en traitement a l'hopital de la Croix Rouge a Boston'.

The late Mrs Merchant and her husband, Victor.

The *Boston Guardian* included a touching eulogy:

> Nurse Merchant, ever since her appointment in 1902, has enjoyed the love and affection of the people of the town, and her death is universally mourned. She was a devout public servant, solicitous to the suffering, and

> most faithful in the discharge of her duty. She performed her duty in the quietest and most unostentatious manner, without the slightest attempt at parade, and in a way that won the admiration of all who knew her. In all weathers we were accustomed to see her visiting the different districts in the town. No one knew whence she came or whither she went. As we walked along the streets, or stood upon the side walk, and saw the little lady cycling on her mission of mercy, we said, 'that is Nurse Merchant', that is all we said, but it was not a fraction of a part of that which was felt. She was beloved by the whole town, and the whole town mourns her death.
>
> In addition to her husband, she left four children, three daughters, Queenie, Evelyn and Grace, and a son Staff Sergeant Victor Merchant, who was at that time serving in the British Expeditionary Force in France or Belgium with the Royal Engineers.[22] [23]

Susan Elizabeth Stephenson, also working with the Red Cross, died on 11 April 1916. She is buried in St Mary's churchyard, Old Leake, and commemorated on the Holy Trinity Church war memorial, Spilsby Road:

> Susan was born in Wrangle in mid-1868 and lived with her family at Lowgate where her father was a farmer with a holding of 20 acres. By 1901 she had trained as a nurse…she returned to Boston and became a district nurse. At the outbreak of the war she was appointed sister-in-charge at Allan House Red Cross Auxiliary Hospital, Carlton Road. At the time of her death she was living at 14, Spilsby Road, and so Holy Trinity was her local parish church and where she was a member of the congregation.
>
> Nurse Stephenson's demise was very sudden. She was taken ill with gastritis in the evening of Thursday, April 6th and an operation was conducted the next morning. She died a few days later at her home. Her funeral took place at Old Leake on Thursday, April

13th… In addition to family mourners there was a large contingent of nurses from Allan House Hospital, the St. John Ambulance Brigade and wounded soldiers from the hospital. A tribute was paid to her in the form of a poem written by one of her former patients:

In Memoriam

A friend in need is a friend indeed,
But now that friend's departed,
We long to hear her cheerful voice,
She's left us grievous hearted,
No call was sent to her in vain,
True sister, to all brothers,
A loving friend to old and young,
She gave her life to others.

From morn till night, she worked so hard,
With cheerful smiling face;
Her love was felt, her every word,
Was never out of place.
It's hard to lose an angel fair,
Whom God has sent to love,
Her work is done, now she has flown,
To God's bright home above.
Sergeant Evans,
Northumberland Fusiliers.[24][25][26]

Many VADs put themselves into dangerous situations to aid sick and wounded soldiers. This bravery resulted in many volunteers receiving awards for their service. The 1914 star was introduced in 1917 for service in France and Flanders between 5 August and 22 November 1914. This award was given to around twenty VADs. In 1919 a clasp bearing the same dates was authorized and given to personnel who had been under fire between those dates.

Authorized in 1918, the 1914/15 star was awarded to personnel who saw service in France and Flanders from 23 November 1914 to 31 December 1915, and to personnel who saw service in any other operational theatre from 5 August 1914 to 31 December 1915. The 1915 star was awarded to around 800 VADs.

It is easy to forget the female role in what was essentially a 'man's war'. The Great War was a catalyst for women's liberation, a drive towards equality and a certain acceptance in areas traditionally dominated by men.

Thank you to all the women of Boston who gave up so much, lest we forget.

Proverbs 31:20: 'She stretcheth out her hand to the poor; Yea, she reacheth forth her hands to the needy.'

CHAPTER FOUR

Fighting on the Land

'Here's to the day, this is the day'

A favourite toast among German officers for some years prior to the war was 'Here's to the day' referring, of course, to the day when war would be declared on Britain: 'this is the day.'

'Now the cloud has burst, the sword drawn and the cannon rattle, Boston like every city, town and hamlet in the British Isles is getting its quota of excitement,' wrote a reporter for the *Boston Standard*.

It was now a chance for two of the greatest powers on earth to pit their military wits against each other so 'this day' dawned on the people of Boston when Britain declared war on Germany on 4 August 1914. At this time Lord Kitchener, Secretary of State for War, believed that manpower was key in winning the war. One famous initiative was the formation of the Pals regiments that were raised locally up and down the country to enable Kitchener's demands to be met and men from the same town or area were able to serve together. Although Boston held regular recruitment drives, a Pals regiment was never formed in the town, the nearest Pals regiments being raised in Grimsby as the 'Grimsby Chums' and the 11th Reserve in Lincoln.

Dissecting regiments and battalions in any major conflict can be complicated. For clarity, this chapter is divided into the roles of the Territorial Force (later known as the Territorial Army) and the men who served with Kitchener's New Army, those who 'answered the country's call'.

The Territorials

In 1914 the fledgling Territorial Force was a direct result of the Haldane Reforms, named after the then Secretary State for War, Sir Richard Burdon Haldane. The reforms required that the regular army should serve overseas and the Territorial Force share in home defence.

Lincolnshire was the home of two volunteer battalions, the 4th forming a brigade with the 5th (each was later assigned the name 1/4th and 1/5th respectively) which was from north Lincolnshire, and the 4th and 5th Leicesters. The second brigade was from Nottinghamshire and Derbyshire, known collectively as the Sherwood Foresters. The third brigade was made up of two battalions, each of the South and North Staffordshires. Grouped together, these were known as the North Midland Division, the lives of its men intrinsically linked forever, both in life and in death.

Sir Richard Burdon Haldane.

The 1/4th Lincolns' companies were based in towns and cities as listed below:

- A Company Lincoln
- B Company Grantham
- C Company Boston (this chapter centres on this company and the Boston men of the 1/5th)
- D Company Stamford
- E Company Lincoln
- F Company Spalding
- G Company Horncastle
- H Company Lincoln

The Boston Company of the Territorial Artillery

The Boston Company of the Territorial Artillery, which was almost unique at the time in being at full strength, had been ordered back to the town from their annual camp at Bridlington where the men would be trained in drilling, company drill, musketry training and range practice. By the night of 4 August they were assembled in the new drill hall on Main Ridge, Boston. Serving with the Territorials was John Stanton Thomas whose grandfather served with the volunteers when they were formed in 1860 and his father who joined in 1888.

The following day sixty soldiers of the East Yorkshire Cycle Corps arrived in the town and were billeted in St John's School.[27] The Boston Company, C Company, was based at the Drill Hall, Main Ridge, Boston (B Troop, Lincolnshire Yeomanry and the 1st Lincolnshire Battery RFA were also based there) and commanded by Captain Meaburn Staniland, the prominent town clerk who was described in the *Boston Guardian* as 'one of the town's gallant eight'[28] by having the distinction of being a Boer War hero, who received orders to march to Lincoln with his men.

On the Thursday the soldiers of Boston paraded through the town with the Excelsior Band leading the way with patriotic

Boston members of the Lincolnshire Imperial Yeomanry, who had been called up.

The rallying-place for the Boston Rifles: Mainridge, Boston.

Boston Territorials in camp at Bridlington.

crowds waving flags. Staniland marched via Sleaford with his men to join the 4th Battalion, Lincolnshire Regiment which was a unit of the Territorial Force with their HQ in Lincoln.

Meanwhile, back in Boston, the town's other volunteer force, the Boston Battery, under the command of Major Lamb, Lieutenants O.B. Giles and S.C. Wright, together with instructors Sergeants Asher and Bodimead, with its six guns, baggage wagons, etc. marched to the Great Northern railway station amid vociferous cheering from the huge crowds that lined the route from beginning to end, via Pen Street, Bargate, Market Place and West Street. In all, the battery numbered 145 men and 150 horses, headed by the brass

Captain Meaburn Staniland, commander of C Company.

C Company passing over Boston Town Bridge, 7 August 1914.

Boston Territorials (group).

band. The Boston Battery would reunite with the 4th in Luton a few weeks later.

On 8 August 543 mobilized reservists joined from the depot at Lincoln, where they had already been fitted out with clothing and equipment. Several days were then spent in strenuous training for service overseas. Men from all over Lincolnshire including Boston eagerly joined up at the depot, 116 of these volunteering to serve overseas. Newspapers from all over the county of Lincolnshire paid tribute to their patriotism. Schools and public buildings within Lincoln had been requisitioned for billeting.

On the afternoon of the 10th, the colours of the 4th Battalion Lincolnshire (Territorial) Regiment had been deposited in the county cathedral for safe-keeping. The two flags were conveyed to the 'mother' church of the diocese by Captain G.R. Sills. At the entrance to the green stretching before the great west doors the company divided and took up positions on either side of the pathway leading to the cathedral. Proud bearers of the colours marched

Boston Artillery (group).

Fighting on the Land 121

The 1/4th Battalion's NCOs. (Photograph from Captain Staniland's Journey*)*

Members of the Reserve Artillery Battery. Left to right: R.W. Marris, J.B. Jessop, A. Pocklington and G. Cressey.

Regimental Colour
4th Battalion TF
The Lincolnshire Regiment
1909-1967

The colours of the 1/4th.

down to the western doors, where they were met by the dean of Lincoln and the chancellor. The dean, Dr Fry, comforted the men by telling them he would pray for them at least three times, especially for any men who were going to the front. The colours would remain there until the battalion wanted them back. At this time, the Territorials were under no obligation to serve overseas; those who did volunteered and were attested at Luton at a later date.

Anticipating a move, the battalion was under orders to leave Lincoln; however, the departure time had not yet been divulged.

On the afternoon of 10 August, the 4th Battalion (and the 5th from Grimsby) reported mobilization complete and on the 11th entrained for Belper, the war station of the Lincolnshire and Leicestershire Brigade. Over the next few days Captain Staniland and his men trained mainly en route, marching with full equipment. Although their stay was short, Belper was hospitable to the Boston lads who poured into the town of an evening. Permission was given to the men to go into town each evening until 9.30 pm, bringing Belper to life with soldiers. When payday arrived, the money flowed freely into the coffers of the local pubs. Public baths were open to the soldiers free of charge; a welcome reward after long training marches in the summer heat. The local cinema admitted soldiers in uniform at half price; they then enjoyed the grounds of the Belper Rowing Club alongside the River Derwent. Complementing the scenery was the band of the 4th serving up an exceptional programme.

On 15 August, Staniland with the rest of the 4th moved to Luton, which for several months was the home of the North Midland Division; the 5th were also billeted in the town. Some billeted in factories, others in empty houses, while a certain proportion of men, to their great delight, were fortunate enough to be billeted in private houses.

Territorials marching through Belper.

At the end of August Captain Staniland went back home to Boston and appealed for fifty more C Company volunteers, enticing men with the highly 'probable' chance that the whole of the Lincolnshire Territorials would be sent to Egypt, Malta or Gibraltar. Inviting the men in person, Staniland was at the drill hall on the last Saturday of the month from 11.00 am to 1.00 pm. An enthusiastic captain fully explained the terms of service to the eighty men in attendance, including the mayor and Sergeant Stephens. More than 170 men rushed forward including 'the best footballers in the town' and were duly examined by the medical officer. Surplus to requirements were a further seventeen men who had passed a medical; however, the quotas had been filled.

Lieutenant J.S. Simons of Willoughby, officer of the 5th Lincolnshires.

Lincolnshire Territorial with a Long Lee-Enfield rifle.

A group of Lincolnshire 1/5th Territorials pictured outside their billets.

Fighting on the Land 125

Boston district recruiting rally with the Wrangle and Kirton boys leaving Boston station for Lincoln.

A letter of thanks was received by the *Lincolnshire and Boston Standard* from Captain Staniland:

4th Lincoln Regt., Luton

September 1st, 1914

Sir, may I make use of your paper to thank all those in Boston who so splendidly responded to the Mayor's appeal issued the other day for 50 recruits for service abroad with 'C' Company, 4th Lincoln Regt.

Although the appeal was only issued for a couple of days, I am proud to say that I not only got the fifty men I required, but could, had they wanted, have had 100 more.

We here are all very proud of Boston's response, and all of the 50 men it has sent us, and are only sorry that there is not much room in the Company for all those others who offered themselves.

Yours, etc.
M. STANILAND
Commanding 'C' Company,
4th Lincoln Regiment.

Second Lieutenant Basil Wood of the 4th Reserve.

Similarly an appeal was made by Lieutenant Giles of the Boston Battery who required another forty-four men to complete establishment.

Eagerly awaiting their next move, the Boston lads were tiring of Luton, especially when given the unpleasant but compulsory anti-typhoid inoculation. In their keenness to get the men ready, the army introduced a new work scheme including night operations, which took the form of trench-digging, ensuring the soldiers were ready for the front. Subsequently, their free time dwindled and with it much of the entertainment raised by the locals died a natural death. Restricting their alcohol intake, it was decided to give public orders

Training for trench warfare: practising rudimentary bayonet work. Charging the trenches, the men endeavoured to transfix scraps of card placed on sacks.

to the Luton landlords that no drink was to be supplied to the Territorials after 9.00 pm. Instead, the church erected marquees along with the local YMCA so that the men could sit down, write letters and read. Earning the football bragging rights, the Boston boys beat the 4th and 5th Leicester Regiments 4–0.

1/5th trench-digging practice in Luton.

The king inspecting a 'perfect' trench...

... the reality was often quite different.

Private F. Jessop in a rare letter to his brother gave a very detailed account of the movements of the 4th and an insight into his short tenure in the army so far:

> We get plenty to eat here [at this point some men had gone back to Lincoln and were staying at the castle], Monday we had roast beef, potatoes, three vegetables, today we had boiled mutton and potatoes. Some days we have stew. We have had plum pudding every day since we have been here.
>
> I thought you would like a diary of what we have done since we left Boston on August 5th:
>
> August 4th – Mobilised.
> August 5th – Left Boston for Lincoln.
> August 10th – Left Lincoln for Belper. Very Hot.
> August 11th – Holiday.
> August 12th – Route march, 10 miles.
> August 13th – Route march, 10 miles.
> August 14th – Marched from Belper to Derby, arrived in Luton.

August 15th – On Sunday morning by train, marched about 15 miles, very hot.

August 16th – Route march, 10 miles, afternoon Company drill.

August 17th – Route march and drill, 8 miles, afternoon Company drill, full equipment, shirt sleeves, very hot.

August 18th – Holiday.

August 19th – Route march, 15 miles, afternoon musketry drill.

August 20th – 8 mile march, shirt sleeves, afternoon Company drill.

August 21st – Route march, 18 miles, shirt sleeves, full equipment, very hot.

August 22nd – Sunday, open air service 2 miles out.

August 23rd – March out 12 miles and drill, afternoon Company drill.

August 24th – March out and drills, 6 miles, afternoon Company drill, shirt sleeves.

August 25th – Route march, got 2 miles out and started raining, turned back, very hot, shirt sleeves. Afternoon inspection by Gen. Ian Hamilton.

August 26th – March out 8 miles and drills, afternoon Company drill.

August 27th – March out 6 miles and drills, afternoon musketry drill.

August 28th – Route march, 18 miles, full dress. Several dropped out, very hot.

August 29th – Open air service, Wardown Park.

August 30th – March out and drills 4 miles. Very hot, shirt sleeves, afternoon Company drill.

August 31st – March out 8 miles and drill, afternoon Company drill.

September 1st – Route march 16 miles.

September 2nd – March out and drill, 7 miles. Afternoon, Company drill.

Standing proudly in front of Major General Sir Stuart-Wortley (see photograph on next page), the men's tiring work paid off when the general praised the 'smart and soldierly' bearing of all ranks. Colonel Jessop later thanked the battalion for their smartness at the inspection.

Buoyed by the comments of Major General Wortley, the men of C Company were bestowed a further tribute when the whole North Midland Division was inspected by Lord Kitchener at the end of September 1914. Although the morning started off cloudy, it did not dampen the spirits of the men whose chests puffed out when Colonel Jessop's voice rang out the command: '4th Lincolns, general salute, present arms.' Breaking through the clouds, the bright sun added lustre to the sight of the Royal Artillery, Royal Garrison Artillery, Royal Army Medical Corps, Northants Yeomanry, Field Transport, Notts and Derby Infantry Brigade, Staffordshire Infantry Brigade and Lincoln and Leicester Infantry Brigade, all in line awaiting the arrival of the revered lord.

The honour of the first corps to be inspected fell to the 4th Lincolns. Kitchener was accompanied by his staff together with General Wortley and Colonel Jessop who inspected the officers formed in strict line in front of the battalion, and then passing along the flank of A and B companies, passed through the proud Boston men of C Company, known affectionately by the people at home as the 'Boston Terriers'.

Major General the Honourable Edward James Montagu-Stuart-Wortley, CB, CMG, DSO, MVO (31 July 1857–19 March 1934) (centre) with his officers.

Commander of the 1/4th Colonel J.W. Jessop.

Sadly the Boston lads suffered their first casualty when 34-year-old Private A.E. Perkins died at Luton after he was taken ill at dinner time and died in the evening in the Wardown Park Hospital, Luton. According to accounts he was a very popular man and prior to the war had worked for Peck and Sons at their Borough Ironworks. He had served in the Territorials for 18 years.

The men were given orders to depart for France and leave was granted; leaving Boston for the 'last time' the men were given a rousing send-off. Disappointingly for the men, that order was cancelled and the expected departure on 30 October never happened. Shortly afterwards the men moved to Stansted, Essex. Bad weather over the next three months deprived the men of the rigorous training they had had in Luton, impeding the structured training schedules. A flu epidemic welcomed the men into the New Year 1915 with hundreds of men being placed on the sick list. Despite these concerns, although anxious to arrive at the front, the men understood the need to protect the coast from any surprise German attacks. Stansted was jocularly described as being 'at the end of the map' but in spite of the humour the men were billeted in houses, schools and local buildings, in better conditions than some of the 5th had been used to in Luton.

Meanwhile in Boston, what work could be found for the unemployed men? Extensive encampment works at Belton Park, Grantham required manpower to complete. Relieving the unemployment problem in the town, 300 workers of all classes had left Boston to work there. Those without jobs were chiefly fitters and turners who had been employed by the Boston Deep Sea Company. Many skilled men, rather than be without work, acquired labouring jobs. This opportunity provided an unexpected income for the families who found their finances impacted by the war.

Boston was also mobilizing a strong and evidently efficient town guard. At the Boston Borough Police Court the magistrate made the usual declaration to act as special constables during the period of the war. Numbering between 200 and 300 strong, the town guard drilled and trained under their respective sergeants, most of whom had already served in the armed forces.

Private A.E. Perkins: the first recorded death of a Boston man from C Company.

The 4th and 5th Lincolnshires were officially formed at Luton in January 1915 and became part of 177 Brigade of the 59th Division which was commanded by Brigadier General H.B. McCall. The next few weeks were devoted principally to the strenuous work of platoon, company and battalion drill.

On 19 February 120 proud men from Boston, part of a full-strength company of 170 officers and men, stood as the king inspected the whole division at Hallingbury Park. Orders for embarkation to the continent arrived; however, the grateful men were given leave to spend time with their families, some saying farewell for the last time, perhaps paying a final visit to the Electric Theatre with their sweethearts to watch the ever-popular cinema artist Charlie Chaplin.

After just seven months' training the Lincolns proceeded to France under the command of J.W. Jessop and in late February/early March of 1915 landed at Le Havre along with the other Lincolnshire Territorials, the 5th Battalion. Both battalions now formed part of 138 Brigade, 46th (North Midland) Division. Two or three days were spent at the rest camp at Le Havre, with some men recovering from severe seasickness while no battles of note were taking place. The contrast between tents on

The newly appointed sergeants had between 200 and 300 men under their direction.

the windswept heights of Normandy in bitterly cold weather in February and the training camp under a hot July sun on the Yorkshire coast at Bridlington can be better imagined than described. The men then travelled to Strazeele, arriving on 9 March. As they passed by, on the roadside were seen several graves marked by little wooden crosses, some of which were roughly painted with the names and regiments of those who had already fallen for their country.

Staggered progress was made by Staniland and his men, along with the rest of the 1/4th and 1/5th as they moved by stages to the front line. On arrival at Ploegsteert they were attached to the 4th Division for instruction in trench duties by the 1st Somerset Light Infantry and the London Rifle Brigade. The 4th Battalion's first casualty of the war occurred when one man was wounded on the 27th. By 1 April, the Boston men were in billets at Le Kirlem and the 1/5th at Steenwerck. A few days later both the 1/4th and 1/5th moved to Dranoutre, Belgium.

Troops waiting to board a ferry for Le Havre.

The time spent at Dranoutre was almost like a holiday camp compared to the horrors to follow, albeit with the usual hallmarks of active soldiering. Dranoutre is very well described in the book *The North Midland Territorials Go to War* by Martin Middlebrook:

SS Empress Queen, *the ship used to transport the men across the Channel.*

Men taking a rest in Ploegsteert Wood in Drocourt-Quéant.

'days were spent resting, drilling, training or on relentless working parties, but there was some free time.' Bailleul was a village just over the French border where a café was available for the purchase of pastries and cakes.

Trench Warfare Begins

Moving on 9 April, the 1/4th entered the front-line trenches just 4 miles away, taking over a portion of the defences for the first time opposite Spanbroekmolen. Finally, their personal war had started.

Standing shoulder-to-shoulder today at Dranoutre are the clean white graves of the fallen men who 100 years ago stood and stared in their 'wretched'[29] trenches over the lines towards the Bavarian regiment. The 1/5th battalion diary gives details of the trenches taken over by the 1/4th and 1/5th battalions. One soldier declared it 'the worst trench of them all', it was also recorded that 'dead bodies are even half exposed in the parados.'[30] Strong smells of sulphur, faeces and rotting flesh permeated the once fresh continental air.

Lance Corporal H.E.J. Sharpe of the 1/4th Battalion wrote to his parents at Rosemount, Witham Bank, Boston the following revealing and amusing letter on 25 April:

Front Line Trenches, Belgium, 'Clifton House'.

My Dear Parents and All,

How do you like my present address? Rather 'high flown', but still you know one cannot be too thankful for even a mud hut just at present, although it is really wonderful how soon one gets accustomed to living (I really mean existing) underground. The little mansion named above is about one yard wide, three yards long and 1½ yards high, built of earth, wood and sheet iron. We (three of us) have a little hole arrangement in one side, with a

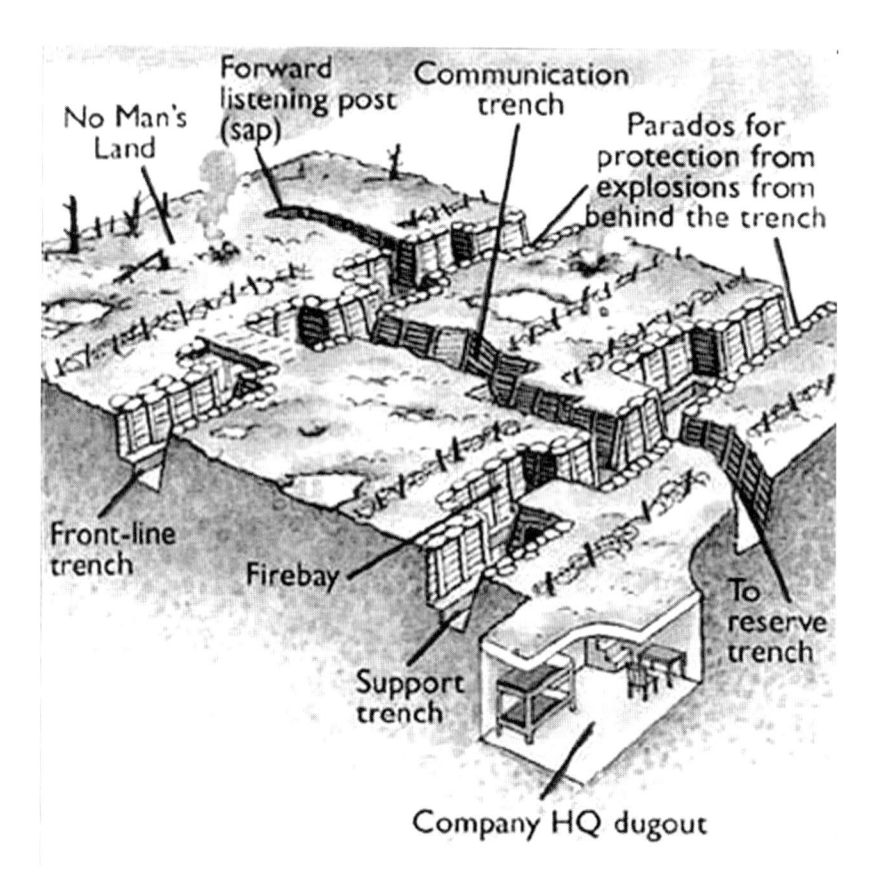

Diagram of a First World War trench.

chimney put up, where we deposit our coke brazier, and in fact we have made ourselves very comfortable, so far as circumstances permit. We took over the house (on a lease, by the way) on Sunday evening about 11.30 pm, together with a small inventory consisting of one saucepan, one empty tin for sugar, one cardboard box and sundry sandbags for bedding.

We are about 120 yards from our old friend 'Mein Herr', but he is not on speaking terms with us at present, although he is very attentive, more especially at dusk and dawn. At dawn he greets us with a tremendous fire of shell ammunition which whizz over us with a great amount of fuss. Our artillery men, naturally, return the compliment, as they consider it one of the virtues of English gentlemen to be under obliga-

Private J.E. Watson who was shot in the buttock during the 1/4th's first tour.

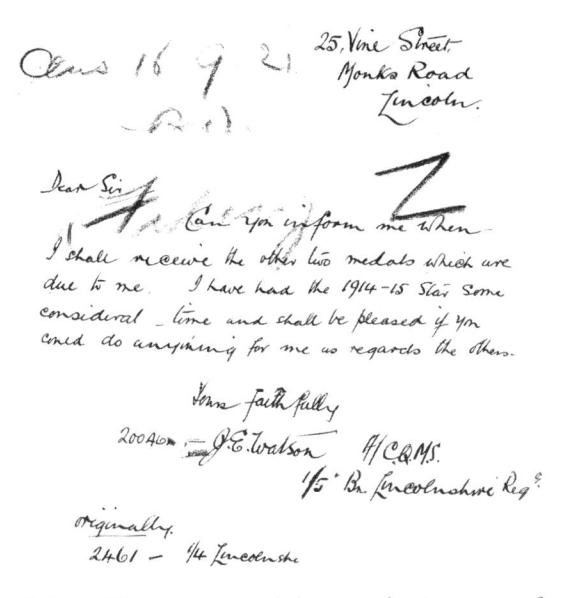

Private Watson survived the war; this is a copy of his letter requesting his war medals.

Private Watson's medical report.

tion to no one. Therefore if the Germans will persist in sending over their little and big 'messengers of love', our fellows reply tenfold on every occasion.

At dusk the 'people over the way' use the small pills by thousands, because, I believe they find their way better and more quickly in the dark.

This, as you are aware, is my first experience of actually being under rifle fire in the trenches, and it reminds me very much of being in the butts down by the river, marking the targets at rifle practice. We had some frightful work since we came up. We are, of course, always working on the improvement of the trench, and when doing so it is quite a recognised thing to find a dead body of a comrade who has to be reburied.

If one uses a most ordinary amount of care here, he is quite safely housed as it were, but what it was at the beginning of the campaign I dare not think. The poor fellows could not have had such elaborate trenches, nor could they have been so looked after in other ways. We have a lot to be thankful for in every way, and no one can imagine how much we feel and appreciate what is done for us now. The experience we are now utilising has been purchased very dearly, and yet one could not possibly meet a more cheerful fellow than a 'Tommy' who has been out here all the while and faced more than his fair share, perhaps, of the music. He has been well-named 'The Incorrigible Tommy'. Were I permitted I could give you instances of men who are out here doing work, cheerfully, which it never occurred to them before to be possible for any human being to accomplish. Yet there it is and always accompanied by a smile and a cigarette, they never omit the 'fag'.

After a few short weeks the Boston men, fresh from home, must have at this time realized the horror of war and the expectation of the misery to follow.

The parents of Private James Chamberlain, C Company and Private E.W. Dallywater, also of C Company, suffered the distress of the 'dreaded' delivery of an official telegram to their home. The parents of these men received graphic, albeit with sympathetic undertones, letters from Major Oliver Cooper and the Reverend J.H. Bateson respectively:

Dear Mr. Chamberlain,

I deeply regret to have to inform you that your son was killed this morning while on sentry duty in the trench. He was firing through a loophole at about 6 a.m. when he was struck by a bullet which passed through his right cheek. I was close by and at first thought that he was not badly injured, but he collapsed at once, and died in a few minutes, and we found that the bullet had also penetrated the right lung and passed right through his body. He was a very good fellow and a good soldier, being always cool and without fear. His comrades in his Platoon and his Officer, Mr. Marris, wish me to express their sympathy with you in your great loss, in which I sincerely join. His personal effects will be sent to you as early as possible. The enclosed notes, value 30 francs, were found in his purse and I thought I had better send these on to you direct.

Yours Faithfully

OLIVER COOPER, Major.

Private James Chamberlain, C Company.

The 18-year-old Private E.W. Dallywater of C Company.

Dear Mr. Dallywater,

I am so sorry to hear through the Rev. A.S. Bishop, our chaplain with the North Midland Division, of the death of your gallant son for his king and country. It may be some consolation to you that he died in doing his duty for his country in the cause of right. You have no doubt had all particulars from Mr. Bishop as to his burial etc. May you have the comfort and help that God alone can supply to bear this heavy trial.

Assuring you of my sincere sympathy and prayers.
Yours Sincerely,

J.H. BATESON (Rev.)

Death swiftly followed at the door of the 1/4th Lincolnshires when on the 13th, two farms held by the 1/4th came under heavy enemy artillery fire. The boys had been caught unawares, with no chance of retaliation. Men from the 1/4th Battalion were in billets near Ypres, their task to keep the men in the trenches well supplied, something that involved frequent journeys across open country exposed to precise enemy fire. A shrapnel shell burst through the roof of the barn one afternoon, quickly followed by another, and the barn was soon under fierce bombardment at Pond Farm. The order was given to head for the dugouts, but Private J.H. Buck, standing outside the door of the barn, Private F. Bridges and Lieutenant G. Staniland of B Company were struck by shells. The latter two were killed outright and Private Buck was so seriously wounded that he had to be taken to hospital where he died the next day.

'Adored by his company' described the affection the men had for Geoffrey Staniland. Private B. Smith, 1/4th Lincs, said in a letter: 'I suppose you will know by now that the battalion has rather tough luck, and we have lost a very valuable officer in Lieut. Staniland. He was such a nice chap.' The Reverend P.O. Ashby presided over a simple burial in a little graveyard, which was pitched on top of the once picturesque hillock, just the other side of the Belgian frontier. At the end of the service the *Last Post* was sounded.

Lieutenant G. Staniland was the son of Robert William Staniland of Hussey House, Boston and the brother of the captain of the Boston Territorial C Company, Meaburn Staniland. Geoffrey Staniland was born around 1881 and he attended Boston Grammar School from the age of 9 from 21 January 1891. His father Robert Staniland was a solicitor and Boston town clerk. Geoffrey moved on to Rugby School and was then articled to his father in Boston. He entered a partnership with Mr S.B. Carnly of Alford and later became a partner in the firm Messrs Allison and Stannard, solicitors at Louth. Geoffrey applied for a commission at the outbreak of war in the 4th Royal Fusiliers and was transferred to the Spalding contingent of the 1/4th Lincolns.[31]

In 1914 Spanbroekmolen was the site of a windmill (*molen* is the Dutch word for 'mill'). At the end of the First

Geoffrey Staniland, brother of C Company commander, Captain Meaburn Staniland.

Battle of Ypres in November 1914 the German front line was established in this location on the high ground of the Messines Ridge. Between then and 7 June 1917 the Germans spent a year and a half developing well-established positions here with concrete bunkers and strong defensive positions. Spanbroekmolen formed a formidable opponent for the Boston men, in stark contrast to their new home just a few hundred yards over the field.

Allied commanders were resolute in their determination to deny the Germans the strategic town of Ypres. Essentially, a salient is a bulge in the forward line and in this case the Boston men were to help defend the saucer-shaped salient of some 15 square miles. Ypres was to the rear of the allies' defensive front-line position in the centre of the 'saucer'. Overlooking the rim, in good higher defensive positions the Germans held the best ground.

Just under a month later on 4 June, Colonel Jessop commanding the 4th Battalion, Major Barrell and Major Cooper left Locre and went to Kemmel village where three Belgian children had been killed by shellfire a week earlier to visit the commander of the 5th Leicesters, Colonel Jones, to arrange the welcome relief of his battalion, including the Boston men in the trenches and those billeted in Dranoutre and Locre.

A German barrage ensued with shells falling in the village and one dropped close to the Leicesters' headquarters. Both colonels left the safety of their HQ as the shells were dropping too close for the comfort of the officers. Exposed in the open, another shell exploded near Colonel Jones and Colonel Jessop, killing Jessop instantly. Major Barrell and an orderly were also hit.

Mourning the death of their commander, the 1/4th Battalion was evidently shaken by the news. Colonel Jessop was a great personality who was missed not just by his own battalion but by the whole brigade. He was buried at Dranoutre on 5 June and his burial was attended by the divisional commander, Major General Wortley, and a large contingent of the Lincoln Territorials.

Arriving at Ouderdom on 22 June and sheltering in bivouac until the 29th, the men moved forward to dugouts in the rat-infested Sanctuary Wood and Maple Cross near the village of Hooge. The next day the 1/4th Lincolnshires relieved the 1st Lincolnshires (regular) and South Lancashires just east of the notorious Sanctuary Wood in trenches known as B4 to B7. Captain

Fighting on the Land 145

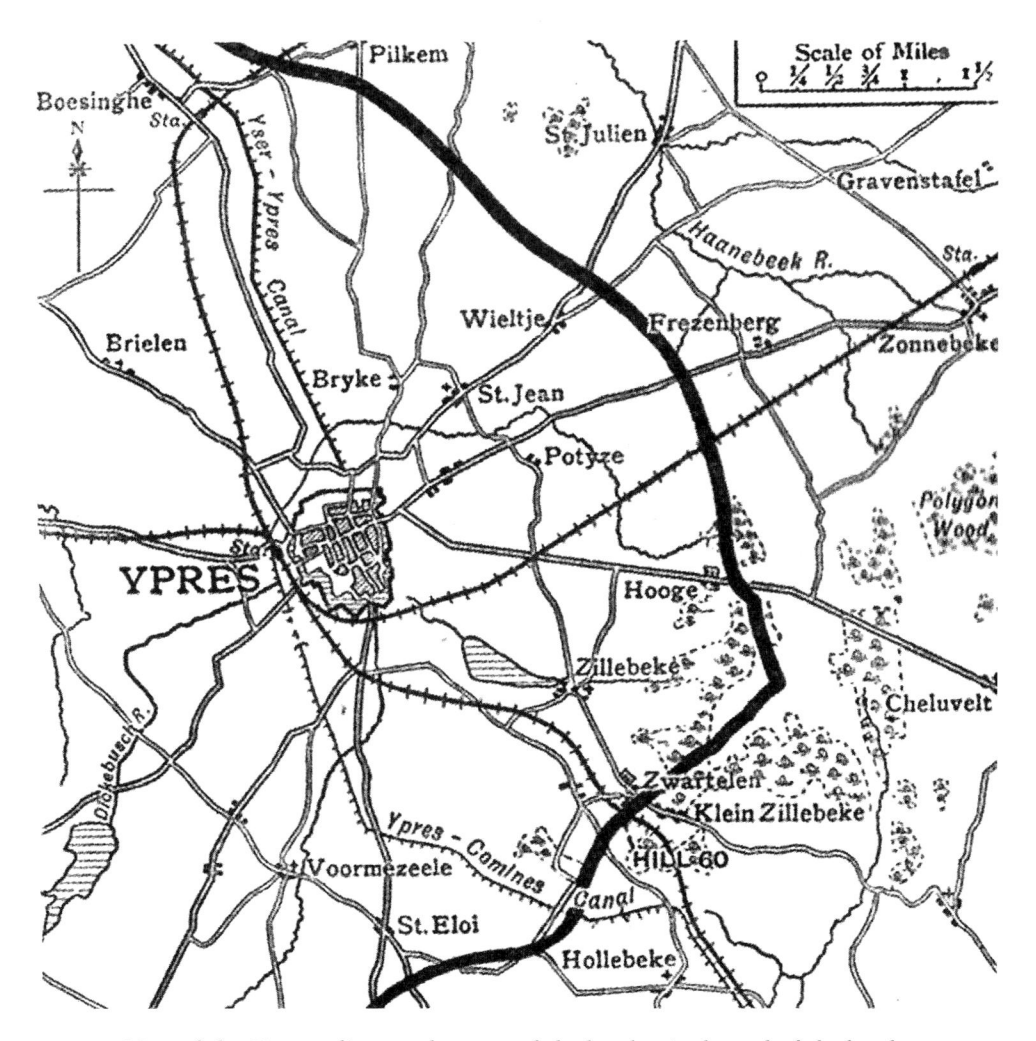

Map of the Ypres salient at the start of the battle. At the end of the battle the salient had been compressed with Ypres itself closer to the front.

Staniland and the Boston men had been assigned to the right-hand front-line trench, B4. According to the diaries, this trench tour was unspectacular for the Terriers; in fact, the next few weeks would see the 1/4th in and out of the front-line trenches. One unfortunate constant for the men was their location, the southern part of Sanctuary Wood or just slightly in front of Armagh Wood.

Boston Battery in Belgium. Top row, left to right: Sergeants G. Smith, F. Stockbridge and H. Hawes. Bottom row: Sergeants G. Hughes, W. Price, S. Emery, T. Preston, A. Hayes, C. Wvendth and Bodimead. The others in the group are Belgian.

Major Barrell, who replaced the popular Colonel Jessop.

A new threat to the wellbeing of the men was the 'whizz-bang', which was the shrieking sound of a 77mm field gun. The peculiar sound of the 'whizz' and the explosion of the 'bang' were simultaneous, catching the men unawares. This was the case with five men from the 1/4th Battalion who were killed near the infamous Hill 60, including Corporal C.H. Burchnall of A Company who lived in Freiston, although in the article 'The Brave Who Are No More' published in the *Boston Standard*, he was presumed to be living at Butterwick.

Corporal Burchnall was commanding a group of men who had been working hard in wretched conditions carrying rations to the front line. By mid-morning

Officers of the 1/4th Lincolns. Back row: Woods(D), G. Staniland(D), C.H. Ellwood, Pennell(W), Newton(W), Marris(W), Dean, Hurst(D), Grunling, Gosling (unconfirmed), Salaman, Ellwood(D), Johnson(D), Bellamy(D), Gray(D), Myers. Middle row: M. Staniland(D), Thompson(D), Sills (unconfirmed), Simpson, Burnell, Jessop(D), Cooper(W), Johnson, Berry, Hart(W), Tetly(W). Front row: Reed(D), Beaulah(W), Burrows, Ellis(W). [D – died; W – wounded.]

Dugouts in Sanctuary Wood, 1915.

the men rested and started to prepare breakfast. The following letter is from Private Woodham, a *Boston Guardian* war reporter:

> The scene at the time was a pleasant one; the men, in various stages of undress, were boiling the water for tea, frying bacon, and making ready for a hearty meal. The morning was sunny and bright, and everyone was in excellent spirits. Corporal Burchnall…was stooping down to pick up a piece of bacon, when a whizz-bang burst some thirty yards away. A piece of shrapnel struck him behind the ear and he fell back unconscious… He only lived half an hour after being hit and never regained consciousness. There seems every reason to believe that his death was a painless one.[32]

His burial was also described by Private Woodham:

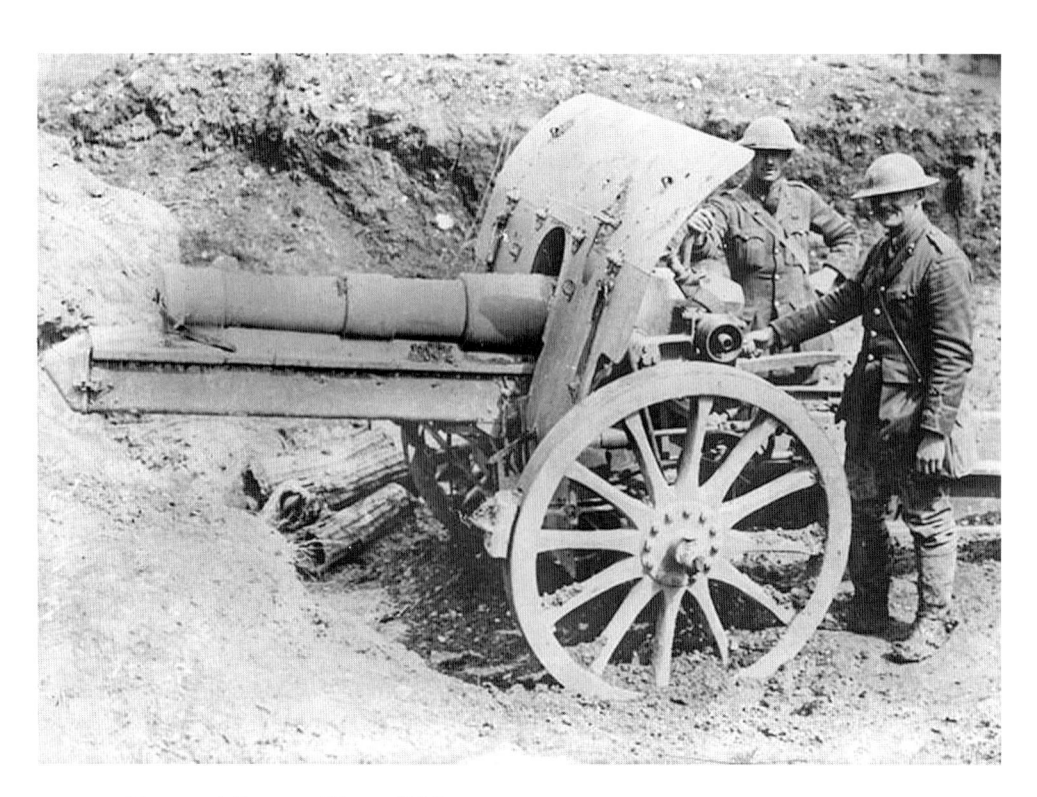

Captured German 77mm field gun.

Fighting on the Land 149

German soldiers at the infamous Hill 60.

In the evening, amid a drizzle of rain, 'Charlie', as he was known to us all, was laid to rest in the little natural cemetery that has grown up by the railway line side, near the spot where he was killed, the last sad ceremony conducted amid the piping of bullets, and the everlasting whirring of shells.

German soldiers blew up a sap in A1 and A2 trenches and mortared the British line at 9.00 am and 6.00 pm on 28 July. Casualties occurred, and then on the 29th at 4.15 pm the 1/4th Battalion was occupying trenches 50 to A7. This was a length of the front line about 650 yards long.

Captain Staniland was inspecting the sentry posts in his company's line; he seemed to be in good spirits as he had been

CORPL. C. H. BURCHNALL.

Corporal C.H. Burchnall, A Company.

on leave a month earlier. The Boston company was holding the extreme right of the battalion frontage when Captain Meaburn Staniland was hit by a German sniper, waiting patiently for his next kill. A lance corporal's letter home, printed in the *Lincolnshire Standard*, describes the moment that Meaburn died:

> I was in charge of a sentry group when the Captain came round. I should say about 3.45am, he stood on the firing platform in order to get a good look over the opposite trenches, as he would invariably have a good look round, and I was getting up at his side when he staggered and fell, a bullet having struck him in the forehead. Myself and two others did all we could for him, but he passed away in the course of about three minutes.

An interview with Rear Admiral Geoffrey Hall adds further intrigue to the death of Meaburn. Rear Admiral Hall was the son of Meaburn's friend and brother-in-law Arthur Hall. He later told his son what really happened: 'It was during the night. He was standing on the step and his last words were "By God, I am going to have a pipe." He struck a match, then came the shot.'[33]

Private W.W. Skinner of the Machine-Gun Section, 7th Lincolnshires, who had been attached to the 1/4th, the son of Mr T.H. Skinner of Church End, Freiston wrote to his mum on 4 August telling her of Meaburn's death:

> I received your letter and paper this morning, you will think me a good long time writing, but I only came out of the trenches early this morning. I have been in a week. We were in with the 4th and 5th Lincolns.
> I expect you will have heard by now about Capt. Staniland being killed. He was killed a few hundred yards from us. Our battalion buried him.

Captain Meaburn Staniland was buried with his brother Geoffrey at Dranoutre, probably at Meaburn's request. In St Botolph's Church in Boston are two memorial plaques, the text on the second reading as follows:

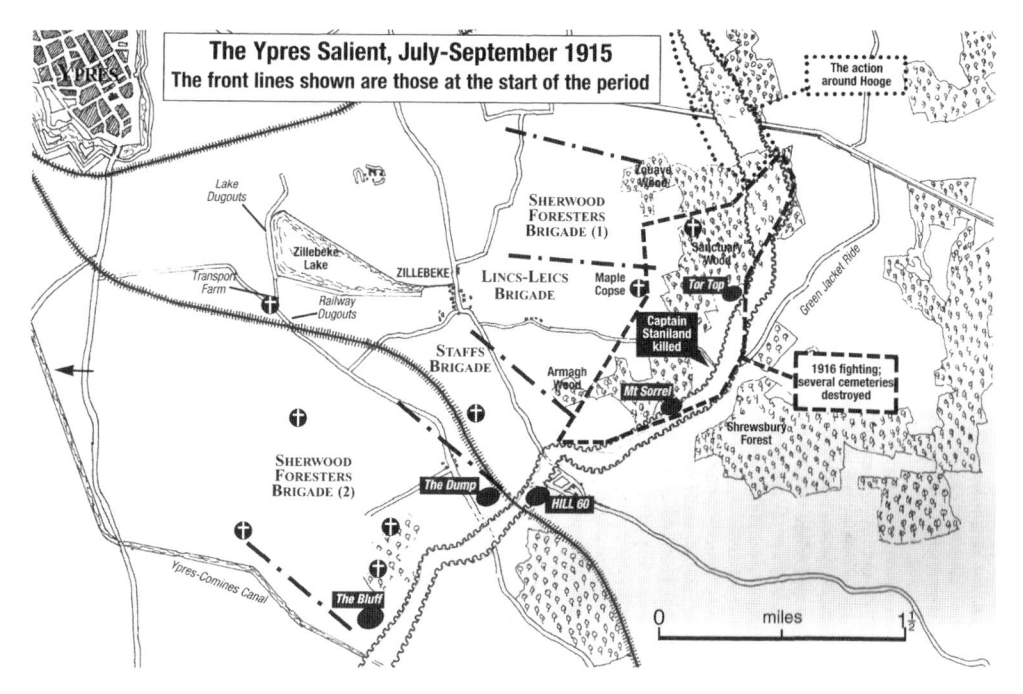

Map courtesy of Martin Middlebrook and Roni Wilkinson.

TO THE GLORY OF GOD AND IN THE LOVING MEMORY OF MEABURN STANILAND CAPTAIN 4TH LINCOLNSHIRE REGIMENT TOWN CLERK OF BOSTON KILLED IN ACTION NEAR HOOGE IN BELGIUM 29TH JULY 1915, AGED 35 YEARS

ALSO OF HIS BROTHER GEOFFREY STANILAND 2ND LIEUT. 4TH LINCOLNSHIRE REGIMENT KILLED IN ACTION AT LINDENHOEK IN BELGIUM 13TH APRIL 1915, AGED 34 YEARS

On a side note, Meaburn's father R.W. Staniland who was the town clerk from 1882 until 1905 when he was succeeded by Meaburn was reappointed town clerk at a special meeting of the Boston Town Council.

    On the 30th the Germans attacked the British line at Hooge and after a ferocious bombardment took some ground from the British. The Lincolnshires, including the Boston men, were kept under heavy bombardment including trench mortar, the shrieking sound of a 77mm field gun and rifle fire. It was also the first time the Germans used the dreaded 'liquid fire' (flame-throwers, German *flammenwerfer*), causing horrific casualties.

It was now time for the Terriers to leave the Ypres Salient for a respite without their inspirational captain, who had recruited some of the men personally and served with others for years previously in the Territorials.

There is one last casualty to mention: that of Sergeant Andrew Crick of Boston, platoon sergeant of No. 1 Platoon, A Company. Some weeks earlier, Sergeant Crick was observing the enemy through a trench periscope when a bullet shattered the glass of the instrument and the splinters flew into his face. He had to go to the hospital to have the shards of glass removed. On 30 September Crick, aged 27, was hit by a 'whizz bang' in the same trench where Captain Staniland had been sniped two months earlier. After five days of pain, he succumbed to his injuries at 7.30 am on 6 October and was buried in Plot 1, Row B of what is now Lijssenthoek Military Cemetery (Remy Siding).

Captain Meaburn Staniland.

By 9 August, the 1/4th found themselves in the Zillebeke dugout (two companies) and the barracks at Ypres (two companies). Records state that the enemy's artillery fire was very heavy as 15in shells were falling on Ypres; avoiding a disaster, the two companies at Ypres joined the other two companies at Zillebeke.

Also on 9 August, the British troops regained some of the lost ground at Hooge by counter-attacking. Describing the German attack, which occurred in the half-light of dawn, a correspondent

Fighting on the Land 153

Captain Meaburn Staniland's father.

Plaque commemorating the Staniland brothers at St Botolph's Church, Boston.

at British HQ said that 'following a heavy bombardment, the German engineers turned the taps of their cylinders and launched a sheet of burning liquid against the enemy.' It was under cover

German soldiers using 'liquid fire' at Hooge.

A captured variant of the German flame-thrower or flammenwerfer.

Sergeant Crick.

of the screen of flame that the German infantry forced an entry into the British first line. The British were shocked at the methods used by the Germans. The same correspondent goes on to write that 'many deeds of heroism were performed during the attack which the Germans delivered with their flame projectors.' Fortunately the 1/4th did not engage with the enemy directly that day.

On the 10th the 1/4th returned to the front line, and then on the 12th Captain Hart was wounded. Another officer, Lieutenant L.A. Reed, was killed on 27 August.

Looking across no man's land at the German-held village of Zillebeke.

Front-line duties occupied the thoughts of the 1/4th when the battalion went back into the soaking trenches. For three days the men were drenched by heavy rain, clogging the mud and making life miserable for the troops. Compounding the dire situation was the relentless shellfire bombarding the line, with Second Lieutenant Edmondson being wounded.

Lieutenant Colonel C.E. Heathcote of the King's Own Yorkshire Light Infantry arrived and assumed command of the 1/4th, replacing the popular Jessop, two days after the 1/4th moved back out of the line on 10 September.

Imminent loss awaited the 1/4th during their next tour in the trenches from 15 to 21 September. Towards the end of their tour

An artist's impression of the charge at Hooge to regain lost ground.

on the 20th, British guns bombarded the German lines as a prelude to the Battle of Loos. German artillery responded with a devastating barrage of their own, killing soldiers along the line. By the 24th the men had some much-needed respite, 'resting' in brigade reserve in Kruistraat dugouts, Railway Embankment and Deeping dugouts.

War diary listings of the casualties of the 4th and 5th battalions between 13 March and 25 September 1915 were as follows:

1/4th Battalion: Killed: Colonel Jessop, Captain M. Staniland, Lieutenants G. Staniland, W.B. Hirst, C.H. Ellwood, W.A. Fox and L.H. Reed; other ranks 10. Wounded: Captains B.C. Thompson and Hart, Second Lieutenant Edmondson; other ranks 22.

1/5th Battalion: Killed: officers 0; other ranks 43. Wounded: Captains Hadfield, Ingoldby, Lowe; Second Lieutenants Disney, Binns and Bott; other ranks 217. Missing: 4.

Private Tom Barber, killed on 9 August 1915 at Gallipoli. Thomas was a soldier with the 6th Lincs and son of Mr F.W. Barber of Hospital Lane. Tom was the second son of Mr Barber to have died, his son Chas of the Terriers being the first.

The Battle of Loos: 25 September to 13 October 1915

British Commander-in-Chief Sir John French had been in talks with the French High Command for a few weeks; however, French regarded the ground south of La Bassée Canal unfavourable for an attack. The ground was also overlooked by German-held slag heaps and colliery towers. Compounding French's concerns was the discovery a few months earlier of a second defensive line behind the front position. Despite his concerns, Kitchener heeded the advice of Ferdinand Foch and General Joffre. Adding to the pressure on French, Joffre required that both the British and French troops be ready for an assault on the German lines by 8 September. Complicating the plan, French preparations for the offensive in Champagne and logistics forced higher command to delay the attack. If the attack was successful a breakthrough was to be followed by a general offensive of all the French and British armies on the Western front intended to compel the Germans to retreat beyond the Meuse and possibly end the war, causing the Franco-British-Belgian armies to join up. If this plan worked, it would force the Germans into open warfare and an overwhelming allied force should, in theory, be enough to beat the Germans.

Actions of the Hohenzollern Redoubt: Boston's Black Week

In 1915 the Hohenzollern Redoubt (*Hohenzollernwerk*) near Auchy-les-Mines in France was considered by the British High Command to be one of the strongest defensive positions on the whole front that was earmarked for attack on the first day of the Battle of Loos. German soldiers had been strengthening their positions across the front throughout the summer, paying particular attention to the redoubt which was essentially a fortified slag heap. Years of spoil deposited by the local mining industry had been tunnelled out on both sides to create a 20ft observation post with excellent views in all directions.

The name 'Hohenzollern', from the House of Hohenzollern (a Prussian/German/Romanian dynasty), would be indelibly etched into the memories of Bostonians just as the Somme is imprinted on the towns that raised Pals regiments who joined the great fallen of 1916. Victory at Hohenzollern could have been a game-changer for the allies; however, the use of outdated tactics in a modern war demonstrated the futility of allied strategy.

As a prelude to the Boston Territorials' involvement in the battle, the redoubt was attacked on 25 September in the first phase of the attack under cover of a gas discharge, a smoke-shell barrage from Stokes mortars and phosphorus grenades. The 46-year-old Major General Thesiger was charged with capturing the redoubt. Initially the attack was a success with the 9th Scottish Division making a good account of themselves by taking the first two positions within one hour. Flanking the soldiers in the first attack were German machine-gun positions that caused immense loss of life over the next few days and hours.

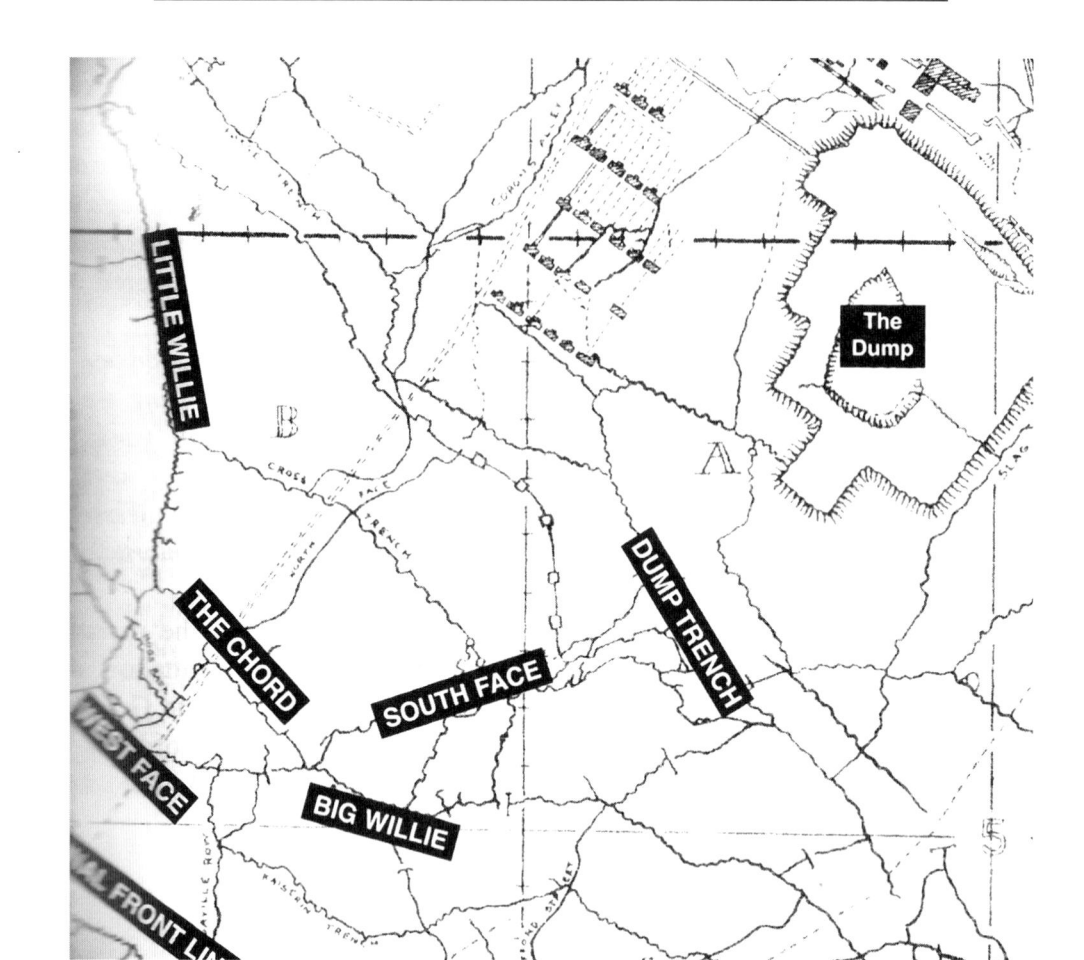

Trench map covering the Hohenzollern Redoubt and the Dump.

After regrouping, the resilient Germans counter-attacked, although each attack was successfully repelled by the plucky British. However, with a scarcity of ammunition and supplies, the British were unable to withstand another counter-attack and they folded as the German forces crept to within 100 yards of the British positions. As dawn approached on the 27th the Germans launched a head-on attack, forcing the defenders to relinquish their positions. Such was the ferocity of this attack, Major General Thesiger who went to assess the situation on the east face of the redoubt was hit by a shell and his body never recovered. It had to

A fosse then looking towards Loos, La Bassée area.

have been exceptional circumstances for his men to leave behind the body of such a high-ranking officer but Thesiger was literally blown to pieces.

Over the next few days both sides attacked, counter-attacked and defended their positions bravely. After eight days of fierce fighting, the only gain made by the British had been one piece of trench attached to the redoubt.

Major General Stuart-Wortley of the 46th (North Midland) Division conducted his own survey of the battlefield at 2.30 pm on 12 October; meanwhile General Haig motored over to visit Stuart-Wortley at the 46th Division's headquarters at Sailly-Labourse. Accounts suggest that Stuart-Wortley disagreed with Haig's plan of attack of 'going over the top' and suggested 'that the best course was to proceed, as in siege warfare, by bombing attacks and approaching the positions trench by trench'. That account was some years after the battle and no official contemporary report exists to substantiate Stuart-Wortley's claim. Haig was determined to ignore his advice and overwhelm the Germans as quickly as possible, despite the excessive risk to the men.

The stage had been set for the Boston men to play their role in this highly ambitious plan. Facing the British line were 153 German

German soldiers on horseback wearing gas masks for protection.

batteries and the 11th Reserve Regiment holding the line facing the British front-line positions. The remaining enemy companies occupied Hulluch Quarries and Cité St Elie.

The following accounts are taken from the war diaries and assembled in part by C.R. Simpson in his book *The History of the Lincolnshire Regiment 1914–1918*.

Prior to the battle, the 46th Division was to relieve the Guards Division opposite the Hohenzollern Redoubt on the night of 12 October. The 1/4th Lincolnshires relieved the 2nd Grenadiers and the Irish Guards. In complete darkness they were led by guides who seemed uncertain as to the exact direction. On 13 October the reliefs were completed.

Major General Thesiger.

Operational orders directed the 46th Division to capture the Hohenzollern Redoubt and Fosse No. 8 ('fosse' meaning a moat or ditch), while the 12th Division was to capture the Hulluch Quarries and establish communication with the 46th at a prearranged point. The 46th Division attacked with 137 Brigade on the right and 138 Brigade on the left.

The division had been promised the use of gas, smoke and a heavy counter artillery bombardment. However, much of the gas just settled in the shell-holes and only alerted the defenders to

B Company, 1st Battalion Scots Guards in Big Willie trench, October 1915. (IWM, Q17390)

the imminent attack. Of 138 Brigade, the 4th Leicesters on the right and 1/5th Lincolnshires on the left formed the first line of the attack; the 1/4th Lincolnshires were in support and the 1st Monmouths in third-line trenches, and the 5th Leicesters were in reserve. The first objective allotted to the 1/5th Lincolnshires was Fosse Trench, behind the western face of the Hohenzollern Redoubt. The latter was an oval-shaped work pushed forward from the German main line (Fosse Trench) and joined to the latter by several communication trenches, of which Big and Little Willie (Big

The British are out of their trenches and are racing towards the Hohenzollern Redoubt on this side of Fosse 8, which can just be made out behind the cloud of smoke to the right.

The gas cloud is seen starting from the left and shells are bursting on the right. The British trenches and approaches can be traced by the chalk that has been excavated. Fosse 8 and the Hohenzollern Redoubt are hidden by smoke and gas.

Hulluch Quarry.

British attack on the Hohenzollern Redoubt, 13 October 1915. Shells are bursting during the attack on the redoubt by the North Midland (TF) 46th Division. Photograph taken from Vermelles.

Fighting on the Land 165

Another view of the German positions near Hulluch.

One of the stone quarries near Hulluch which, due to its strong natural fortifications, the Germans imagined being an impregnable position.

and Little Willie Trenches were a reference to the Kaiser and his son) were the chief trenches. North of the redoubt was a strategic German strongpoint nicknamed 'Mad Point'. The redoubt itself was situated on slightly rising ground of which the near portion dipped towards Fosse Trench and was the only part of the objective allotted to the 1/5th visible from the trenches of the latter.

The attack of the two front-line battalions was to pass straight over to the redoubt without pause and proceed without a check to secure Fosse Trench. The assaulting line was to advance from the trenches under cover of gas and smoke at 1.50 pm and go forward as far as possible without approaching too near the fire of the divisional artillery which would still be firing on the redoubt. At 2.00 pm the guns were to lift their fire and the infantry attack was to begin.

The 1/4th Lincolnshires, in support, were to follow the assaulting battalions 100 yards in rear of the last line of the attack so that their flanks were covered; they were to clear, by bombing, all trenches passed over by the front line.

The 1st Monmouths, in rear of the 1/4th Lincolnshires, were to occupy the Hohenzollern Redoubt and organize it at once as a strong supporting point for all-round defence, as well as connecting

The 5th Lincs with a Maxim machine gun in action.

the redoubt to the present British front line by 'Big Willie'. The 5th Leicesters were to occupy the front-line British trenches after the attacking troops had left them, affording covering fire to the men slowly moving forward.

At 12 noon the artillery bombardment began and for the first half-hour the enemy's reply was confined to considerable numbers of 'whizz-bangs'. From 12.30 pm onwards, bombs dropped on the

Aerial photograph of the Hohenzollern Redoubt.

reserve trenches, fortunately doing little damage. Next, precisely at 1.00 pm with the wind becoming favourable, gas was projected onto the German lines and smoke bombs were thrown, producing clouds of smoke to hide the advance of the infantry.

As soon as the enemy observed the discharge of gas and smoke clouds, they began in earnest to bombard the British trenches and the first, support and reserve lines were heavily shelled; violent machine-gun fire also swept the ground over which the Boston lads were to advance, especially from 'Mad Point'.

At 2.00 pm the first, second, third and fourth lines (1/4th Leicesters and 1/5th Lincolnshires) of attacking infantry left the trenches and advanced against the enemy; the fifth and sixth lines (1/4th Lincolnshires) filed up through the second support line and advanced from the first support trench; the Monmouths and 5th Leicesters followed in that order. All accounts agree that the 4th Leicesters and 1/5th Lincolnshires (Lieutenant Colonel T.E. Sandall commanding) advanced with great gallantry; however, they reached their first objective just as the smoke was clearing. Immediately, heavy machine-gun fire cut down the Lincolnshires, including some of the 'Terriers'. Tangled wire in front of the redoubt had been well cut by the artillery and both battalions swept over the West Face with few casualties. 'We reached the redoubt,' said Captain R.E. Madge, who commanded the machine-gun section. A further advance was impossible, as the brigade on the right was held up on the wire in front of 'Big Willie', and the British were being bombarded heavily on their right flank. Attempts were made to get to Fosse 8, both over the open and along communication trenches, but the intensity of German machine-gun fire made these efforts impossible. Managing to get one Vickers gun, without tripod, into the redoubt, some effective work was done with this in repelling minor counter-attacks. Captain Madge was the only officer left to bring the 1/5th out of the action.

Several small bombing parties attempted to go over the top and were at once wiped out. The redoubt was so knocked about that two officers were killed in that trench while talking to Captain Madge, both by machine-gun bullets. Madge discovered in the evening that he was the only officer left in his battalion and that the 1/4th Leicesters had none, so he informed brigade. Later the 1st Monmouths (pioneer battalion attached to the division) came up to help consolidate the position. A fresh trench was dug in front and it was wired:

> Things were very quiet during the early part of the night, but the Germans brought up guns later that night and on the 14th shelled the original front line heavily. At 8 am, they were relieved by the 1/8th Sherwood Foresters... They went into the show with about twenty-three officers and eight hundred and fifty men and came out with one officer and about one hundred and ten men.

Captain Madge provided an excellent summary of what actually happened to the 1/5th Battalion: 'The attackers got across No Man's Land and into the Redoubt splendidly and then advanced on Fosse Trench, only to be mown down by violent machine-gun and rifle-fire.'

Another account states that an advance by bombing was made up the north face and a post formed in that trench. On the night the casualties among officers of the 1/5th Lincolnshires was irreparable, as the following casualty list shows; it bears eloquent testimony to the gallant leadership of the battalion

After the four-day barrage, the wire was still impassable in some places. (IWM, Q28969)

in attack. Killed in action: Major H.I. Robinson, Captain and Adjutant V. de Hoghton, Captains H.S. Scorer, H.W. Nicholson and G.H.J. Sowter, Lieutenant W.L. Hartley, Second Lieutenants P.K. Brown, E.E. Early, J.A.B. Jollye, C.B. Shrewsbury and T. Wright. Died of wounds: Second Lieutenant J. Blunt. Wounded: Lieutenant Colonel T.E. Sandall, Major H.G. Wilson, Lieutenants B.C. Hall, C.F.W. Haseldine, F.L. Jones, H.D. Mountain, J.S. Nichols, D.F. Underwood, Second Lieutenants R.L. Hett and W.H.G. Smyth.

On 13/14 October the 1/5th Battalion as a whole held the west face of the Hohenzollern Redoubt. Although to the reader this may seem good news, the enormous sacrifice of life in reaching this point was unnecessary. A contemporary report reads: 'The fighting on the 13th and 14th October had not improved the general situation in any way and had brought nothing but useless slaughter of infantry.'

The 1/4th Lincolnshires (Lieutenant Colonel C. Heathcote commanding), supporting the Leicesters and 1/5th Battalion, crossed the front-line trenches and went forward to the redoubt in four lines. Their diary records describe the situation like this: 'Redoubt taken, but at heavy cost. Incessant bombing, machine-gun and rifle-fire all the evening, also shelling. Gas and smoke were used to cover the advance but apparently with little damage to the enemy.' They also were relieved on the morning of the 14th and came out of the line having suffered terribly. Distressed, tired men had to walk past their friends, many of whom had died in the first ten minutes of the battle. One account describes how 'bits of limbs and clothes hung from shreds of barbed wire'. Their casualties were 10 officers and 385 other ranks, killed, wounded or missing.

Many gallant deeds were performed on that day of hard fighting, but only a few are recorded. Corporal C. Leadbeater, 1/5th Lincolnshires, who had been awarded a DCM for gallantry at Ypres on 30 September, won a bar to his decoration. He was most conspicuous among many brave non-commissioned officers who had to take charge when their officers had been shot down. Leadbeater, on 13 October, took charge of a point on the north face and, when the bombers were unable to advance further up that trench, he built a barricade and consolidated the trench. He spent that night in bombing fights with the enemy and when daylight came

A German view of the British line with exposed land in front. (IWM, Q28978)

on the 14th, regardless of all personal danger, acted as a stretcher-bearer.

Company Sergeant Major A. Peasgood of the 1/4th Lincolnshires was another NCO who was awarded the DCM for conspicuous gallantry on the 13th and 14th. When in charge of a party of about twenty men 'in the south part' [south face is probably meant here] he organized bombing parties and, with the greatest courage and resource, held his position from 3.00 pm on the 13th throughout the night and until after midday on the 14th, and during the afternoon he was still holding the same position, although his party had been reduced to six. He refused to relinquish his post when the rest of his battalion was relieved by fresh troops. At the time he was suffering from a wound in the chest received on the afternoon of the 13th.

Two more men of the 1/4th, one Corporal C.W. Jackson and the other Private F. Hibbs, were awarded the DCM for conspicuous gallantry during the attack on the Hohenzollern Redoubt. Corporal Jackson organized bombing parties to hold back the Germans, who were bombing from 'Big Willie'. When darkness had fallen he collected six more men and held the enemy till dawn, by which time both he and all his party

The Dump viewed from the British front line on the first day.

had been either killed or wounded. Hibbs was a signaller at battalion headquarters and carried out his duties most gallantly, making perilous journeys between the old British front line and the redoubt in an endeavour to run a telephone wire across. Eventually his efforts were successful. His coolness set a fine example throughout.

Private C.A. Hocknall of the 1/5th Lincolnshires, who remained in a shell-hole under heavy shell- and machine-gun fire in order to tend a wounded officer whom he carried back to the British line when darkness fell, was awarded a Military Medal (MM). Sergeant W.E. Hamp and Lance Corporal A.C. Ingamells, both of the 1/5th Battalion, were also awarded the MM for showing great personal gallantry.

Both battalions fought most gallantly in the operations of 13 and 14 October; they captured a position powerfully and Adjutant E.J. Grinling of the 1/4th Lincolnshires was awarded the MC for gallantry during the attack on the Hohenzollern Redoubt on 13 October.

Survivors of the two battalions, though shaken by their experiences in their first great battle, then set about the task of reorganization with undiminished spirit.

The 46th Division was congratulated by the corps commander (Lieutenant General Sir R. Haking) on the manner in which the attack against the Hohenzollern Redoubt and fosse had been carried out.

On 1 October both the 1/4th and 1/5th Lincolnshires were relieved, the 1/4th marching back to Dickebusch huts and the 1/5th to huts near Ouderdom. One officer of the 1/5th remarked: 'We turned our back on the Ypres Salient with great satisfaction.'[34]

The 1/4th and 1/5th, on relief on the 14th, withdrew to the second-line trenches but during the evening they were again relieved and moved back to the Lancashire trenches. On the 15th they proceeded to Vermelles, then by bus to their old billets in Hesdigneul.

'Boston's Black Week' was the headline describing the role of the Terriers. Private George Rear of A Company, 1/4th Lincolns returned home to Boston and gave this account of the action:

> I have been cooking for the machine section and did not take part personally in the attack on the Hohenzollern Redoubt, but I saw our fellows when they came out of it – those who did. Three hours before the attack I was ordered not to go into the trenches, and it was lucky for me too, because out of 31 men of my section who went over the parapet into the charge, only nine came back, and 21 were down. Yes, that actually happened. We relieved the Guards Division, consisting of the Grenadiers, the Scots Guards, the Irish Guards, and the Coldstreams to charge this position, which embraced five lines of trenches and the village of Hulluch. Our men found the Germans very strong. We easily captured two lines of trenches and the redoubt, but when we got to the third line of trenches they drove us back. That was where most of our losses took place. There was an enormous number of Germans there.

More stories crept across the Channel, all recounting the brave exploits of the men, some of them sad. Poignant photographs appeared in the *Boston Guardian* of soldiers still missing with anxious families waiting for any news. It was rumoured in the town that Sergeant T. Bailey of 22 Oxford Street was injured in the charge and was lying in a ward at a Lincoln hospital. When his wife made a visit to Lincoln to see him the news had been incorrect and the soldier lying there was a wounded man also called Bailey. Sergeant T. Bailey had died during the battle.

The *Lincolnshire Standard* offices were besieged by anxious inquiries from relatives and friends of the soldiers. After the 'great charge', some of the men returned home on leave, one such man being the Boston Sergeant Wallis Smith of A Company. Arriving home, he presented a 'very war-worn appearance' as well he might, for he had come straight from the scene of the great fighting. The sergeant brought home a formidable-looking revolver which he had acquired from a German.

An article in the *Leeds Mercury* of Thursday, 4 November 1915 described the Hohenzollern Redoubt victory as 'the most enthralling epic of the war'. Some contemporary reports today refer to the battle as one of the bloodiest battles in history. The recovery of the Hohenzollern Redoubt was one of the final acts in the great Battle of Loos. Illustrating the ferocious fighting, of the 399 casualties of the 1/4th and 1/5th Lincolnshires, 97 per cent have no known graves. In total 1,308 men lost their lives: 74 officers and 1,234 other ranks, hardly 'enthralling' to the men who were there!

A Change of Scenery: Embarking for Egypt

Still reeling from the carnage at Hohenzollern, the 1/4th and 1/5th Lincolnshires moved to Hesdigneul on 15 October. Training was carried out and drafts received to bulk out the numbers, and eleven days later on the 26th they moved to Verquin (2 miles south of Béthune). Here a composite brigade, which included the 1/4th Battalion, was formed from the 46th Division for inspection by His Majesty the King. The diary of the 4th Battalion mentions an accident to His Majesty: 'The King was crushed by his horse rolling on him shortly after inspecting the Composite Brigade of the 46th Division.' Fortunately the consequences of this alarming accident were not as serious as they might have been.

November was spent on the front line near Neuve Chapelle in appalling conditions. Incessant rain and shellfire reduced the trenches to uninhabitable quagmires and each painful step eked out their last vestiges of energy. Fortunately, only two days were spent at the front in December with the remaining time spent at Le Sart and Thiennes (11 miles south-east of St. Omer).

Imagine the relief of the men when orders were issued to the 46th Division to embark for Egypt, thus avoiding a long winter in

STILL MISSING.

Uncertain Fate of Popular Young Boston Territorial.

REPORTED MISSING.

Sergeant who was in the Grena Section of Boston Company.

PTE. J. FOSTER.

SERGT. T. BAILEY.

'Still Missing': anxious families awaiting news of their loved ones. These two Boston men never returned.

SERGT. WALLIS SMITH.

the trenches. After a fifty-five-hour ride, thirty-three of those spent in a truck from northern France, the men arrived in the south of France. Both battalions left Marseilles on the TSS *Anchises* on 7/8 January 1916. On the way they enjoyed porridge, stewed steak and fruit, a welcome relief from the bully beef and dry biscuits of their time in the trenches. Excited by the change of scenery and warm weather, the men reached Alexandria on the 13th and left by rail for El Shalufa, a few mud huts on the Suez Canal 2 miles south of the Bitter Lakes where, after detraining, they crossed the Suez Canal by ferry. The men were to strengthen the defence force on the Suez Canal against possible Turkish attack.

Their camp at Shalufa was miles away from any town and life was quiet. Private Meeds of the 1/4th wasn't happy with their allocation of bread and biscuits. It seems that the men could not buy anything from the native canteen as the place was always besieged by the 'Staffords' who were also guests at Shalufa. Accounts say that the next two weeks passed peacefully, although the work was similar to that of England, including the dreaded route-marching, now in the heat of the desert. To the east of the men's lines were a few shallow trenches and then about 60 miles of gently undulating rock-strewn desert, ending on the horizon in a range of mountains of which every detail stood out with surprising clarity. To the west of the canal another range about 5 miles away seemed only about as many hundred yards distant, rising very steeply from the desert and apparently absolutely sterile and arid.

Some days were cooler than others, with normal temperatures being very hot during the daytime and cold at night. It was a

VOLUNTEER !

(Tune, "March of the Men of Harlech.")

Englishmen! be up and doing,
See that Belgium has fair play,
One and all come rally round her,
   Help her win the day.
Ev'ry able man is needed;
Come then at stern Duty's call:
Englishmen can fight for others
    And, when needs be, fall.
France and Russia nobly
War's dread burdens bear,
If England's sons are true to her
    Then she can do her share.
   Volunteer then for your Country;
   Answer to the call for men;
   England claims her sons' allegiance,
    Shall she claim in vain?

Honour calls us loudly, clearly,
To redeem our given word;
Not till Honour's wrongs are righted
   Can we sheathe the sword.
At the call sons offer freely
From "Dominions Overseas,"
Which of you then values honour
    One whit less than these?
Never shall a tyrant
Crush and rule the free,
If ye but heed your country's call,
    And let your answer be:—
   We will fight for King and Country;
   We will act as Englishmen;
   Right o'er Might shall once mo triumph,
    Peace return again.
                  G. ELSEY.
38, Sleaford-road, Boston.

A patriotic poem by G. Elsey of Boston.

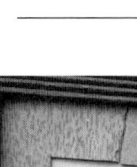

standing order that heavy greatcoats should be worn after sunset. The occasional dust cloud was no match for the German gas clouds endured by the men a few weeks earlier during the 'Black Week'.

Corporal F. Maltby of the 1/5th wrote a letter to his parents, including a funny description of the natives: '...you would laugh at the natives here. You cannot tell men from women. I laughed at one of our men, he thought he was getting on fine with a "girl" when he suddenly found out "she" was a man.'

A touching home-made memorial to Private Arthur Caborn including his casualty form.

Orders abruptly interrupted their short 'holiday' and on 4 February 1916 the 1/4th embarked at Alexandria on the *Minnewaska* and on the 5th on the *Megantic*, disembarking at

A troopship that carried the men to Alexandria.

Marseilles on the 9th. The premature stay in Egypt was due to the evacuation of the Gallipoli Peninsula which liberated a large number of troops for service in Egypt.

On 19 February 1916 the *Boston Guardian* printed an interim Roll of Honour, informing readers that the war had accounted for twenty-three men either killed or missing from the 4th and 5th Territorials of Boston. Incidentally, in all theatres of war where Boston men had fought, seventy-four had been killed in total.

The action at the Hohenzollern Redoubt and the early action in the Belgian trenches accounted for twenty-three men from Boston. Remarkably only six other men from the 1/4th died in the remaining years of the war. After Captain Staniland died, the other two officers from Boston, the Marris brothers who had served pre-war with the battalion, survived the conflict. Harold served a total of twenty-one months before surrendering to 'shock and neurasthenia' and was invalided out of the army before the war ended in 1918 and died in 1966. Both Geoffrey and Harold Marris achieved the rank of captain.

Snow was falling by the time both battalions travelled by rail to Pont-Remy (south-east of Abbeville) and after several changes reached Doullens, in heavy snow, on 2 March. Orders were given to the 46th to relieve French troops in the sector south of Souchez (5 miles west by south-west of Lens), and on 10 March the 1/5th Lincolnshires took over the front-line trenches near Villers-au-Bois with the 1/4th moving into the support line in the Talus des Zouaves.

Private J. Meeds, a soldier with the 1/4th who worked for the Lincolnshire Standard.

Corporal F. Maltby of the 1/5th.

Men of the 1/5th encountered their first incursion since arriving back in France when the Germans exploded a mine under the parapet, followed up by a bombing attack. Sergeant Warren showed great coolness and resource under enemy fire in repelling the attack and was later awarded the MM.

Not escaping the action, the 1/4th went into the front line on the 14th and lost two officers during the tour. Further lives were lost on 20 April when the Germans, again using mining technology, blew a mine nearly under the front-line trench, killing Lieutenant W.R. Wright and fifteen other ranks who were buried by 8ft or more.

Good news arrived on 6 April when Lieutenant Colonel Sandall, wounded in the attack on the Hohenzollern Redoubt, rejoined the

Three Boston soldiers in Egypt serving with A Company, 21st Midland Battalion. From left to right: Privates G. Boyce, C.H. Atkin and F. Wilson.

5th after convalescing for six months, delighting all ranks and injecting some much-needed morale.

Arras welcomed the men for carrying duties with 51 Brigade until 9 May and then at Sus-St.-Léger making fascines and similar work. From Sus-St.-Léger, the 4th moved to Foncquevillers and the 5th to Bienvillers, keeping busy by digging communication trenches in preparation for a planned attack on the German positions. An unusual casualty was Lieutenant Colonel Gardner of the 1/4th who was knocked on the head while watching the work. So serious was his injury that Gardner was replaced by Lieutenant Colonel Barrel on 8 June.

On the night of 8 June a covering party of two platoons with Lewis guns was pushed well forward, while one and a half companies and the whole of the 1/4th Lincolnshire Regiment dug about 400 yards of the new trench down to a depth of 3ft 6in during the night. The enemy was evidently aware of the proceedings to some extent and the work was carried on under heavy shrapnel and machine-gun fire, causing fifteen casualties. The 1/4th Lincolnshire Battalion suffered somewhat heavily, with their commanding officer, Lieutenant Colonel H. Gardner being dangerously wounded.

Harold Marris in his lieutenant's uniform on his wedding day.

On the next two nights, 9 and 10 June, with the usual covering parties out, the digging was completed and the trench sufficiently wired to enable it to be occupied for observation purposes, the garrison consisting of one platoon by day and three platoons by night. By day work continued on the assembly trenches, trench mortar positions and ammunition stores were prepared, small-arms ammunition (SAA) and bomb stores were constructed in the front line and communication trenches were improved; by night the 1/5th supplied covering parties, while working parties of the 1/4th Lincolnshire Regiment continued the wiring and improvement of the advanced trench, known as Bush Trench. Meanwhile it was evident that the enemy by this time had observed the immense amount of work being done and the days of the 'quiet sector' were over, the enemy shelling daily growing heavier and more persistent, and it was therefore with considerable satisfaction that after a spell of fourteen days' continuous work in the front line the men were informed that they were to be relieved on the night of 18 June.

A surviving officer of C Company, Geoffrey Marris as a second lieutenant.

Warmer weather and the front-line trenches opposite Gommecourt welcomed the troops where no man's land was wide. A raiding party of thirty-six men was sent over the top on the night of the 29th to take prisoners. They were discovered by the Germans, who attempted to surround them but were repulsed. No prisoners were taken by either side; however, the commander of the raiding party, Lieutenant Bond, was wounded in the neck. Meanwhile, the 1/5th Battalion was in divisional reserve at Warlincourt on the night of 30 June.

The Somme and the Battle of Gommecourt

Accounts of the Battle of the Somme have graced bookshelves for decades, describing hideous acts and accounts of remarkable bravery; stories that still defy human logic and affection and love that could only be understood by men who had experienced the same. The Somme still ranks as the bloodiest battle in the history of warfare. In 141 days between 1 July and 18 November 1916, a total of approximately 1.2 million men were killed or wounded.

Our account of the Boston Territorials picks up again at Gommecourt on the night of 30 June/1 July. Although little activity was found in the trenches during the day, the night was a hive of activity. Troops moved to their assembly points, stores being carried forward for the formation of dumps, artillery ammunition collected in huge quantities near the guns, ration parties and medical units moving to their allotted positions. More activity was found behind the lines with roads, railways and trams cramming the space.

Zero hour for the attack was 7.30 am on 1 July; within the trenches excitement mixed with tangible apprehension as the men approached their destiny. The ferocious allied bombardment of the enemy trenches had lulled some of the men into an almost false sense of security, believing that the enemy's defensive positions were completely destroyed, including the men taking shelter. It was therefore anticipated that the crossing of no man's land would be easy and with that the capitulation of the enemy was inevitable.

Dawn broke with a slight mist mixing with the smoke that was discharged along the front. Enormous explosions were heard as huge mines were detonated, expelling great dust clouds into the air and producing a settled blanket of smog. As the final intense bombardment stopped, the ladders and trench bridges were placed in position, ready for the infantry assault. Whistles blew in relay along the trench lines, tin hats bobbing in anticipation of the expected victory to follow…and the rest is history.

The 1/4th Lincolnshires, although they made no attack, were in the front-line trenches, for on the night of 30 June/1 July they had dug a false trench in front of the main line to draw the enemy's fire. The parapet was made as obvious as possible to lure the German artillery towards it. During the first night the 1/4th was relieved by the London Scottish moving to the Hennes camp trenches.

Lieutenant Colonel T.E. Sandall and the 1/5th were relatively safe and away from the action in reserve in the corps line just east of Souastre. At 8.30 am the battalion was moved to Midland Trench, west of Foncquevillers. Although the whole day was spent in the trench, only two casualties were suffered.

Colonel Sandall received orders to send two officers per company to assess the German lines before Gommecourt Wood, which had been unsuccessfully attacked by 137 Brigade. There was a suspicion that elements of 139 Brigade were still holding out in enemy trenches and at 11.00 pm the 1/5th were ordered to attack and join up with the Sherwood Foresters who might still be in the hostile trenches.

Just before receiving the orders the 1/5th left Midland Trench for the front line, passing through Foncquevillers. Horrific sights greeted the men as they progressed down the communication trenches. Dead bodies were strewn over the floor with some hanging on their backs over the side, stragglers and wounded congesting the trenches coming back from no man's land. Orders were received at 11.00 pm to attack in four lines of platoons on a four-pronged company attack. Suddenly there was an abrupt change of plan as the battalion was ordered not to consolidate the enemy trench but to meet up with the Foresters and bring them back. Consolidating the trench was now not an option. At midnight on 1/2 July, the 1/5th went forward, but the darkness disoriented some of the men with only two platoons reaching the enemy line. To their horror, the wires were found to be uncut and the Germans, waiting in force, opened up on the 1/5th, while flares lit up the whole front line. Common sense prevailed when the men were ordered to lie down, as the situation made any further advance impossible. Further deliberation by the GOC Division nearly condemned the men to their deaths when the order was almost given to regroup and advance. Fortunately the 1/5th was ordered to return to the British lines. It was deemed – rightly so – that the German position was too strong for just one battalion to attack successfully.

This order also saved the lives of some Sherwood Foresters who lay wounded in between the German positions and the 1/5th. Acts of gallantry are recorded from this attack; numerous accounts of bravery that will live long in the memory of those who saved and those who were saved.

Two days into the attack, the 1/5th were relieved and moved to Foncquevillers where they relieved the Royal Warwickshire Regiment in the front-line trenches immediately north of those previously occupied. By 13 July, both the 1/4th and the 1/5th were out of the line, the former at La Cauchie and the latter in huts north of Bavincourt.

In August the men were in the Bienvillers-Berles sub-sector with the 1/4th and 1/5th assigned the unpleasant job of installing 1,244 gas cylinders in the front-line trenches in anticipation of a favourable wind. The sight of these cylinders winding their way into position was not welcome to the trench garrisons due to possible leakage or a rogue German shell hitting the gas casing. Their fears came to fruition when a German shell hit six cylinders on 22 August. Second Lieutenant Coles and fourteen other ranks of the Lincolnshires were badly gassed, one of them dying

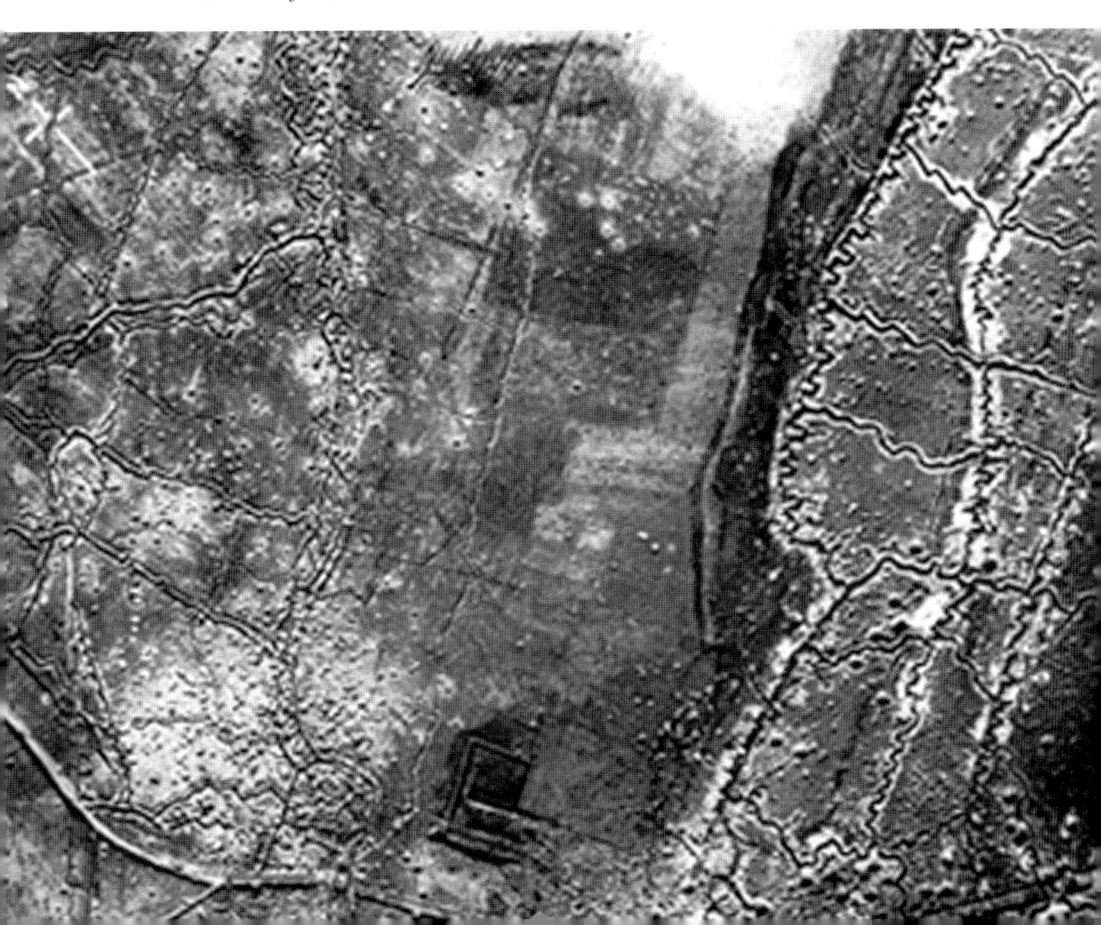

Aerial view of the trenches at Gommecourt.

later at Berles. The hero of the hour was Lance Corporal B. Hill who, although badly gassed himself, remained in the trench and warned all the other men in the vicinity to put on their gas masks, including waking up men asleep in the dugouts. Eventually, the gas was released on 30 August when the wind changed in favour of the British.

More gas cylinders were installed, making the garrison in the trenches very nervous. There was a feeling of déjà vu when the enemy scored a direct hit on the cylinders on 30 September but this time the wind was blowing towards the German lines. Realizing that the Germans knew the gas cylinders were there, the last of the cylinders were removed by a weary party of the Lincolnshires.

Both battalions carried out raids: the 1/4th Lincolnshires on 5 October and the 1/5th Lincolnshires on the 18th. During the second operation, A Company infiltrated the German trenches, bringing back a shoulder strap and a helmet; this intelligence was sufficient to establish the identity of the German unit holding the

The ruins of Gommecourt, 30 June 1917. (IWM, Q78396)

line. The divisional GOC delivered congratulations via wire: 'Well done 5th Lincolns.'

The German Retreat and the British Advance to the Hindenburg Line

German tactics changed significantly after their major losses, first at Verdun and then on the Somme, left them with no choice but to shorten their line. Preparations were made to evacuate the line from opposite Arras to the Aisne Valley, north-west of Reims. The Hindenburg Line, a powerful defensive system, awaited the Territorials. Hindenburg ran from the defences at Arras in a south-easterly direction for 12 miles to Quéant, then west of Cambrai to St. Quentin, La Fère, St. Gobain to the northern banks of the Aisne, east of Crouy. Some of these sectors contained some of the Lincolnshire battalions who chased the enemy across the shattered, devastated area they were leaving behind.

At the end of February the number of Lincolnshire battalions rose from eight to ten with the arrival of the 2/4th and 2/5th as part of 177 Brigade, 59th Division.

January through to the middle of March saw the 1/4th and 1/5th near Gommecourt taking up front-line duties in the wet, muddy trenches of Foncquevillers. After heavy snow during the first week of March, conditions in the trenches were so bad that the men had to sleep outside the dugouts with the rats on the firing steps. In one sector the water came up so high that it overflowed into the men's boots. Both the right and company sector trenches had to be abandoned and then wired in. Hard work by the men in pumping, draining and clearing the trenches finally made them bearable.

Nothing much is recorded in January, simply because not much occurred. That changed on 28 February when the 5th Lincolnshires received news that the 1/4th Leicesters had, during the night of 27/28 February, occupied Gommecourt, the Germans having evacuated the park, village and château. Attempts to occupy 'Z' trench by the Lincolnshires opposite the 1/5th line were repulsed by the incumbent Germans.

Both battalions were out of the line on 13 March at St. Amand (4 miles north-west of Gommecourt). News was received of the

The complex set-up of gas cylinders and pipes in the front-line trenches. The men in the trench belong to B Company, 1/6th Battalion, Gloucestershire Regiment.

enemy's retreat from Grevillers and the trenches in front of Achiet-le-Petit. All existing orders were cancelled and the Lincolnshires ordered to be ready to march at short notice.

On the night of 13 March the battalions in the front line in support or reserve between Damery on the Roye-Amiens road and Arras were the 2/4th in support at Belloy-en-Santerre and the 2/5th in dugouts in Triangle Wood. Both the 1/4th and the 1/5th were in reserve at St. Amand but kept busy by supplying working parties for the Gommecourt-Foncquevillers sector.

Evacuation of Grevillers and the trenches west of Achiet-le-Petit was reported by the 1/4th on 13 March. That night 137 Brigade attacked the enemy; however, the Bucquoy Graben trench was strongly held, resulting in a failed attack. Three days later on the 16th the brigade was ordered to attack again with the 1/4th Lincolnshires on the left and, after taking Bucquoy Graben, to pass on to Preussen Graben and Hill 155. While practising the forthcoming attack on prepared ground at Château de la Haie, counter-orders cancelled the attack as the enemy had retired.

The 1/4th Lincolnshires marched off at 3.00 pm on the 16th to relieve the left battalion of 139 Brigade in posts running roughly

Fighting on the Land 189

The grim reality of Verdun in 1916.

east to west through Quesnoy Farm, where preparations were made to continue the advance at dawn as contact with the enemy had been lost. On the night of the 17th/18th the 1/5th also moved forward to Rettemoy Farm.

Red flares from the German lines on 16 March 1917 signalled the withdrawal to the east of the Somme to take up their new defensive positions. Two sorties were carried out north and south of the Estrées-Villers-Carbonnel road and each raiding party found the trenches empty. Realizing there was easy ground to be gained, the advance began immediately. By noon the Germans were reported clear of the eastern bank of the River Somme.

German soldiers were quickly retiring to the Hindenburg Line; the British patrols sent out early on the 18th still had no sight of the retreating enemy. That night the 1/4th had formed an outpost line from Douchy to Adinfer, the 1/5th on the right of the 1/4th, holding a spur between Ayette and Moyenneville. Arriving at Ayette the soldiers found an 'absolute wreck' with no shelter or water to be found. Douchy fared no better, with the 1/4th recording that 'the whole village is a mass of ruins. Houses have been demolished, trees cut down and roads damaged by mines. Surrounding villages present a similar appearance and the whole country bears the smear of Hun Kultur.'

Corps troops now took up the pursuit and the 1/4th moved back to billets in St. Amand, then at Estrée-Blanche, the 1/5th returning to Souastre and then marching to Bourecq.

Just beyond the old German line, the retreating Germans destroyed the road to such an extent that it was almost impassable. Both the 2/4th and 2/5th Lincolnshires were hard at work repairing the road until the 20th. Next day on the 21st both these battalions went to Foucaucourt for a few days' rest.

Falling back rapidly, the Germans took up position at Hervilly where snipers had been posted on the east ridge. At daybreak on the 27th German snipers from Hervilly fired on the Lincolnshire piquets and killed one man. That night the 2/4th sent two companies to Roisel, where they relieved two companies of the 1st Bucks (TF). The 2/5th marched to Nobescourt Farm, placing an outpost on the Bernes-Hamelet road.

On the 31st the 2/5th Leicesters, supported by the 2/4th Lincolnshires, attacked Hesbecourt and cleared the enemy from the village. The 2/5th Lincolnshires also supplied forty-eight Lewis-gunners and twenty-four scouts and snipers to take part in the operation.

The 2/4th Battalion moved to Roisel on 1 April, where they worked to clear up the village and helped in the preparation of the corps line. The 2/5th still remained at Nobescourt Farm. Two days later on the 3rd, the battalion had sent out some working parties in the morning in preparation for an attack. At 10.45 am the attack order was cancelled as an attack on Fervaque Farm and Bosse Wood was deemed a priority. At 6.45 pm the Lincolnshires paraded and marched under cover to a point south of Hesbecourt.

Company commanders reported their men in position at 8.15 pm, moving forward ready for the attack. The British barrage lifted and the assaulting columns A and D advanced. Wire of 12 to 30ft, rifle and machine-gun fire thumped into the British lines. The enemy's 77mm, 4.2in and 5.9in as well as *minenwerfer* also opened fire, and the attack was brought to a standstill. The Hindenburg Line was very near and the Germans had no intention of relinquishing their new defensive line. Second Lieutenant W.K. Carruthers and five other ranks were killed. The battalion spent the 4th resting in Roisel and on the 5th moved to Templeux, taking up an outpost line between that village and Hargicourt. Heavy shellfire on the 6th resulted in three other ranks being killed. False reports on the 9th enticed further probing of Hargicourt, but the Germans were still occupying the village. Later in the day, the Germans were seen moving back from their trenches north of Fervaque Farm. At 5.00 pm the 1/4th, under brigade orders, entered the enemy's trenches north of Fervaque Farm through a quarry and took possession of them up to the Hargicourt-Villeret road, then west to Hargicourt. The 2/5th Lincolnshires took over the 1/4th positions during the night of 9/10 April.

German defenders were busy on their line while the British shored up their own defences utilizing the old German trenches wherever possible. The 2/4th and the 2/5th Lincolnshires passed the summer of 1917 on the Somme with the 1/4th established in a camp at Winnezeele. A tented camp at Proven was the temporary home of the 1/5th.

After a fairly long period away from front-line training, the 1/4th and 1/5th returned to the forward area during the third week of April. The 1/5th went into the front line east of Cité St. Pierre, north-west of Lens, and on 19 April they occupied the old German front and support-line trenches. Simpson says about this:

> The method of holding the line in this sector was entirely new to these Lincolnshire battalions: trenches served only as a means of approach to advanced posts, which consisted mostly of houses recently vacated by the enemy. There was little protection in the way of wire or other obstacles, so that super-alertness was imperative. Except the garrisons in the advanced posts, the greater part of the battalion was kept in cellars behind the front line. Apart from the usual patrol work and intermittent shellfire the tour was uneventful, and on the 23rd the 1/4th took over the line.

Respite was never achieved by the men during May as attack was met by counter-attack with the incessant boom of the guns both

Minenwerfer (flame-thrower) crew in action. Note the length of the lethal discharge.

day and night. Men were in constant fear of death from a bomb, a sniper's bullet or enemy machine guns. The diaries have frequent entries such as 'enemy shelling and trench-mortaring incessant' or 'enemy put down heavy barrage'. On 1 May the 1/4th took over part of the front line between Fosse 11 de Lens and Hart's Crater. German *Sturmtruppen* (stormtroopers) raided a bombing post in Netley Street and the battalion suffered sixteen casualties. Second Lieutenant J. Rickey was killed by a sniper. It was time for the 1/5th to take over the line just before the enemy raided the 1/4th. The 1/5th's turn did indeed come when the Germans raided them on the 5th. About thirty Germans tried to rush a bombing post with rifle grenades and trench mortar bombs. The NCO commanding was killed in the bombardment and another seriously wounded. Private A.F. Foster assumed command, ordering the survivors of the garrison to retreat, carrying the dead NCO and wounded men with them. Foster was a hero that day, covering the retirement and holding the enemy. He disrupted the enemy's advance, obtaining support from Lewis guns, and the raid was repulsed with considerable loss to the enemy. Foster was awarded the DCM.

Private G.P. Rawson was the embodiment of the fighting spirit of the battalion when events unfolded on the night of 17 May during a seemingly routine mission. Two men were sent out as a connecting patrol to visit the advanced posts. They were attacked with bombs by a patrol of six Germans. Both men were wounded, but Private Rawson fired at once into the enemy; killing two, he then charged the remainder with his bayonet, forcing them to beat a hasty retreat. He was awarded the MM.

There is in the diary of the 1/4th Lincolnshires the following entry for 28 May. On that day 138 Brigade (Lincolnshire and Leicestershire) was withdrawn from the line, the 1/4th Battalion, Lincolnshires taking up billets at Bouvigny-Boyeffles. Here it was that stirring news reached them. The battalion was honoured by the command to take part in an extensive enterprise on a 2,000-yard front north-west, west and south-west of Lens.

The next day (29 May) training began in earnest over a replica of the ground over which the attack was to be launched. On 6 June the commanding officer announced on parade that the plans had been altered and instead of the proposed operations, the attack was to be a series of raids: zero hour was 8.30 pm on 8 June. That evening the 1/4th Lincolnshires (Lieutenant Colonel G.A. Yool commanding) marched out of Bouvigny and billeted in the ruins of Liévin.

The story of the attack that took place is recorded in the battalion diary:

> The 8th of June arrived – a perfect summer day. The afternoon was spent in moving up to cellars in Cité de Riaumont, adjoining the assembly trenches. All companies reached these without mishap except D Company, which lost the services of 2nd Lieutenant E.A. Dennis (13 Platoon) wounded by one of the enemy's shells, which were already finding our stationary zone. Time crept on towards zero. 'Sausages' enlivened the waiting period, as they crashed on and around the ruins which sheltered us. Well before 8 p.m., C, D and B Companies were in position in their respective assembly trenches. In some way the enemy seems to have known our timed movements and intentions.
>
> The intensity of the barrage to which the assembled troops were subjected was an experience no one on the spot is likely to forget. D Company fared worst, as, while the bombardment of their sector was accurate to a degree, on the flank sectors it was sufficiently 'plus' to miss the assembled platoons.
>
> At zero–3, Captain R.D. Ellis, commanding D Company, and Captain Wakeley, commanding 4th Leicesters 'mopping up' company, were caught by the same shell as they came into position in the rear trench. Both were killed outright.
>
> At 8.30 p.m. the synchronized signal to advance was given. C Company on the right got away without mishap, two platoons south of the Cutting and one under 2nd Lieutenant A.B. Hardy, who was wounded almost immediately, to bring covering fire from the Cutting. D Company, in the centre, as soon as they 'jumped off' by serried ranks and increased intervals to lessen gaps, showed the effects of their experience in the assembly

trenches. B Company, on the left, were a joy to behold as they went over in line. The Cutting was reached.

D Company, by this time reduced by half its numbers, and B Company, already caught by the enemy's guns, scaled the further slopes of the Cutting together and advanced to their objectives. Captain E.J.S. Maples, commanding B Company, was at this juncture struck in the forearm by an ugly piece of shell case, but continued the advance with his men. Owing to a portion of their line being oblique to the 'A' barrage and the Stokes mortars, which were to deal with this sector, being put out of action, the enemy tried to man his trenches from his dugouts. C Company, with the platoon of the 5th Leicesters on their right, were completely held up. When the first wave of D and B Companies reached the front German trench his barrage was already on it, and a temporary check occurred until the reinforcing waves came up. Owing to this check, we were unable to keep up with our barrage and the enemy lined his second trench before our arrival there. Hand-to-hand fighting ensued and after a further advance by D Company to the south and B Company to the east, the odds became overwhelming. We fell back first to Ahead, and then to the Cutting.

Meantime Sergeant E. Quinton with his platoon got further afield than the rest. It was during this stage of the fight that B Company lost 2nd Lieutenant R.T. Thomson and 2nd Lieutenant H.C. Chase, both of them died gloriously, the former as the result of a second wound and the latter from a shell-burst. Sergeant E. Quinton, B Company, and his platoon, after several attempts to rejoin their comrades, in which they repeatedly bumped up against strong parties of the enemy, finally succeeded in rushing an opposition post and fighting their way back to our line after having been in the German lines for four hours – a triumph of leadership on the part of Sergeant E. Quinton. The demolished bridge on the right flank was at once manned and, under 2nd Lieutenant

W.F. Maskell (D Company, 14 Platoon), kept the enemy at respectful distance, telling work being done by the Lewis guns. The front of the Cutting was lined by the remnant of B and D Companies under Captain E.J.S. Maples, and was held until orders for withdrawal to assembly trenches were received, A Company having manned our original line of posts. It was not till then that Captain E.J.S. Maples withdrew from the fight and had his arm properly dressed, some three hours after he was wounded.

The greatest assistance had been rendered throughout by the 138th Machine-Gun Company under Major A.A. Ellwood, a 4th Lincolnshire officer, and particularly by a detachment of two of his guns under Lieutenant Stentiford, manned by the 4th Lincolnshires. The attack on the right had gone well, A Company, 4th Leicesters, having reached their objective easily, and sent back twenty-seven prisoners.

The Attacks towards Lens: 3 June to 26 August 1917

Throughout the 9th, companies reorganized and at night the 1/4th were relieved by the 1/5th Lincolnshires, the former taking a well-earned rest at Liévin in support.

On the 15th the 1/5th were informed that they were to attack the enemy as a prelude to a bigger operation. A daylight attack was the first operation in which four companies took part. This operation was to be carried out at 2.30 pm on the 19th.

Prior to the attack on the 19th the 18th battalion moved up to the front line, relieving the 1/5th Leicesters at Cité de Riaumont. Relief companies had been working through the day and into the night bringing up bombs, rations, rockets, wire and water. The next morning the exhausted men were equipped for attack and moved to their assembly positions. A Company (2 officers, 89 other ranks) and B Company (2 officers, 75 other ranks) were to assault the enemy's trenches, C Company (1 officer, 80 other ranks) was detailed to wire the position when captured, and D Company (2 officers, 80 other ranks) for carrying duties.

The whistle blew just after the barrage fell at 2.30 pm and the two assaulting companies advanced to the attack in two waves. Entering the left trench relatively easy, the Germans were waiting and ready to put up a stiff fight. The German casualties were high and some thirty prisoners were taken. Other Germans had been pushed towards the Canadians who were attacking on the right. Tenaciously the men advanced under vicious machine-gun and rifle fire and bombs were also flung at the attackers. After a brief check the advance was resumed and with rifle fire and rifle grenades the Germans were driven out of their trenches, objective complete.

Three brave counter-attacks were thrown at the British lines with the first at 4.45 pm, the second at 7.00 pm and the last attack at 10.00 pm. All were broken up by artillery, Lewis gun and rifle fire and the Germans lost heavily.

A rather quiet remainder of June ensued, as the 1/4th and 1/5th lent assistance to the 1/5th Leicesters and 1/5th South Staffords who assaulted the German trenches on 28 June 1917. Of the 1/4th, A Company was detailed to carry bombs etc. for the Leicesters, while B, C and D companies jointly supplied five parties of one officer and thirty men each for wiring. Of the 1/5th, B Company carried wire from Quarry Dump to the foot of the slag heap.

A large operation was planned for 1 July, in which all three brigades of the 46th Division were to take part with the Canadians attacking on the right. No. 138 Brigade was to be on the right, the two assaulting battalions being the 1/4th and 1/5th Lincolnshires, right and left respectively.

A whistle at 2.47 am on 1 July heralded the advance. On the extreme right of the divisional front, with their right resting on the Souchez River, they were advancing in a north-easterly direction. A and C companies were in the front line, supported by B and D companies. Using a rolling barrage, which remained stationary for seven minutes, the two companies reached their objectives with few casualties and light resistance. Cité de Moulin, where fortified houses were surrounded by wire, was the objective; owing to the darkness the 1/5th veered off to the right, inadvertently linking up with the 1/4th but losing it with the left company.

Meanwhile, the 1/5th company on the right had a more difficult crossing of no man's land and having to negotiate the 'fortress' like houses of the Cité, they were unable to get forward before the barrage left them behind. They were forced to fall back. Exposing the left flank of the 1/4th, they too were found to be in a very difficult position. The advantage fell to the Germans when dawn broke, exposing the position of the Lincolnshires. Almost immediately, the enemy turned its attention on to the outpost and piquet lines formed by the battalion. Inevitably, their defences were destroyed and the men were forced to withdraw, taking shelter in the ready-made cover of existing shell-holes. At 10.00 am Captain Elliot bravely crawled forward and established his advanced posts in their original positions. For forty-eight hours they endured a bombardment with only a few short intervals of respite. Hundreds of tons of explosives were hurled by the enemy, clinging with great courage and tenacity to their vulnerable positions. The 1/5th, with their flanks open, had been unable to capture their objectives.

A further attack ordered for the night of 1/2 July was cancelled. On the 2nd the Canadians took over the line from 138 Brigade and the 1/4th moved back to Houvelin and the 1/5th to Bailleul-aux-Cornailles.

Lance Corporal W. Wakefield of the Boston Terriers.

The Battle of Polygon Wood: 26 September to 3 October 1917

Much of the woodland that made up Polygon Wood had been destroyed by the huge quantities of shellfire from both sides since 16 July and the area had changed hands several times. Previous operations from 20 to 25 September gave the allies the whole of the Menin Ridge, but the next battle was pivotal to achieve the next objective: to push the line further east to a position from which a direct attack could be made on the ridge near Broodseinde. The date of 26 September was earmarked for the attack.

Nightfall heralded the lining up of the 1/4th and 1/5th from Zevencote to Elms

Corner with the Leicesters just in front. Two hours before zero (5.50 am) the guns opened with a heavy bombardment on the German positions. Leading up to the attack, the area had been soaked in sunshine and the bursting shells threw up clouds of dust that naturally obscured the attackers from the enemy.

Successfully achieving the first objective, the Leicesters stood as the 2/4th Lincolnshires passed through at zero plus 135 minutes, the formation of the battalion being a line of men who moved about 50 yards in rear of the barrage. A Company was on the right, C on the left and B in support, while D was used for carrying and mopping-up duties. The support company moved in artillery formation.

The Germans' fighting spirit deserted them: some surrendered and came out of their pillboxes as soon as the first line approached. Outflanking the next two concrete bunkers, the garrisons gave in. The creeping barrage held up the 2/4th, under cover of which deep narrow trenches were dug in irregular formation. Patrols were dispatched to round up more enemy troops, some secured from Dochy Farm.

Finally the Germans countered with a heavy barrage inflicting many casualties, principally on the support line. Following this, enemy infantry attacks were quickly broken up; however, the shellfire was continuous.

Equally successful, the 1/4th and 2/5th Lincolnshires captured their objective. The battalion attacked on a two-company frontage with B Company on the right, D on the left, C in support and A in reserve, with orders to provide carrying parties.

Reserving a strong position north of Dochy Farm to a strongpoint constructed by D Company, the men made use of connected shell-holes for cover. Futile attempts to shell the British were made by the Germans as the attacking troops had passed beyond it. The final objective sustained the heaviest casualties with the aggressive artillery placed on the pillboxes.

Diaries record the following: 'The men behaved with the greatest gallantry throughout, and on several occasions had to be checked from passing through our own barrage to their objectives, especially during the wait behind the 2/5th Leicesters until zero plus one hundred minutes.'

Both the 2/4th and 2/5th Lincolnshires passed a comparatively peaceful night, but on the 27th the enemy's shellfire was again

Western section of Polygon Wood.

heavy, though only a few casualties were suffered. At 1.00 pm the 2/5th were relieved and moved back to trenches west of Pommern Castle. The 2/4th, however, held the same position until the night of the 29th, when they were relieved by New Zealand troops and marched back to Red Rose Camp, Vlamertinghe, the 2/5th moving back the same night to Derby Camp. Although the Lincolnshire Territorials had captured their objectives without encountering a great deal of opposition, the casualties in both battalions were heavy. The 2/4th lost Captain E.W. Hall and 36 other ranks killed; Lieutenant Colonel A.B. Johnson, Captains E.G. Hooper, G.D. Fox, E.G.V. Knox and M.J.M. Gale, Lieutenant F.R. Coulson, Second Lieutenants H.R. Smith, R. Scott, G.G. Hillery, E.W. Barker and 144 other ranks were wounded and 18 other ranks missing. The losses of the 2/5th were even heavier: Captains G.L. Hill and C.N. Newsum, Second Lieutenants E.J. Lowe, P. Grantham and 12 other ranks were killed; Second Lieutenants R.H. Turner, R.C. Ingram, H.C.W. Charles, G.H. Gouldby, R.J. Brooke, W. Parvin, G. Houlden and 202 other ranks were wounded and 74 other ranks were missing, of whom the majority, no doubt, were killed. The battalion diary states that out of 21 officers and 563 other ranks who went into action on the 26th, only 10 officers and 275 other ranks marched out of the trenches; a heavy price to pay for victory.

After the battle the 2/4th and 2/5th Lincolnshires were withdrawn from the Ypres Salient and a few days later moved south with other units of the brigade and the 59th Division. On 13 October 177 Brigade relieved Canadian troops in the Avion sector, the 2/5th going into the front line and the 2/4th remaining in reserve in the Zouave Valley. Further tragedy befell the 2/4th who lost one officer, Second Lieutenant W.H. Owston who was wounded on 21 October and then died on the 24th.

The 59th Division was then in corps reserve, but on 27 October the 2/5th marched to Trescault. At Trescault the men were billeted in tents and bivouacs at the northern end of Havrincourt Wood, the 2/4th marching on the 28th to Flesquières, where during the day they were joined by the 2/5th Battalion.

The Battle of Cambrai: 20 November to 7 December 1917

The Battle of Cambrai, fought in November and December 1917, proved to be a significant event in the First World War. Cambrai was the first battle in which tanks were used en masse, part of a mixture of tanks, heavy artillery and air power. Mobility, lacking for the previous three years of the conflict, suddenly found a place on the battlefield, although it was not to last for the duration of the battle.

The objective was to gain a local success at a point where the enemy did not expect it. At 6.20 am on 20 November, tanks and infantry attacked on the front about 6 miles from east of Gonnelieu to the Canal du Nord opposite Hermies. The success of the first attack was astonishing compared to other attacks such as that on the Somme. The main system of the Hindenburg Line was overrun and even the Hindenburg Reserve Line was attacked. On the evening of 21 November, it was decided to continue with the attack in order to gain possession of the Bourlon Ridge.

The 2/5th took over a section of the Hindenburg Line (Support) south-west of Flesquières. German artillery counter-attacked with several shells scoring direct hits in the 2/5th trench, hitting a shelter with a number of officers – one was killed and seven wounded –

and immediately taking out some of the leadership team.

Between 7.00 am and 8.00 am on 30 November the Germans attacked the right of the British line, preceded by intense shellfire. Neither the 2/4th nor the 2/5th made any move on 30 November; nonetheless, both battalions were industriously digging trenches round Flesquières and setting up stout defences in case of a breakthrough by the nearby Germans. Continuing the hard work into 1 December, the Lincolnshires moved to the forward trenches. The 2/5th North Staffords made way for the 2/5th Lincolnshire Battalion on a line that went from Bourlon Wood, just east of the quarry, for about 1,000 yards. Moving in support, the 2/4th moved to the old German line north-east of Anneux and two in the sunken road running from Graincourt.

Heavy losses and stubborn resistance from the British prevented the Germans from breaking through, localized attacks continuing along the lines with little impact on the British holding the front.

Gas-shelling intensified during the evening of the 3rd causing distress to the 1/4th Lincolnshires who relieved the 2/4th Leicesters in Bourlon Wood. On the right the 2/5th Lincolnshires suffered equally from the gas that lay thick and heavy in the valley, creating a death trap in the wood. Sir Douglas Haig realized the danger and withdrew his men on the night of the 4th/5th to a position roughly corresponding with the old Hindenburg Reserve Line. Pack ponies and limbers were brought up, and ammunition and stores were removed before the withdrawal commenced in good order without any casualties. The 2/5th then held a line of trenches north and north-west of Flesquières with the 2/4th and the 2/4th Sherwood Foresters acted as rearguard. Discovering the retreat, the Germans began to advance along the line evacuated. Consequently, as far as the Lincolnshire Regiment was concerned, this ended the Battle of Cambrai.

The Final Year: 1918

A belated Christmas dinner was enjoyed by the 1/4th Lincolnshires in Beuvry on 3 January before relieving the 1/5th in the front line on the 7th south of the La Bassée Canal. Appalling conditions greeted the men, but fortunately the tour was comparatively short.

Morale dipped on 24 January when the battalion was acquainted with the drastic reorganization of the army. 'In each brigade,' records the battalion diary, 'one battalion is to be disbanded, and no outsider can appreciate the gloom that is cast over the battalion when we hear that we are to make the sacrifice.'

The 1/4th was to be divided as follows: battalion headquarters, 12 officers and 200 other ranks to the 2/4th Battalion, and 12 officers and 250 other ranks to the 2/5th Battalion. Most of the officers of the 1/4th had joined the battalion since the war began, but there were still numbers of warrant officers and men who had served in no other battalion and could look back on years of camp training in pre-war days. It was a sad business.

The actual break-up began on the 29th when the party detailed to join the 2/5th Lincolnshires, then at Ambrines, left Busnes. The commanding officer (Lieutenant Colonel G.A. Yool), adjutant, quartermaster and 9 other officers with 200 other ranks joined the 2/4th Lincolnshires with whom they were to amalgamate and form the 4th Battalion, Lincolnshire Regiment.

Lieutenant Colonel N.M.S. Irwin relinquished command of the battalion on 21 February and Lieutenant Colonel E.P. Lloyd assumed command. The commanding officer of the 1/5th (Lieutenant Colonel H.A. Watkins) called for a voluntary parade to give the 1/4th a send-off, which was attended by every available man:

> The spirit which prompted this voluntary parade to see us off was very much appreciated, demonstrating as it did the splendid feeling of kinship which has always existed between us and our sister battalion, a feeling which the two colonels had always done their best to foster. (Battalion diary, 1 Lincolnshires, January 1918.)

The 1/4th Lincolnshires left the 46th Division. The 1/5th began the year in the Cambrin sector and on 20 March the battalion was at Sailly-Labourse, in support.

Maizières was the temporary home of the 2/5th Lincolnshires engaged in training when they were informed of the impending change. Lieutenant Colonel Yool, together with other officers of the 1/4th, arrived and then the reorganization began. The diary stated that 'the battalion from the date of the amalgamation will be called the 4th Battalion Lincolnshire Regiment.' Lieutenant

Colonel T.H.S. Swanton, who had previously commanded the 2/4th, became second-in-command of the new 4th Battalion.

On 9 February the battalion left Maizières for Barly, then via Hendecourt and Boiry to Hamelincourt. The 59th Division relieved the 40th in the front line on the 13th, 177 Brigade taking over the Bullecourt sector, the 4th Lincolnshires going into camp at Mory l'Abbaye.

The front-line trenches were immediately east of Bullecourt and overlooked Riencourt. On 2 March the battalion was ordered to raid two hostile posts and obtain an identification of the Germans manning the line. A raiding party of forty other ranks, with Captain H. Ward who was to train them and Second Lieutenant H.R. Greenwood to lead, then proceeded to Mory Camp to prepare.

The operation took place on the night of the 5th/6th. The raiders entered the German posts, but the time taken to explode Bangalore torpedoes beneath the enemy's wire warned the latter and the posts were found empty. Two other attempts by Lieutenant J.R. Neave and six scouts on the 13th and 14th to enter the hostile posts were similarly unsuccessful in obtaining an identification. During the second attempt Private W.H. Evans' brave conduct won for him the MM.

The diary of the 4th Battalion for March contains many references to the prevailing feeling that the enemy was preparing for a great offensive. A German deserter taken on the 10th, 3.5 miles south-east of Béthune, reported that a great attack was to take place on the 13th, but nothing materialized.

On the 20th the 4th Battalion was in Mory Camp and 'stood to' during the morning 'in view of the expected enemy'. For the whole of January the 2/5th were out of the line in training at Ambrines. On the 29th their diary records the arrival of 260 other ranks and 12 officers from the 1/4th Lincolnshires. The battalion was now very strong and at the conclusion of their seven weeks' training, which ended on 9 February, was well-equipped with men in good condition and a good proportion of Lewis guns, bombers, rifle-grenadiers, etc.

On 9 February the battalion marched to Gouy-en-Artois and billeted for the night. The march was continued during the 10th, 11th and 12th, the Lincolnshires reaching Bullecourt on the latter date. They then relieved the 20th Middlesex in the front line. The guns of both sides were continually active, but the enemy's infantry was extraordinarily inactive and rarely showed themselves.

On 20 February there is a statement that the Germans were using gas shells. This is the earliest mention of a new kind of insidious gas used by the enemy before his offensives with the idea of thinning out the allied line. In some parts of the line, gas casualties were extremely heavy and the fighting strength of divisions was greatly affected.

The 2/5th was with the 4th in divisional reserve in Mory on the eve of the German offensive.

The German Spring Offensive of 1918: The Somme, 21 March to 5 April

The German Spring Offensive or *Kaiserschlacht* (Kaiser's Battle), also known as the Ludendorff Offensive, comprised a series of German attacks along the Western Front beginning on 21 March 1918, which marked the deepest advances by either side since 1914. The Germans had realized that their only remaining chance of victory was to defeat the allies before the overwhelming human and matériel resources of the United States could be fully deployed. They also had the temporary advantage in numbers afforded by almost fifty divisions freed by the Russian surrender (the Treaty of Brest-Litovsk).

The trenches reeked with a 'certain apprehension difficult to diagnose, there is a general restlessness all round'. This was the description in the battalion diary. Tension in the front-line trenches had for several days and nights been almost unbearable.

The 4th and 2/5th entered the plan while still in Mory Camp. Breakfast was hurried and with half-full plates still on the table the soldiers were ordered to 'stand to'. Orders quickly came to move immediately with other units of the brigade across country in artillery formation to their allotted positions in the support line third system, which ran just east of the Vraucourt-St. Léger road. The 4th Lincolnshires had the 2/5th on their right front and 4th Leicesters on their left front.

Mist obscured the view as all three battalions laid in these positions until noon, although the roar of the bursting shells could be heard.

At 12 noon the 2/5th Lincolnshires and 4th Leicesters were ordered to occupy the second-system trenches, the 4th Lincolnshires to remain in reserve in the third system. However, the two leading battalions, on passing the third-system trenches, discovered that the enemy had overrun the Ecoust Ridge and was already occupying the second system. Indeed, their troops were climbing over the ridge in large numbers and before the 2/5th Lincolnshires could extend, three companies were cut off and the brigade narrative states: 'What happened to these companies is not known, as they were never seen again.'

The remaining company took up position in the front line of the third system, with the 4th Lincolnshires on the left and 4th Leicesters on the left of the 4th Lincolnshires. The enemy's machine-gun fire was terrific, as his troops carried large numbers of guns. The enemy's plan of attack appeared to be the capture of all high ground from which he could enfilade the allied line, right and left.

The third system, in which the Lincolnshires were located, was merely a line of split-blocked trenches affording little or no cover. Tools were, therefore, collected from a neighbouring dump and the men dug themselves in with a will. No change, apparently, took place in the position during the remainder of the 21st.

Survivors of the 2/5th Lincolnshires had been found on the 22nd in the third system support line north-west of Vraucourt.

A little respite was enjoyed in the morning and then, like locusts swarming, the Germans advanced round the far side of Vraucourt, turning right of the 4th Lincolnshires who were forced to withdraw to the army line in front of Mory, taking with them the remnants of the 2/5th Lincolnshires. Tired men dug in, worn out and cold as they were.

News of the situation was presented to the battalion headquarters by an officer from the 2/4th Leicesters. Mory was in danger of being overrun by the Germans, firing on the Leicesters, the 2/5th and the 4th Lincolnshires from both front and rear. The battalion diary describes how the men fared: 'Though the men were becoming very tired they fought every inch of the way and obeyed all the orders of their officers and NCOs in a most exemplary and cheerful manner.'

All three battalions of 177 Brigade then fell back to positions south-west and west of Mory and patrols were sent out but found that the enemy had penetrated the village in considerable numbers. During the night B Company of the 4th Lincolnshires occupied the southern edge of Mory and held up the enemy with almost continuous Lewis gun and rifle fire. The Leicesters also, holding the western outskirts of the village, drove back the enemy in hand-to-hand fighting.

Early on the morning of 23 March the commander of 177 Brigade, seeing that the enemy was holding the high ground north of Mory and that the positions of the 4th and 2/5th Lincolnshires were untenable, ordered a withdrawal to a position on the high ground south-east of Ervillers and east of the Ervillers-Béhagnies road. This necessitated a retirement across 500 to 600 yards of open country and was carried out under very heavy close-range machine-gun fire with further casualties being suffered.

'The extended line of our men moved back in splendid order with the greatest steadiness until they arrived at the position where they dug in.' (Battalion diary, Lincolnshire Regiment.) The 4th Lincolnshires had the 2/5th on their left. Here the welcome news was received that the 40th Division would relieve the Lincolnshires. For two days the two battalions had been fighting almost continuously, during which time for sleep or rest had been practically impossible but relief seemed to have been very unlikely.

After St. Quentin and the close of the first Battle of Bapaume in 1918, this period saw practically the end of the fighting on the Somme in March 1918 as far as the Lincolnshire Regiment was concerned. The six battalions, as the records show, had fought most gallantly, and had worthily upheld the fine traditions of the regiment. Their losses had been heavy, as far as can be gathered from the records (necessarily brief, as they were written during a period of great strain).

The 4th Battalion lost Second Lieutenants M.S. Page, H.J. Eynes, A.M.H. Bain and 27 other ranks killed; Major H.G. Dean, Captain S. Lee, Second Lieutenant G. Tolson and 114 other ranks wounded; and 58 other ranks missing.

The casualties of the 2/5th were Major H. Ward (4th Battalion, attached 2/5th) and Lieutenant G.V. Butler, Army Service Corps, killed; Lieutenant R.H. Turner, Second Lieutenants R.G. Eedes,

R.E. Creasey, E.B. Smith, C. Taylor, Captain L.M. Webber, Royal Army Medical Corps, and Regimental Sergeant Major W. Coldwell wounded; Captain E.J.R. Hett, Lieutenant B.H. Challenor, Second Lieutenants A. Begg, H J. Gale, F. Sharpe, F.R Gibbons, F.J. Levi, P.E. Cottis, L.G. Moss, C.W. Allen and A.J. Elston missing; in other ranks the losses were approximately 490 killed, wounded and missing.

So far as the Somme was concerned, the German offensive had practically come to an end on 27 March, the enemy had failed to break a way through the allied front and Amiens, one of their objectives, remained in allied hands.

There is little further to record of the regiment during the closing days of that momentous month except that the battalions both assisted in the formation of composite battalions but, apart from taking up defensive positions at Baisieux and Bonnay, were not actively engaged. The 1st Battalion on 31 March was at Bourbon, and the 2nd at Hangest. The 7th Lincolnshires took up an outpost line north of Millencourt on the 27th, and on the 31st relieved the 10th West Yorks in the left sector of the divisional front east of Bouzincourt. Both the 4th and 2/5th Lincolnshires marched to Sus-St.-Léger on the 27th and to Houdain on the 31st. The 10th Battalion had gone north to join the First Army and on 31 March took over front-line trenches in Wez Macquart, covering Armentières from the south-east.

The 4th and 2/5th Lincolnshires entrained at Brandhoek during the early afternoon of 13 April and on arriving at Godewaersvelde marched to Mont des Cats and billeted in huts. After just a little rest the men were moved again, this time to Locre where they were temporarily accommodated in huts until 11.00 am when they again moved along the Locre-Dranoutre road and stood ready while the company commanders reconnoitred the reserve line south of Dranoutre.

Again, the men were responsible for holding a line of four advanced posts on the forward slope of the Ravetsberg Ridge. Two hostile patrols approached one of the right posts but were driven off. Three prisoners had been taken by the Lincolnshires and seventeen dead and wounded were lying out in front. Twelve more prisoners were taken by the 2/5th when the Germans advanced against a machine-gun post on the right. During that morning, eight German deserters gave themselves up.

The tenacity of the Lincolnshires was evident at noon when heavy German artillery was laid on the entrenched men for two and a half hours. Infantry attacked twice and each time the Germans had no answer to the Lincolnshires' determined defence.

At 4.30 pm it was perceived that the 4th Lincolnshires had fallen back. The 4th Battalion had simply formed a defensive flank, still keeping in touch with the left of the 2/5th. By 5.25 pm the line of the 4th was north of the Ravetsberg Road and along the railway cutting between Keersebrom and Hill 75. A few minutes later the Germans forced their way over the crest of the hill and, breaking the line of the 4th, got behind the left flank of the 2/5th and one platoon of the 4th, which had maintained touch with the left of the former. At the same time another attack was made on the 2/5th, and the left company (D) was seen in its original position fighting at close quarters. The bravery of the Lewis-gun section was recorded as 'fighting to the bitter end, having emptied its magazines into the closely-packed ranks of the enemy at very close range'.

Heavy machine-gun fire rained down on the remaining companies of the 2/5th from the left and they suffered heavy casualties. Forming a flank facing east, the survivors were gradually driven back to a line taken up by 177 Brigade north-east of Bailleul. Battalion HQ sent out a patrol to find the companies but only found the enemy. The Battalion HQ was ordered to withdraw back to Locre.

The 2/5th sustained heavy casualties in this action: Lieutenant Colonel H.B. Roffey was killed, Second Lieutenant L.G. Dickinson was wounded and Second Lieutenants W.G. Fenton and J.C. Myers were missing. The losses among other ranks killed, wounded and missing were 352.

Meanwhile, the 4th Lincolnshires had been involved in heavy fighting. On taking over from 102 Brigade, A Company was on the right, B in the centre and C on the left, D being in reserve behind Crucifix Hill. These positions were well down the forward slope of the Ravetsberg Ridge under observation from the enemy and movement was impossible.

At 12 noon the bombardment began, Crucifix Corner (behind the left flank of the battalion) receiving marked attention. At 2.45 pm a local attack developed against the latter place, the enemy obtaining a footing in the battalion's line, but they were driven out by the counter-attack platoon of the left company. Again and again the Germans attacked and twice reached the high ground in the neighbourhood of Crucifix Corner, but on each occasion were driven off with severe losses. This barrage was then shortened to the position, but these attempts were still frustrated in the most gallant manner. A heavy frontal attack against the whole line then developed. On the right, rifle and Lewis-gun fire forced the enemy back. On the left, however, troops on the left of the 4th Lincolnshires had been forced to retire and at last the enemy broke through and captured the crest of Crucifix Hill from the eastern side. They were now able to dominate the whole of the 4th Battalion line with machine-gun fire and the Lincolnshires were forced to withdraw. The action then developed into a series of stands and retirements, in which hand-to-hand fighting was a frequent occurrence. Eventually a line was dug north of the railway in rear of Hill 75, where at about 10.00 pm troops of the 34th Division, having arrived at 7.30 pm to take over and reorganize the line, received orders to retire to Locre, which was reached at about 2.30 am on the 16th.

The losses of the 4th Lincolnshires were Second Lieutenants G.W. Pacey and H.L. Hubble killed, Captains R.B. Wilmshurst, A.E. Stephenson, G. Fleming (Royal Army Medical Corps) and Second Lieutenants W. Paypers, G.S. Lakeman, S.R. Slidel, L.E. Squirrel and E.R. Beecroft wounded, and Second Lieutenant C.E. Blamires missing. Among other ranks the casualties were 12 killed and 120 wounded.

Months passed, culminating in the breakthrough of the Hindenburg Line and then the surrender of the German army. Years of hard fighting had taken their toll on the men who had entrained for Luton in the early months of 1915.

Two years before the war at the 1912 mayor's banquet particular attention was given to the Territorials who were affectionately described as 'very zealous' and 'efficient'. Some 170 of these men came forward to serve and die for their country in time of need. Zealous and efficient are just two qualities describing the men of the 'Boston Terriers' who endured so much on behalf of their country.

Lincolnshire Regiment: Kitchener's Men

Restricted by the Pals initiative, only four men came forward on the first day of the recruiting campaign in Boston, despite passionate and patriotic speeches. The local press reported on slow recruitment, with the recruiting Sergeant Shaw encouraging men to 'take the King's shilling', stressing that those men who made enquiries were under no obligation to join.

Local and national newspapers enthusiastically encouraged men to join, Kitchener applying the pressure with blatant anti-German propaganda. By October 1914, it was reported in the *Lincolnshire Echo* that as many as 700 local men were serving in the armed forces. Records showed that 70 were in the regular army, about 390 in the Territorials and 250 were volunteers for Kitchener's New Army. Joining the New Army was an alternative to being vilified as a 'skulking parasite', 'a curse to the country' or a member of the 'White Feather Brigade'.[35]

One such 'shirker' was George William Cook, farm servant of Punchbowl Lane, who was charged under the Reserve Forces

Advertisement in the Boston Standard *encouraging men to join up.*

Act with absenting himself without leave when called up for permanent service. His over-protective mother claimed that he was 18 years of age but witnesses found he was 20, having been born on 19 May 1896. He was fined £2 13s and ordered to be handed over to a military escort. His mother need not have worried though; George was one of the fortunate lads who survived the war and was discharged in 1918 in Exeter due to injury. George was serving in Ypres when a shell exploded by the side of his trench and he was wounded by shrapnel. The dubious discharge certificate had a note written by a suspicious doctor – underlined in pen, it said 'X-ray, no damage to arm' – but at least his mum got him back!

"LEND A HAND."

Play a Man's part, and enlist to-day.
You will learn the address of the nearest Recruiting Office at any Post Office.

THE LINCOLNSHIRE STANDARD. SATURDAY, JAN. 23, 1915.

NOW THEN, YOU.

Look here, my lad, if you're old enough to walk out with my daughter, you are old enough to fight for her and your Country.

At any Post Office you can obtain the address of the nearest Recruiting Office.

Advertisements in the Boston Guardian *and* Lincolnshire Standard *designed to prick the conscience of men trying to avoid the call-up.*

The Parliamentary recruiting campaign pulled out all the stops when it sent the Pipers' Band to play at the Assembly Rooms where Mayor Alderman C. Lucas welcomed them. Lieutenant West, the articulate speaker who was getting quite a reputation for recruiting from the Boston district, held a meeting near the Five Lamps followed by a similar gathering at the town football ground.

Boston's Kitchener men dispersed themselves to different regiments throughout the country, with the Lincolnshire Regiment being the main beneficiary. Seven service battalions, the correct term for Kitchener's men, were raised for the war, and at its conclusion their short history ended. Of the seven battalions raised, two – numbered 9 and 11 – were kept for service in the United Kingdom and one – numbered 12 – was a labour battalion.

Men were allocated to a battalion depending on requirements and due to the diaspora of men it would require another book to describe every noteworthy event. For ease of reference, the battalions are described below.

Battalions of the New Army

6th (Service) Battalion
Formed at Lincoln in August 1914 as part of K1 and came under command of 33 Brigade in 11th (Northern) Division. Moved to Gallipoli in July 1915. Landed at Suvla Bay 7 August 1915. Went to Egypt in January 1916 and thence to France in July 1916.

7th (Service) Battalion
Formed at Lincoln in September 1914 as part of K2 and came under command of 51 Brigade in 17th (Northern) Division. Landed at Boulogne 14 July 1915.

8th (Service) Battalion
Formed at Lincoln in September 1914 as part of K3 and came under command of 63 Brigade in 21st Division. Landed at Boulogne 10 September 1915; 8 July 1916 transferred with brigade to 37th Division.

9th (Reserve) Battalion
Formed in Lincoln in November 1914 as service battalion, part of K4. November 1914: came under command of 91 Brigade, original 30th Division. Became a reserve battalion 10 April 1915. Converted into 11th Training Reserve Battalion in 3rd Reserve Brigade 1 September 1916.

10th (Service) Battalion (Grimsby)
Often known by its original name of the 'Grimsby Chums'. Formed at Grimsby on 9 September 1914 by the mayor and town. June 1915: came under command of 101 Brigade, 34th Division. Transferred to 103 Brigade in same division on 3 February 1918; 18 May 1918, reduced to cadre strength after suffering heavy casualties; 17 June 1918, transferred to 116 Brigade, 39th Division; 16 August 1918, transferred to 197 Brigade, 66th (2nd East Lancashire) Division.

Fighting on the Land 215

Pipers' visit to Boston by the Pipers Band sent out by the Parliamentary Recruiting Committee.

Second Lieutenant N.D. Rice of the Buffs, son of Mr B.F. Rice of the firm of Messrs Rice and Waite, solicitors of Boston.

Private Herbert Gobey was a soldier in the London Regiment who died of spotted fever in 1915 and was buried at Watford.

Not all Boston soldiers went to the front, as in the case of John Donaldson-Hudson of Tawney Street, Boston who joined the Army Service Corps.

Lieutenant G.H. Payne of Sleaford Road. Part of the Suffolk Regiment, he fell during fierce fighting at Le Cateau.

Second Lieutenant G.R. Holland, formerly a private with C Company, 4th Battalion and later a commissioned officer in the Army Service Corps.

Former recruitment committee member H. Sawyer, who recruited himself into the Army Ordnance Corps.

SERVE YOUR COUNTRY

MEN URGENTLY NEEDED.

Men between 19 and 30 for the new Regular Army for 3 years or duration of War. Ex-soldiers between 30 and 42 may join Special Reserve for one year or duration of war. Must have had a character of fair or better on discharge.

Apply to Col.-Sergt. Wright, Recruiting Sergeant, C Company Drill Hall, Main Ridge, between the hours of 9 and 12 in the Morning, 2 and 4 in the Afternoon, and 7 and 8 in the Evening.

Men who are not eligible for the Regular Army or Special Reserve who wish to join the Territorials may have their names placed on the Waiting List by applying to Mr. G. E. Nash, Church Close, Boston.

Battalions of the Regular Army

1st Battalion

August 1914: in Portsmouth, part of 9 Brigade, 3rd Division. Landed at Le Havre on 14 August 1914. The brigade was attached to 28th Division between 17 February and 2 April 1915; 14 November 1915 transferred to 62 Brigade, 21st Division. The Bermuda Rifle Volunteer Corps sent a contingent of 2 officers and 125 men who served with the 1st Lincolns from June 1915 onwards. They had suffered 75 per cent casualties by the end of the war.

2nd Battalion

August 1914: in Bermuda and moved to Halifax, Nova Scotia. Returned to England 3 October 1914 and on arrival came under command of 25 Brigade in 8th Division; 6 November 1914, landed at Le Havre; 4 February 1918, transferred to 62 Brigade, 21st Division.

3rd (Reserve) Battalion
August 1914: in Lincoln. A training unit, it remained in the UK throughout the war. Moved to Grimsby in August 1914 and remained there until early 1918 when moved to Cork.

Other Battalions

12th (Labour) Battalion
Formed in Brocklesby in July 1916. August 1916: landed in France and moved to lines of communication. April 1917: transferred to Labour Corps as 16th and 17th Labour Companies.

Brothers in khaki: Private J.W. Mills with the 7th Lincolns and his proud little brother, 3-year-old Henry Walter.

1st Garrison Battalion
Formed in September 1915. Moved next month to India and then remained there, under command of the Presidency Brigade in 8th (Indian) Division.

2nd (Home Service) Garrison Battalion
Formed at North Coates near Grimsby in May 1916. August 1917: converted into the 4th Battalion, Royal Defence Corps.

As the war of attrition dragged on into 1916, the government introduced conscription to replenish some of those units decimated on the front line. Prior to this the Derby Scheme was introduced in

Private William Baines of the 1st Lincolnshires who was shot through the head at Ypres. Standing at only 5ft 4in, William survived his horrific injury and returned to the front.

the autumn of 1915 by Kitchener's new Director General of Recruiting, Edward Stanley, 17th Earl of Derby. They would demonstrate whether British manpower goals could be met by volunteers or whether conscription was necessary. Derby required each eligible man aged 18 to 41 who was not in a 'starred' (essential) occupation to make a public declaration. When the scheme was announced many men went to the recruiting office without waiting to be 'fetched'. It was an enormous enterprise. Each eligible man's pink card from the recently-completed National Register was copied onto a blue card, which was sent to his local Parliamentary recruiting committee. How did the men of Boston respond to this? About 1,000 men from Boston and 500 from the local villages went to the Drill Hall to demonstrate their willingness to comply with the scheme before the deadline.

The Great War was a war of attrition, chiefly determined by the outdated or forced tactics used at the time. If the men of the service battalions had not joined the throngs of men heading for the front, Europe might now quite likely be a different place.

Ambulance Men Go

The Boston Division of the St John's Ambulance Brigade assembled in the town to make their final arrangements for the departure of its contingency to Aldershot with the Military Home Hospital Reserves. The council of the Boston Institute loaned their offices as a temporary headquarters. Fifteen men entrained for Aldershot with Chief Officer Stanley Dickinson heading the men to the station. These men, although not fighting on the front, played an equal part in bringing victory to Britain and her allies.

The Last Post

The news of the armistice and cessation of hostilities reached Boston before 10.30 am on Monday, 11 November 1918 through Messrs A.H. Read & Son, who obtained it over the telephone from shipping agents in London. The good news quickly spread and at 11 o'clock the flag was hoisted on the parish church tower and the joy bells started to ring. The public rejoicings that followed were on a scale not witnessed in Boston for many years. On official confirmation of the news reaching the Post Office by wire, the staff cheered and sang *God Save the King* and the enthusiasm was taken up outside and communicated itself to hundreds of people in the town.

On all hands flags were put out, and before noon Boston presented a 'gay and animated scene'. Strait Bargate, High Street and West Street were festooned with bunting and the euphoria was almost tangible. Local schools joined the enthusiasm in the afternoon when they were closed, as did many working people. The market place became crowded with demonstrations and the public generally, including soldiers, sailors, women and girls, 'entering with zest into the celebration'. A band was set up in the corner of the market place with the 2/6th Suffolk cyclists playing music that encouraged people in the Scala balcony to cheer and sing. Effigies were displayed on the streets, then fireworks were discharged and maroons sent up from the fire station in West Street. Countless more flags, bunting and coloured ribbons immersed the market place in the patriotic red, white and blue. To quench the thirst of the partygoers a barrel of beer was rolled to the Five Lamps from the Still Hotel and there consumed by the festival crowd.

Such scenes, long absent during the war years, continued into the night when many coloured flares were sent up, scores of people lingering in the streets until a late hour. By Home Office order the

Former Boston Grammar School pupil Lieutenant E.N. Marris, who was awarded the Military Cross.

The Boston St John's Ambulance Brigade.

lighting restrictions were in large measure removed and for the first time, with the threat of the dreaded Zeppelin removed, shops re-opened brightly illuminated. Later that night, another bonfire was started on Bargate Green and star-shells were fired by the military, encouraged by the excited crowd. A glee party near the Five Lamps aided by a merry crowd at about 10 o'clock sang patriotic songs, concluding with the national anthem.

Spiritual Need

Sombre scenes at the parish church reminded people of the possible futility of the past four years. A great congregation including Mayor Alderman A. Cooke-Yarborough, Deputy Mayor Councillor E. Richardson and other members of the Corporation attended the service. Conducting the proceedings was the vicar, the Reverend R.O Hutchinson and the choirs of St Botolph, Skirbeck Parish Church and the Holy Trinity, Skirbeck took part. After prayers, comforting words from Psalms 124 and 150 were chanted, with a song from David describing how if Jehovah had not been with Israel when men rose up to attack them, like raging waters overwhelming them, they would not have escaped the hunters' trap. Yet the trap was broken and they escaped. This was by way of confirmation to the crowd that this had been a righteous war with God on their side. One can only wonder what words of consolation were offered by the German clergy to their flock! The remarkable words within Revelations 21 were read out by Reverend A.M Cook, offering at least some consolation to those who had lost someone in the war. *The Magnificat* and *Te Deum* were sung, followed by *Onward Christian Soldiers*, further assuring the congregation that the war had been ordained by God and was therefore righteous. Miss M. Oldrid was the organist, assisted by Lieutenant Middleton of the Suffolks, who played out the service with *God Save the King*.

In keeping with tradition, several war memorials were unveiled in Boston after the war once sufficient funds had been raised. On 2 October 1921 the St Thomas Memorial was unveiled by Major S.C. Wright, DSO who as an officer had gone to France in 1915 with the Boston Royal Field Artillery battery. The respectful audience heard Major Wright remind them of the debt owed to those whose names had been engraved. The cross, surmounting a shaft

FLAGS

and where to get them.

Union Jacks, **St. George's Cross,**
American, **French,**
Belgian, etc.

ROPED AND TOGGLED READY TO FLY.

5d. to £5 each.

J. OLDRID and Co.,
TEL. 109.   BOSTON.

Boston shop advertising flags for sale to the patriotic public.

springing from a stone pedestal and steps, was designed by Mr Temple Moore, the church architect. The front panel of the cross bears the inscription: 'The Gallant Dead: 1914–1918', with the other three panels containing the names of the fallen men.

A procession of ex-servicemen walked from St Thomas's School to the churchyard accompanied by the Salvation Army Band playing Chopin's *Funeral March*. Lieutenant A. Clift was in command of the parade, with soldiers carrying their arms reversed. Poignantly, Major Clarke reminded the assembly that one of the greatest battles of the war was fought and the greatest victory was won. 'To those who mourn the loss of a brave man I would commend these lines':

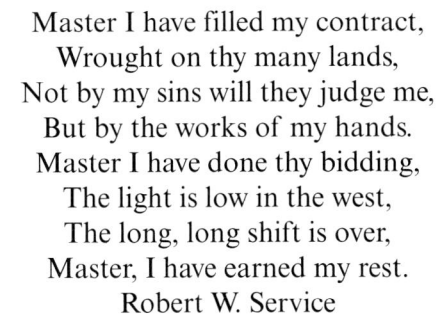

Reverend J. Beanland, vicar of the Holy Trinity, Skirbeck.

> Master I have filled my contract,
> Wrought on thy many lands,
> Not by my sins will they judge me,
> But by the works of my hands.
> Master I have done thy bidding,
> The light is low in the west,
> The long, long shift is over,
> Master, I have earned my rest.
> Robert W. Service

Boston people erected other memorials such as the Bridge Street Memorial, Centenary Church Memorial, the parish church of St James, Freiston and the Holy Trinity Church Memorial, each one a timeless tribute to those who had paid the ultimate sacrifice. The memorial on Bargate Green was unveiled on Sunday, 25 September 1921 by the Lord Lieutenant

Lieutenant J.W. Beanland, son of the vicar of the Holy Trinity Skirbeck, killed in the Dardanelles at 'Chocolate Hill'.

of the County, the Right Honourable the Earl of Yarborough. Inscribed on the monument was: 'TO THE GLORY OF GOD AND IN GRATEFUL REMEMBRANCE OF THE MEN OF

"God Punish England!"

As remarkable as Herr Ernst Lissauer's "Hymn of Hate" was the form of greeting adopted in Germany. "God punish England!" (Gott strafe England!) was the form of address, to which the reply was: "May God punish her!" (Gott mög'es strafen!) This formula, which was used all over Germany, was celebrated in a set of verses by Herr Hochstetter. These appeared in the well-known German weekly "Lustige Blätter." We give Mr. G. Valentine Williams's translation:

This is the German greeting
When men their fellows meet,
The merchants in the market-place.
The beggars in the street,
A pledge of bitter enmity
Thus runs the winged word:
"God punish England, brother!—
Yea! Punish her, O Lord!"

With raucous voice, brass-throated,
Our German shells shall bear
This curse that is our greeting
To the "cousin" in his lair.
This be our German battle-cry,
The motto on our sword:
"God punish England, brother!—
Yea! Punish her, O Lord!"

By shell from sea, by bomb from air,
Our greeting shall be sped,
Making each English homestead
A mansion of the dead.
And even Grey will tremble
As falls each iron word:
"God punish England, brother!—
Yea! Punish her, O Lord!"

This is the German greeting
When men their fellows meet,
The merchants in the market-place,
The beggars in the street,
A pledge of bitter enmity
Thus runs the winged word:
"God punish England, brother!—
Yea! Punish her, O Lord!"

A translation of a German hymn, claiming that God was also fighting for them.

A poignant burial at a German grave.

BOSTON WHO GAVE THEIR LIVES IN THE GREAT WAR 1914–1918.'

'There is but one task for all – One life for each to give. What stands if Freedom fall? Who dies if England live?' (*For All We Have and Are*, Rudyard Kipling). 'Went the day well? We died and never knew. But, well or ill, Freedom, we died for you.' (J.M. Edmonds). 'He died the noblest death a man may die, Fighting for God, and Right, and Liberty;- And such a death is Immortality.' (*All's Well*, John Oxenham).

'Their name liveth for evermore' (Ecclesiasticus 44:14, King James Bible). 'I with uncovered head, Salute the sacred dead, Who went, and who return not.–Say not so! 'Tis not the grapes of Canaan that repay, But the high faith that failed not by the way; Virtue treads paths that end not in the grave; No bar of endless night exiles the brave; And to the saner mind, We rather seem the dead that stayed behind.' (James Russell Lowell).

Gunner W. Robinson of the 1st Lincolnshire Battery, who died of meningitis just before deployment to France.

This chapter is dedicated to the men of the Boston Territorials, service battalions and

Holy Trinity Church, Skirbeck memorial.

Procession of people marching to the unveiling of the war memorial in 1921.

The unveiling of the war memorial.

battalions of the regular army and the families who suffered after being left behind. Lest we forget.

> John 5:28-29 (New International Version)
>
> (28) 'Do not be amazed at this, for a time is coming when all who are in their graves will hear his voice (29) and come out – those who have done what is good will rise to live...'

The Battle Honours of the Lincolnshire Regiment

The Great War[36] – nineteen battalions:

MONS, Le Cateau, Retreat from Mons, MARNE, 1914, Aisne, 1914, 1918, La Bassée, 1914, MESSINES, 1914, 1917, 1918, Armentières, 1914, YPRES, 1914, 1915, 1917, Nonne Bosschen, NEUVE CHAPELLE, Gravenstafel, St. Julien, Frezenberg, Bellewaarde, Aubers, LOOS, SOMME, 1916, 1918, Albert,

1916, 1918, Bazentin, Delville Wood, Pozières, Flers-Courcelette, Morval, Thiepval, Ancre, 1916, 1918, Arras, 1917, 1918, Scarpe, 1917, 1918, Arleux, Pilckem, Langemark, 1917, Menin Road, Polygon Wood, Broodseinde, Poelcapelle, Passchendaele, Cambrai, 1917, 1918, St. Quentin, Bapaume, 1918, LYS, Estaires, Bailleul, Kemmel, Amiens, Drocourt-Quéant, 1918, HINDENBURG LINE, Épehy, Canal du Nord, St. Quentin Canal, Beaurevoir, Selle, Sambre, France and Flanders, 1914–18, SUVLA, Landing at Suvla, Scimitar Hill, Gallipoli, 1915, Egypt, 1916.

The Battle Honours of the First World War listed above are emblazoned on the Regimental Colours, sitting proudly together with existing honours from BLENHEIM to SOUTH AFRICA.

Ten of the Battle Honours in the Great War are printed in capital letters in the list. They are emblazoned on the King's Colour.

They were recommended for that distinction to the Army Council for submission to His Majesty the King by a regimental committee on which each of the battalions that helped to earn them was represented.

'THE WHITE COMRADE – "LO, I AM WITH YOU ALWAYS"'
Following the Battle of Loos this painting by G. Hillyard Swinstead was reproduced in the *Illustrated London News* and *The Illustrated War News*, (6 October edition) also it was on display at the War Exhibition at Prince's Skating Rink, London, in 1915. Thus all the death and maiming being suffered was made to appear as divinely sanctioned.

Meanwhile Jesus was brought in to favour all the German soldiers in this postcard depicting a blessing underway:
For Thine is the Kingdom and the power and the glory forever – Amen!

Endnotes

Chapter One:
1. Admiral Reinhard Scheer, *Germany's High Sea Fleet in the World War* (London, Cassell and Company Ltd, 1920).
2. *Boston Guardian and Lincolnshire Independent*, 26 September 1914.
3. Henry Charles Mahoney and Frederick Arthur Ambrose Talbot, *Sixteen Months in Four German Prisons: Wesel, Sennelager, Klingelputz, Ruhleben* (1917).
4. Dr Katherine Storr, *South Holland Life*.
5. *Lincolnshire Standard*, 17 July 1915, 13 February 1915.
6. *Lincolnshire Echo*, Monday, 23 June 1919.
7. Paul Meyer and John C. Revell, *Boston: Its Fishermen and the First World War*.
8. Leslie Cope Cornford, *The Merchant Seaman in War* (1918).
9. *Nottingham Evening Post*, Thursday, 18 March 1915.

Chapter Two:
10. Alastair Goodrum, *No Place for Chivalry: RAF Night Fighters Defend the East of England Against the German Air Force in Two World Wars*.

Chapter Three:
11. *Lincolnshire Echo*, 5 August 1914.
12. Dr Katherine Storr, *South Holland Life*.
13. *Lincolnshire Echo*, Tuesday, 15 February 1916.
14. Ibid., Saturday, 21 October 1916.
15. Ibid., Wednesday, 30 August 1916.
16. Ibid., Wednesday, 1 March 1916.
17. Scarletfinders.co.uk
18. Scarletfinders.co.uk
19. *Lincolnshire Echo*, Sunday, 18 August 1918.
20. Ibid., Friday, 15 August 1919.
21. Joint War Committee of the British Red Cross Society and the Order of St John of Jerusalem in England. London, HMSO, 1921.

22. Quoted in both the *Lincolnshire Standard and Boston* edition and the *Boston Guardian*, 31 October 1914.
23. William M. Hunt, M.Phil, Ph.D, *A Town Remembers*, Vol. III, Part 2.
24. Ibid.
25. *Lincolnshire Standard*, 15 April 1916.
26. *Boston Guardian*, 15 April 1916.

Chapter Four

27. Richard Gurnham, *The Story of Boston*.
28. *Boston Guardian*, 5 August 1914.
29. *The History of the Lincoln Regiment, 1914–1918*.
30. Ibid., p.182.
31. *The Grantham Journal*, Saturday, 24 April 1915.
32. Dr William M. Hunt, *A Town Remembers*.
33. Martin Middlebrook, *Captain Staniland's Journey: The North Midland Territorials go to War*.
34. *The History of the Lincolnshire Regiment*.
35. Richard Gurnham, *The Story of Boston*.
36. C.R. Simpson, *The History of the Lincolnshire Regiment 1914–1918*.

APPENDIX

Location of Boston's War Casualties

(With kind permission of Dr William M. Hunt Ph.D for allowing me to use the information below from his book *A Town Remembers* in association with *The History of Boston Project*, Richard Kay.)

GREAT BRITAIN

BOSTON CEMETERY, BOSTON: ATKINS, T.L.B.; BATTERHAM, F.; BEARDSALL, E.; BOYCE, G.W.; BRACKENBURY, B.; BREWELL, H. (S.544); BURBIDGE, G.A. (S.609); BURRELL, H. (G.268); CHESTER, C.; CLARK, H.H.; CLAYTON, G.H.; CRUNKHURN, H.; DAMMS, G.L.; DENCH, S.E.; GOODACRE, E.; HEPPENSTALL, G.H.; HORRY, T.A.; HUMBERSTONE, W.G.; JACKSON, J.R; KIRK, J.T.; LADDS, L.; MAWER, R.N.; MOODY, C.; MORALEE, H.; MOYER, W.; MUSTON, F.; PEARSON, W.; PERKINS, A.E.; PORTER, A.; PRIESTLEY, T.; RASTALL, A.; REESON, A.; ROBINSON, J.T.; ROBINSON, W.; SANDERS, E.W.; SLINGSBY, T.E.; SMITH, J.H.; SPEIGHT, A.; STAINES, W.J.; WELLS, S.; WILLIAMS, G.; WILSON, J.C.; WINTER, W.H.R.

BOSTON, HOLY TRINITY CHURCHYARD, SPILSBY ROAD: COPPING, J.W.; THOMPSON, J.S.T.

BOSTON, ST NICHOLAS' CHURCHYARD, SKIRBECK: MALTBY, C.W.; WELBERRY, A.J.

BOSTON, ST THOMAS'S CHURCHYARD, LONDON ROAD: RANSOME, J.E.

BOSTON, ST GUTHLAC'S CHURCHYARD, FISHTOFT: ALLEN, H.K.

DOVER (ST JAMES'S) CEMETERY, KENT: HOLLAND, C.

LYNESS ROYAL NAVAL CEMETERY, WALLS AND FLOTTA: HARRISON, J.W.

NETLEY MILITARY CEMETERY, SOUTHAMPTON, HAMPSHIRE: CHESTER, A.

PAINSWICK PARISH CEMETERY, GLOUCESTERSHIRE: POCKLINGTON, J.

MEMORIALS TO THE MISSING IN GREAT BRITAIN

CHATHAM NAVAL MEMORIAL: BENTON, C.W; BONTOFT, J.; BREWSTER, C.T.B.; BURSNALL, F.G.; COOK, F.; COUSENS, A.; DAMMS, T.; DIXON, F.W.; ELLERBY, R.H.; HACK, J.C.; HILEY, H.; LADDS, D.F.; LADDS, W.; PARKER, W.G.; SHARP, R.; STRICKLAND, T.; WINGATE, J.H.

PLYMOUTH NAVAL MEMORIAL: DONNISON, R.

PORTSMOUTH NAVAL MEMORIAL: ATKINSON, L.H.; HALL, J.T.; TURNER, C.E.; WOOD, C.S.

TOWER HILL MERCHANT NAVY MEMORIAL, LONDON: FOLLOWS, A.; LADDS, F.; MOSS, J.; SMITH, A.R.H.; TAYLOR, H.; WARNER, G.; WELBERRY, A.J.

BELGIUM

CANADA FARM CEMETERY: FEATHERSTONE, E. (3,D,19).

CEMENT HOUSE CEMETERY, LANGEMARK: MITCHAM, L. (13,A,24).

COXYDE MILITARY CEMETERY: WILKINSON, A.W. (3,A,16).

DOZINGHEM MILITARY CEMETERY: WARD, W.H. (9,D,5).

DRANOUTRE CHURCHYARD: STANILAND, G. (6,1); STANILAND, M. (6,15).

DUHALLOW ADS CEMETERY, YPRES: BROWN, A. (1,E,9).

HARINGHE (BANDAGHAM) MILITARY CEMETERY: POVEY, A. (2,F,17).

HARLEBEKE NEW BRITISH CEMETERY: KIRTON, J.W. (14,C,5).

HOOGE CRATER CEMETERY: WILKINSON, W. (1,C,2).

HOP STORE MILITARY CEMETERY, VLAMERTINGHE: ROBSON, F. (1,A,43).

KEMMEL CHÂTEAU MILITARY CEMETERY: ARMITAGE, R. (E,43); TRUELOVE, C. (C,14).

KLEIN VIERSTRAAT BRITISH CEMETERY: MCGUIRE, W.M. (5,E,3).

LARCH WOOD (RAILWAY CUTTING) CEMETERY, ZILLEBEKE: BURCHNALL, C.H. (1,B,6).

LIJSSENTHOEK MILITARY CEMETERY: ASHBERRY, T. (7,C,37); CHEESEWRIGHT, J.F. (26,A,20A); COMER, T. (3,A,41); CRICK, A. (1,B,1A); MORLEY, A.W. (4,B,34); WILSON, G. (3,D,23).

LINDENHOEK CHALET MILITARY CEMETERY, KEMMEL: CHAMBERLAIN, J.H. (2,J,9); DALLYWATERS, E.W. (2,J,8).

NINE ELMS BRITISH CEMETERY, POPERINGHE: AIREY, A. (14,E,17).

OXFORD ROAD CEMETERY, YPRES: BARBER, A.C. (2,C,17).

PACKHORSE FARM SHRINE CEMETERY: ROBINSON, G. (A,10); WILSON, H. (C,4).

RAILWAY DUGOUTS BUR. GROUNDS (TRANSPORT FARM), ZILLEBEKE: GROCOCK, W.H. (1,E,21); PARKER, R. (1,E,18); PRESTON, A.J. (1,E,19); SHORT, J. (1,E,16).

RENINGSHELT NEW MILITARY CEMETERY: HERRINGSHAW, W. (1,H,17).

SANCTUARY WOOD CEMETERY, ZILLEBEKE: BARBER, C. (2,M,18); GOODACRE, A. (4,P,2).

TYNE COT CEMETERY, PASSCHENDAELE: WHITEWAY, F.R. (54,C,6).

WYTSCHAETE MILITARY CEMETERY: WRIGHT, R.R. (4,E,9).

YPRES RESERVOIR CEMETERY: UPCRAFT, B. (7,A,8).

MEMORIALS TO THE MISSING IN BELGIUM

PLOEGSTEERT MEMORIAL: BASKETTER, A.E.; CARROTT. J.; EAST, J.; LAMBERT, J.; MOTLEY, C.; REAR, W.; TODD, R.

TYNE COT MEMORIAL, PASSCHENDAELE: BOSWORTHIC, W.H.; CHAPMAN, R.L.; FORMAN, L.L.; MABLESON, E.; MANNING, C.; MOWBRAY, G.; PERRIN, A.; ROBERTS, A.; ROGERS, E.G.; SMEDLEY, G.H.; WHITEHEAD, C.J.; WRIGHT, R.

YPRES (MENIN GATE) MEMORIAL: GASH, J.E.; HAGUE, C.B.; HOLMES, W.R.; HOYLES, J.T.; MADDISON, T.; MARTIN, A.; MARTIN, A.L.; MEYER, G.E.; MORTON, A.; NORMAN, W.; ROGERS, W.E.; SUTTERFIELD, G.

EGYPT

CAIRO WAR MEMORIAL CEMETERY: AKRILL, G.G. (Q,192).

KANTARA WAR MEMORIAL CEMETERY: WILSON, F. (E,298).

SUEZ WAR MEMORIAL CEMETERY: HARRISON, D.J. (D,10).

FRANCE

AIRE COMMUNAL CEMETERY: BRADLEY, J. (2,A,11).

ALBERT COMMUNAL CEMETERY EXTENSION: JACKSON, G. (1,P,17).

ASSEVILLERS NEW BRITISH CEMETERY: PARKINSON, T. (1,D,3).

Private A. Goodacre, who was shot through the heart by a shrapnel bullet and died instantly.

Private G. Robinson of the 5th Lincs who lived on Norfolk Street and was killed by a German mine.

BAGNEUX BRITISH CEMETERY: MORALEE, J.W. (4,C,8).

BAILLEUL COMMUNAL CEMETERY: NORTON, W. (C,23).

BAILLEUL COMMUNAL CEMETERY EXTENSION: BEST, C. (2,D,216).

BEAUVAL COMMUNAL CEMETERY: JARY, R.E. (G,17).

BELLICOURT BRITISH CEMETERY: MITCHAM, T.H. (3,B,3); RAMM, J.T. (2,B,3); SIMPSON, W.H. (Sp. Mem. B.2).

BERLES-AU-BOIS CHURCHYARD EXTENSION: HOPPERTON, R.E. (L,5).

BIENVILLERS MILITARY CEMETERY: STUBLEY, L.M. (18,E,14).

BOULOGNE EASTERN CEMETERY: ALLIWELL, W.E. (8,C,68).

BRANCOURT-LE-GRAND MILITARY CEMETERY: KING, T. (B,13).

BUCQUOY ROAD CEMETERY, FICHEUX: DARLING, T. (1,J,14); KEMP, S. (2,C,6).

BULLY-GRENAY COMMUNAL CEMETERY EXTENSION: TURNER, A. (1,F,9).

BUSIGNY COMMUNAL CEMETERY EXTENSION: CREASEY, C.E. (5,B,2).

CABARET ROUGE BRITISH CEMETERY: BAILEY, T. (27,G,16); CHRISTY, W.H. (14,A,1).

CAMBRIN MILITARY CEMETERY: DAY, T. (M,11); DOUGHTY, J.G. (N,18); LEDGER, F. (N,19).

CANADIAN CEMETERY NO.2, NEUVILLE-ST. VAAST: COLE, A.W. (1,C,12).

Private J.T. Hoyles of the 1st Battalion Lincolnshire Regiment, who died on 4 June 1915.

CHOCQUES MILITARY CEMETERY: GUNBY, C.D. (4,A,13).

CITÉ BONJEAN MILITARY CEMETERY, ARMENTIÈRES: WHELBOURN, F.W. (9,A,95).

DELVILLE WOOD CEMETERY, LONGUEVAL: TROTT, J.J. (22,Q,7).

DENAIN COMMUNAL CEMETERY: WHITE, G.A. (D,61).

DERNANCOURT COMMUNAL CEMETERY EXTENSION: BAKER, S. (2,D,15).

ECOIVRES MILITARY CEMETERY, MONT-ST. ÉLOI: GARRILL, H.E. (1,E,14).

ÉTAPLES MILITARY CEMETERY: DAVEY, C.R. (48,D,1); HORTON, W. (20,J,4); INGRAM, G.A. (11,C,15); JORDAN, B. (18,K,17A); UPSALL, H. (66,E,5).

ÉTRETAT CHURCHYARD EXTENSION: BARTON, C. (1,A,7).

FAUBOURG D'AMIENS MILITARY CEMETERY, ARRAS: EDWARDS, G.E. (2,F,21).

FAVREUIL BRITISH CEMETERY: CLARKE, A.E. (1,F,22).

FONCQUEVILLERS MILITARY CEMETERY: ENDERBY, H. (1,G,23).

FOUQUIÈRES CHURCHYARD EXTENSION: SMITH, H. (2,A,4).

FRANVILLERS COMMUNITY CEMETERY EXTENSION: KING, G. (2,A,17).

FRESNOY-LE-GRAND COMMUNAL CEMETERY EXTENSION: WELBOURN, C. (B,15).

GLAGEON COMMUNAL CEMETERY EXTENSION: GOOR, J.T. (2,B,1).

GOUY-EN-ARTOIS COMMUNAL CEMETERY EXTENSION: AYRE, H. (A.15).

HANNESCAMPS NEW MILITARY CEMETERY: PARSONS, F. (E,17); WILLIAMS, J.R. (B,6).

HEATH CEMETERY, HARBONNIERS: TROOPS, F.C. (5,J,5).

HEILLY STATION CEMETERY, MÉRICOURT-L'ABBÉ: WOOD, W.H. (4,E,74).

HENINEL COMMUNAL CEMETERY EXTENSION: BOGG, C. (C,12).

HERMIES HILL BRITISH CEMETERY: ANDREWS, W.B. (2,B,37); GREGORY, A.W. (4,J,5); SPECK, W. (4,D,5).

HIGHLAND CEMETERY, LE CATEAU: GREEN, J.H. (2,B,5).

JEANCOURT COMMUNAL CEMETERY EXTENSION: BARTON, T.Y. (2,D,20).

LA CHAPELETTE BRITISH CEMETERY, PÉRONNE: AYRE, F. (1,D,10).

LE CATEAU MILITARY CEMETERY: PAYNE, G.H. (3,C,3).

LE GRAND BEAUMART BRITISH CEMETERY, STEENWERCK: CADE, T.B. (3,D,11).

LES BARAQUES MILITARY CEMETERY: BURROWS, J.W. (6,A,4A); WHITE, L. (4,F,9).

LONGUENESSE (ST. OMER) SOUVENIR CEMETERY: EASTICK, G. (5,C,22).

MERVILLE COMMUNAL CEMETERY: WILLIAMS, J.R. (4,N,4); WOODS, H.(4,N,10).

MILLENCOURT COMMUNAL CEMETERY EXTENSION: TOOLEY, G. de G. (C,29).

MONT-BERNANCHON BRITISH CEMETERY, GONNEHEM: WALMSLEY, P. (1,C,8).

MONT HOUN MILITARY CEMETERY: FARROW, J.C. (3,H,2B); WARWICK, R. (7,A,7A).

MONT-NOIR MILITARY CEMETERY: LAND, T. (1,F,6).

MORY-ABBEY MILITARY CEMETERY: WHITE, G.L. (2,H,4).

NOEUX-LES-MINES COMMUNAL CEMETERY EXTENSION: UPSALL, A. (4,B,3).

OWL TRENCH CEMETERY: MCGUIRE, T.O.P. (A).

PERNES BRITISH CEMETERY: BURN, J. (2,A,34).

PÉRONNE COMMUNAL CEMETERY EXTENSION: GARRILL, W.H. (3,B,16).

PÉRONNE ROAD CEMETERY, MARICOURT: WOODS, R.S. (3,B,11).

PUCHEVILLERS BRITISH CEMETERY: DENNISON, J. (4,F,18).

QUARRY CEMETERY, MONTAUBAN: TRIGG, C.R.D. (4,E,6).

QUÉANT COMMUNAL CEMETERY BRITISH EXTENSION: WRIGHT, H. (C,25).

RAMICOURT BRITISH CEMETERY: FARRAM, A.T. (B,38).

ROCQUIGNY-ÉQUANCOURT ROAD BRITISH CEMETERY: DENCH, G. (4,C,28); GREEN, A. (8,A,5).

ROISEL COMMUNAL CEMETERY EXTENSION: PAGE, G.W. (1,J,4).

ROMERIES COMMUNAL CEMETERY EXTENSION: WILLIAMSON, R. (9,B,4).

SERRE ROAD CEMETERY, NO.1, BEAUMONT HAMEL: CLARKSON, S. (1,J,1).

ST. AUBERT BRITISH CEMETERY: GILCHRIST, F. (2,A,9); KEAL, H. (1,B,10).

ST. PATRICK'S CEMETERY, LOOS: ALLISON, H.H. (1,C,2).

ST SEVER CEMETERY, ROUEN: CABORN, J.W.A. (A,14,42); CARBY, H. (A,17,35); SIMPSON, H.(i) (B,15,49).

ST SEVER CEMETERY EXTENSION, ROUEN: CARROTT, J. (O,7,J,6); LOTE, S. (S,3,J,5).

ST. SOUPLET BRITISH CEMETERY: MITCHAM, F. (3,D,11).

TEMPLEUX-LE GUERARD COMMUNAL CEMETERY EXTENSION: APPLEBY, F. (A,9).

THÉLUS MILITARY CEMETERY: DAVY, W.H. (3,A,3).

TINCOURT NEW BRITISH CEMETERY: DANBY, H. (5,H,3).

VADENCOURT BRITISH MILITARY CEMETERY: BARTON, F.P. (3,A,31).

VALENCIENNES COMMUNAL CEMETERY: GOODMAN, F. (5,B,7).

VARENNES MILITARY CEMETERY: WEBBER, A. (1,F,7).

VERMELLES BRITISH CEMETERY: HORREY, A. (5,F,7).

VILLERS-FAUCON COMMUNAL CEMETERY: BELL, D. (D,56).

VILLERS-FAUCON COMMUNAL CEMETERY EXTENSION: WHITE, J.W. (2,C,9).

WANCOURT BRITISH CEMETERY: FAUNT, G.K. (6,G,2).

WIMEROUX COMMUNAL CEMETERY: STRAY, J.W. (1,H,29).

'Y' FARM MILITARY CEMETERY, BOIS GRENIER: FOLLOWS, H. (F,21); PITTS, G.C. (F,36).

MEMORIALS TO THE MISSING IN FRANCE

ARRAS MEMORIAL: BELL, S.; BENTON, A.C.; BITTIN, F.; BLYTHE, W.; CARTWRIGHT, W.; DEACON, S.G.; DICKINSON, W.S.; DRACASS, F.; KIRK, C.H.; LOVELEY, G.T.; MORALEE, M.H.; NORTON, H.; PANTON, F.E.; RUSHTON, J.; SCARGALL, C.S.; SIMPSON, H.(ii); SPRATT, F.V.; STORR, H.; WATSON, H.E.; WELBOURN, W.; WEST, H.

CAMBRAI MEMORIAL: MUNTON, A.W.; OVERTON, F.

LE TOURET MEMORIAL: ATTERBY, A.; MYERS, A.E.

LOOS MEMORIAL: BARLOW, H.P.; BLAND, L.; COE, E.; DAVIES, J.H.; FOSTER, J.H.; FREEMAN, J.; GARNHAM, R.H.; HOPKINS, C.J.; LEE, W.; LILLEY, W.F.; PINNER, H.G.; ROBINSON, S.; SHERWOOD, F.; WOOD, T.B.

POZIÈRES MEMORIAL: BERRY, W.; BURTON, R.; CHRISTIAN, W.; GOODMAN, J.; JACKSON, F.; LUCAS, A.E.; ROSSINGTON, J.F.; SMITH, J.R.; SYMONDS, C.P.; WATLING, J.W.

SOISSONS MEMORIAL: BROCKELSBY, W.; JONES, W.H.

THIEPVAL MEMORIAL: BEECHAM, H.H.W.; BLYTHE, D.; BRACKENBURY, E.; BROWN, M.W.; CLAYPOOLE, C.G.S.; COPPING, E.J.; DERRICK, A.J.; DOUGHTY, R.; ELSOM, E.; FORREST, T.; JACKSON, T.; LONGFORD, H.; LUCAS, W.; SIMPSON, J.; SOUTH, J.; STOPPER, S.; TOSLER, R.A.; WATERFIELD, T.A.

VIS-EN-ARTOIS MEMORIAL: GOODRICK, J.W.

GERMANY

COLOGNE SOUTHERN CEMETERY, COLOGNE: MASON, F. (13,G,4); MCCANN, J.F. (15,A,57).

NIEDERZWEHREN CEMETERY, KASSEL: BAKER, J. (5,B,6); HANDS, G.B. (1,C,6).

GREECE
STRUMA MILITARY CEMETERY: HUNWICK, F. (3,D,4).

INDIA
KIRKEE MEMORIAL: LOCKWOOD, W.E.E.

ST. SEPULCHRE'S CEMETERY, POONA: LOCKWOOD, W.E.E. (C,401).

IRAQ
BAGHDAD NORTH GATE WAR CEMETERY, BAGHDAD: GOOSE, J.R. (16,N,8); RASTALL, T. (7,D,7).

ISRAEL
JERUSALEM MEMORIAL, JERUSALEM: MALTBY, A.P.

ITALY
SAVONA MEMORIAL: PEARSON, J.M.

MALTA
PIETA MILITARY CEMETERY: CHARLTON, S.F. (D,16,2).

REPUBLIC OF SOUTH AFRICA
ELLIS, E.G. (location of grave not known).

Private Matthew Henry Moralee, killed on 20 April 1916.

TUNISIA
BIZERTA CEMETERY: COCHRANE, W. (Grave 2).

TURKEY
HELLES MEMORIAL, GALLIPOLI: BARBER, T.; BEANLAND, J.W.; COLE, J.W.; FREEMAN, W.; GREEN, P.A.; HARDING, E.; SCULTHORPE, G.H.

DISTRIBUTION OF THE OMITTED CASUALTIES BY LOCATION (FIRST WORLD WAR)

GREAT BRITAIN

BOSTON CEMETERY, BOSTON: BASTOW, H. (S.588); BUNTING, J. (S.486); CLARK, C.W. (P.147); DICKINSON, W.G.B. (U.490); DILLMORE, G.E. (T.910); FLANNIGAN, A. (I.605); KEIGHTLEY, C.G. (S.390); LANG, J. (T.933); MARSHALL, H.M. (S.7); MCINTOSH, A.F. (S.456); MERCHANT, F. (U.492); OUGHTON, H. (T.801); ROBINSON, E.A. (S.560); ROGERS, E. (S.750); SWINN, W.E. (T.876); TAYLOR, R. (S.415); TURNER, G. (G.306); WILLIAMS, W.H. (S.841).

BOSTON, HOLY TRINITY CHURCHYARD, SPILSBY ROAD: BEANLAND, M.R., PALMER, V.C., SARGISSON, M.S.

BOSTON, ST NICHOLAS' CHURCHYARD, SKIRBECK: BARRAND, P.W.; CLARKE, J.R.; RANDALL, J.W.

BOSTON, ST THOMAS'S CHURCHYARD, LONDON ROAD: CRAWFORD, F.

BUTTERWICK, LINCS, ST ANDREW'S CHURCHYARD: LEGGETT, F.W.

LEEDS (LAWN WOOD) CEMETERY, YORKSHIRE: JOBSON, D.E. (T.58).

LOUGHBOROUGH (LEICESTER ROAD) CEMETERY: ANGRAVE, H.

OLD LEAKE, LINCS, ST MARY'S CHURCHYARD: STEPHENSON, S.E.

SCARBOROUGH (MANOR ROAD) CEMETERY: RYALLS, J.S. (A.99).

STROMNESS CHURCHYARD, ORKNEY: PARSONS, W.H.

MEMORIALS TO THE MISSING IN GREAT BRITAIN

CHATHAM NAVAL MEMORIAL: BRAIME, W.; BROCKLESBY, P.; HUTTON, W.R.; LAWRENCE, A.W.; LUCAS, W.T.; SMALLEY, H.; WHITEHEAD, C.

PORTSMOUTH NAVAL MEMORIAL: CROSS, G.; DOLBY, S.; SUTTON, J.T.; WARD, J.W.

TOWER HILL MERCHANT NAVY MEMORIAL, LONDON: AISTHORPE, F.; ANDERSON, G.; ANSLOW, E.W.; ARMITAGE, W.H.; BAYES, T.W.; BEECHAM, A.D.; BIGGADIKE, W.; BIGGADYKE, B.; BLAKEY, G.F.; BRAIME, F.; BROWN, F.H.; BRUNNING, W.T.; BUCK, A.J.; BUTTERFIELD, H.W.; CAMMACK, W.T.; CLARKE, A.P.; CLARKE, W.R.; COATES, W.D.; CORBIN, F.; DARBY, W.A.; DOBSON, T.; DRAPER, G.; DUFFIELD, A.J.; EASTICK, J.A.; EVANS, J.A.; FORWOOD, H.V.; FRANCIS, D.R.; FULLER, W.; GOWER, J.H.; GRANT, G.; GREENACRE, J.; HACK, T.R.F.; HADDINOTT, T.; HANCOCK, P.M.; HARMAN, W.T.; HARRISON, W.; HAWKINS, G.H.; HILEY, T.E.; HOLLIS, J.J.; HOWARD, E.F.; JOHNSON, W.A.; KEMP, W.J.; KIERTON, R.A.; LAWRENCE, C.E.; LEWIS, A.V.; LEWIS, F.C.; MACE, W.C.A.; MARTIN, C.; MEEDS, T.;

Private Tom Barber, killed on 9 August 1915 at Gallipoli. Thomas was a soldier with the 6th Lincs and son of Mr F.W. Barber of Hospital Lane. Tom was the second son of Mr Barber to have died, his son Chas of the Terriers being the first.

MILLINS, H.; MITCHELL, H.C.; MOODY, E.; MOORE, C.J.; NEWMAN, J.S.; NORMAN, F.; NORTON, J.W.; OGILVIE, J.; PAGE, W.J.; PARVIN, T.S.; PASSON, H.W.; PAWLETT, J.R.; PESTERFIELD, E.W.; PICK, T.; PRATT, W.C.E.; PRIESTLEY, W.; PROCTOR, E.; READ, W.A.; REVELL, J.W.; RICE, S.; RICHARDS, J.C.; RINGWOOD, J.W.; RODGERS, J.; ROSE, A.E.; SANDERSON, A.; SAUNDERS, J.W.; SCOTRICK, G.H.; SMITH, C.C.; SMITH, E.C.; SMITH, J.; SMITH, W.; SPINK, J.; SULLIVAN, P.; TAYLOR, J.; THOMAS, A.; THOMPSON, J.W.; THORGRIMSEN, C.; TIMBY, E.; TIMBY, E.B.; TIMMATH, W.H.; TODD, C.C.; TURNER, G.; TYLER, W.; UPCRAFT, C.W.; WEATHERHOGG, C.; WEBB, C.A.; W(H)ISKING, T.; WHITTLE, E.; WILLOWS, S.G.; WILSON, J.H.; WOOD, F.; WRACK, T.; YOUNGS, W.C.

BELGIUM

BARD COTTAGE CEMETERY, YPRES: JACKSON, W. (2,M,9).

COXYDE MILITARY CEMETERY: LEACHMAN, C. (2,J,17).

DUHALLOW ADS CEMETERY, YPRES: BANISTER, J.J.E. (7,G,3).

FRAMERIES COMMUNAL CEMETERY: KENNEDY, T.H. (3,A,3).

HUTS CEMETERY: SUTCLIFFE, E. (4,A,8).

LIJSSENTHOEK MILITARY CEMETERY: LEGGOTT, A. (7,A,39); TAYLOR, J.E. (19,B,20).

MENIN ROAD SOUTH MILITARY CEMETERY, YPRES: MASON, W. (1,R,16).

Bert Biggadyke, second engineer on the Fijian.

NINE ELMS BRITISH CEMETERY, POPERINGHE: TONGE, G.W.S. (14,B,21).

RAILWAY DUGOUTS BURIAL GROUNDS (TRANSPORT FARM), ZILLEBEKE: ANDREWS, A.M. (Sp. Mem. B.10.); REED, L.A. (1,C,6).

VLAMERTINGHE NEW MILITARY CEMETERY: HOLEHOUSE, A.H. (6,G,3); WELLS, G.F. (1,B,1).

MEMORIALS TO THE MISSING IN BELGIUM

PLOEGSTEERT MEMORIAL: CAMMACK, A.E.; JOHNSON, H.; LUFF, W.E.

Thomas Dobson, deck hand on the Fijian.

TYNE COT MEMORIAL, PASSCHENDAELE: ABLEWHITE, C.; ADCOCK, A.; BOURNE, A.; CLAY, W.F.; GREENFIELD, W.H.; HINDS, J.E.; LIMBERT, W.; MARRIOTT, F.W.; NEWTON, G.

YPRES (MENIN GATE) MEMORIAL: CAVILL, H.; GILLETT, E.; RASON, C.F.; SMITH, W.E.; SMITHBONE, R.P.; TREDINNICK, W.P.; WALTHAM, A.

CANADA
UNKNOWN LOCATION: RAWLING, J.R.

EGYPT
ALEXANDRIA (CHATBY) MILITARY CEMETERY: CHAMBERS, W.E. (A,7).

W.J. Page, mate on the trawler Carrington.

Skipper T. Storr Parvin of the trawler Holland.

C.C. Smith, an apprentice on the trawler Carrington.

FRANCE

AIX NOULETTE CEMETERY EXTENSION: BEDFORD, F. (1,O,13).

ANCRE BRITISH CEMETERY: BARLOW, J. (1,A,40).

AUBIGNY COMMUNAL CEMETERY EXTENSION: HALL, G.E. (5,B,14).

AWOINGT BRITISH CEMETERY: DODDS, J.L. (5,E,1).

BAILLEUL COMMUNAL CEMETERY EXTENSION: BENNETT, T.R. (1,E,83).

BEAUCOURT BRITISH CEMETERY: HARWOOD, C.J. (A,6).

BLIGHTY VALLEY CEMETERY: WARD, A.E. (5,H,15).

BRAY VALE BRITISH CEMETERY: DAWSON, F. (4,B,3).

CABARET ROUGE BRITISH CEMETERY: BRINKLEY, H. (15,L,8).

CAUDRY BRITISH CEMETERY: GREEN, F.S. (2,E,7).

250 BOSTON IN THE GREAT WAR

CHOCQUES MILITARY CEMETERY: BRIGHT, N.H. (1,G,39).

CITÉ BONJEAN MILITARY CEMETERY: MITCHELL, J.E.L. (7,B,23).

CONTAY BRITISH CEMETERY: CLARKE, J.W. (7,D,7).

DAOURS COMMUNAL CEMETERY EXTENSION: DAY, F. (7,B,30).

DELVILLE WOOD CEMETERY, LONGUEVAL: QUEENBOROUGH, S.H. (28,O,7).

DUISANS BRITISH CEMETERY: GLEDHILL, B. (3,K,47).

ERQUINGHEM-LYS CHURCHYARD EXTENSION CEMETERY: WILLOWS, B.H. (2,G,18).

Chief engineer Thomas Wrack was a survivor of the trawler Arctic (see Chapter One); unfortunately he was not so lucky on the Fijian.

ÉTRETAT CHURCHYARD EXTENSION: HARRIS, J.T. (2,B,8A).

FONCQUEVILLERS MILITARY CEMETERY: HOUGHTON, H.J. (1,L,2).

FORCEVILLE COMMUNAL CEMETERY AND EXTENSION: LEGGOTT, R. (4,C,2).

GORDON DUMP CEMETERY: SYMONS, T.R. (Sp. Mem. B,21).

GOUZEAUCOURT NEW BRITISH CEMETERY: BRINKLEY, W.A. (2,H,18).

HARGICOURT BRITISH CEMETERY: SMITH, H.R. (1,E,12).

HÉBUTERNE MILITARY CEMETERY: ABLEWHITE, S. (4,J,3).

HEILLY STATION CEMETERY, MÉRICOURT-L'ABBÉ: SIMPSON, H. (1,C,15).

HERMONVILLE MILITARY CEMETERY: GREEN, J. (2,C,8).

LEVEL CROSSING CEMETERY: WILSON, A.F. (1,A,48).

LOOS BRITISH CEMETERY: PRESGRAVE, S. (19,D,2).

MARFAUX BRITISH CEMETERY: PENTELOW, A.L. (5,H,10).

MAZINGARBE COMMUNAL CEMETERY EXTENSION: GILLIATT, F.R. (2,D,1).

MINDEL TRENCH BRITISH CEMETERY: WEDD, H. (B,50).

PÉRONNE COMMUNAL CEMETERY EXTENSION: MARKWICK, W.P. (5,M,9).

PIGEON RAVINE CEMETERY: HOWDEN, C.H. (3,A,8).

PUCHEVILLERS BRITISH CEMETERY: MARTIN, A.E. (6,C,17).

REGINA TRENCH CEMETERY: SEARS, H.R. (7,D,2).

ROCQUIGNY-ÉQUANCOURT ROAD BRITISH CEMETERY: BRITTIN, E.G. (4,C,28).

ROEUX BRITISH CEMETERY: WALTHAM, E. (Sp. Mem. H.3).

STE. MARGUERITE CHURCHYARD, AISNE: PAULSON, J.S.

ST. SEVER CEMETERY EXTENSION, ROUEN: RAWLINGS, R.F. (S,3,S,21).

ST. SOUPLET BRITISH CEMETERY: SHARMAN, L. (3,D,13).

ST. VAAST POST MILITARY CEMETERY: CRAWFORD, A.B. (3,F,8).

TEMPLEUX-LE GUERARD COMMUNAL CEMETERY EXTENSION: COOK, A.J. (1,E,6).

VALENCIENNES (ST. ROCH) COMMUNAL CEMETERY: WHITE, C.W. (4,B,12).

VITTEL COMMUNAL CEMETERY, VOSGES: COLEMAN, J.G.

WANCOURT BRITISH CEMETERY: ELLIS, J.E. (Sp. Mem. 60).

WARVILLERS CHURCHYARD EXTENSION: JACKSON, W. (A,1A).

WIMEREUX COMMUNAL CEMETERY: HUTTON, H. (2,E,8A); MARSHALL, A. (6,D,29A).

MEMORIALS TO THE MISSING IN FRANCE

ARRAS MEMORIAL: CHEAVIN, S.R.; DRURY, R.; FLINTHAM, S.W.; OSTLER, A.; PRESGRAVE, W.; ROBERTS, A.; SEXTON, E.J.; SHARMAN, H.; SIMPSON, H.; SKINNER, H.I.; TITHERLEY, O.R.; WILSON, W.; WOODS, A.E.

CAMBRAI MEMORIAL: QUIRKE, G.A.L.; WILKINSON, W.P.

LA FERTÉ-SOUS-JOUARRE MEMORIAL: MYDDLETON, E.G.; ROBERTS, W.; WOODTHORPE, G.

LOOS MEMORIAL: CRAWLEY, C.W.; DAWSON, E.; DAY, P.W.; GOLDSMITH, J.; MARTIN, W.; STEPHENSON, G.D.

POZIÈRES MEMORIAL: BORMAN, F.; GOSLING, W.

THIEPVAL MEMORIAL: BANISTER. G.A.; FORREST, J.; GREENFIELD, F.; LUCAS, G.W.; MOONEY, W.; POTTER, C.; SIMSON, S.; VURLEY, W.; WARD, C.H.

VIMY MEMORIAL: LEGGOTT, R.J.

VIS-EN-ARTOIS MEMORIAL: GREENFIELD, J.E.

GERMANY

NIEDERZWEHREN CEMETERY, KASSEL: CHRISTIAN, G. (5,A,6); MARSDEN, H. (5,B,5).

STAHNSDORF CEMETERY, BERLIN: HAZELL, W. 'Charlottenberg' (civilian) section.

IRAQ
AMARA WAR CEMETERY: SIMPSON, E.M. (21,C,20).

BAGHDAD NORTH GATE WAR CEMETERY, BAGHDAD: JACKSON, C. (15,M,21); STEPHENSON, C.W. (9,D,3).

MEMORIAL TO THE MISSING IN IRAQ
BASRA MEMORIAL: OSBORNE, A.

ISRAEL
JERUSALEM WAR CEMETERY: ADAMS, L.E. (K,17).

ITALY
BOSCON BRITISH CEMETERY: GASH, E.E. (2,B,18).

TURKEY
ARI BURNU CEMETERY, ANZAC: STEPHENSON, J.W. (J,3).

REDOUBT CEMETERY, HELLES: HALL, C.B. (Sp. Mem. A.154); WRIGHT, A. (Sp. Mem. B.173).

MEMORIAL TO THE MISSING IN TURKEY
HELLES MEMORIAL, GALLIPOLI: BLYTH, R.T.; SHARP, P.; WILSON, J.A.

UNKNOWN
SMITH, G.H.; WALKER, J.

DEATHS AT SEA

Below is a list of the men who sailed from Boston who were drowned and have no known grave but the sea:

ARTIC: SUNK 5 JUNE 1915

FULLER, WILLIAM, age unknown
MACE, WALTER CHARLES, age 40
PESTERFIELD, ERNEST WILLIAM, age 40
TAYLOR, JAMES, age 22

FIJIAN: SUNK 16 OCTOBER 1915

BIGGADYKE, BERTIE, age 20
DOBSON, THOMAS, age 38
FOLLOWS, A., age 20
HAWKINS, GEORGE HENRY, age 64
HILEY, THOMAS E., age 57
MOSS, JAMES, age 45
PASSON, HENRY, age 48
TIMMATH, W., age unknown
WRACK, THOMAS, age 42

CARRINGTON: SUNK 14 MARCH 1916

ANSLOW, EDWARD, age 28
GREENACRE, JOB, age 59
LADDS, FREDERICK, age 54
PAGE, WALTER, age 55
PICK, THOMAS, age 43
SMITH, CHARLES CHRISTOPHER, age 18

Eric J. Sexton, the youngest son of the Reverend and Mrs W. Sexton of Spilsby Road.

Lance Corporal Percy W. Day. Having enlisted in the 1/4th Lincolns, Percy died in the charge at the Hohenzollern Redoubt.

TYLER, WALTER, age 37
WILLOWS, SYDNEY, age 31

***BROTHERTOFT*: SUNK 9 APRIL 1917**
HACK, T., age 30
HANCOCK, P., age unknown
KEIRTON, RUPERT ALEC, age 36
NEWMAN, JOHN SPENCER, age 18
NORMAN, F., age 36
RINGWOOD, J., age 40
SANDERSON, A., age 17
SMITH, J., age 16
SULLIVAN, P., age 30
UPCRAFT, C.W., age 62

***DALMATION*: SUNK 14 APRIL 1917**
BRAIME, FRED, age unknown
CORBIN, FREDERICK, age unknown
DRAPER, G., age unknown
NORTON, JOHN WILLIAM, age unknown
PRIESTLEY, WALTER, age unknown
RICHARDS, J.C., age unknown
SPINK, JAMES, age unknown
WEBB, CHARLES, age unknown
WISKING, THOMAS, age unknown

***SUTTERTON*: SUNK 17 APRIL 1917**
HADDINOTT, T., age 45

***DERWENT*: SUNK 26 JANUARY 1920**

BAYES, THOMAS W., age 23
BUCK, ALBERT JOHN, age 24
CLARKE, WALTER RICHARD, age 28
DARBY, WILLIAM ALFRED, age 55
FRANCIS, DANIEL ROBERT, age 24
GOWER, JAMES HENRY, age 18
OGILVIE, JAMES, age 26
RODGERS, JOSEPH, age 23
ROSE, ALBERT EDWARD, age 18
SAUNDERS, JOSEPH W., age 22

BOSTONIAN: SUNK 14 JANUARY 1938

ANDERSON, GEORGE, age 21
BLAKEY, GEORGE F., age 30
CLARKE, ALBERT PERCY, age 40
HOWARD, E., age 20
JOHNSON, W. ALFRED, age 45
MARTIN, C., age 57
MOORE, C.J., age 20
THORGRIMSEN, CHRIS, age 36
TIMBY, EDWARD, age 17
TIMBY, EDWARD BERESFORD, age 38

LINDSEY: SUNK 10 SEPTEMBER 1920

BROWN, FREDERICK HANSARD, age 21
BUTTERFIELD, H.W., age 33
DUFFIELD, A., age 21
EASON, J.J., age 27
FORWOOD, HENRY VICTOR, age 19

Alfred Fellows, fireman on the Fijian.

Harry Passon, cook on the Fijian.

GRANT, G., age 43
LEWIS, FRED, age 31
REVELL, JOHN WILLIAM, age 22
WARNER, GEORGE, age 45

The following list gives the names of local fishermen who lost their lives while sailing from other ports (these are listed by name, vessel, date sunk and age at death):

S. RICE, ST *LORD HOWICK*, 14 SEPTEMBER 1914, age 22

JOHN W. THOMPSON, ST *SALVIA*, 29 SEPTEMBER 1914, age 31

JOHN R. PAWLETT, ST *ST LAWRENCE*, 3 OCTOBER 1914, age 41

G. SCOTERICK, ST *CYGNUS*, NOVEMBER 1914, age unknown

WILLIAM COMMACK, ST *EARL HOWARD*, 11 DECEMBER 1914, age 30

FRED AISTHORPE, ST *RECOLO*, 26 APRIL 1915, age 23

WALTER J. KEMP, ST *DON*, 6 MAY 1915, age 29

JOSEPH A. EVANS, ST *VENTNOR*, 24 JULY 1915, age 52

HENRY MILLINS, ST *VENTNOR*, 24 JULY 1915, age 50

ERNEST C. SMITH, ST *FITZROY*, 11 OCTOBER 1915, age 24

ARTHUR BEECHAM, ST *CASSIOPEIA*, 6 NOVEMBER 1915, age 27

WILLIAM READ, ST *VICEROY*, 7 DECEMBER 1915, age 54

W.D. COATES, ST *EARL*, 21 JANUARY 1916, age 20

W. HARRISON, ST *QUAIR*, 3 NOVEMBER 1916, age 36

W. BRAIME, HMT *BURNLEY*, 25 NOVEMBER 1916, age unknown

ALFRED LAWRANCE, HMT *HOLDENE*, 2 FEBRUARY 1917, age unknown

CHARLES LAWRENCE, ST *SHAKESPEAR*, 7 FEBRUARY 1917, age 31

THOMAS MEEDS, ST *BEL LILY*, 14 MAY 1917, age 45

WILLIAM T. LUCAS, HMT *EARL LENNOX*, 23 DECEMBER 1918, age unknown

WILLIAM SMITH, ST *EGRET*, 1 MARCH 1919, age 43

WILLIAM C. PRATT, ST *T.W. MOULD*, 1 JULY 1919, age 44

ENOS MOODY, ST *SCOTLAND*, 13 JULY 1919, age 25

WILLIAM ARMITAGE, ST *SUNLAND*, 8 AUGUST 1919, age 42

CHARLES C. TODD, ST *SUNCLOUD*, 8 JULY 1919, age 43

GEORGE TURNER, ST *CYRANO*, 15 AUGUST 1919, age 30

JOHN H. WILSON, ST *KING GEORGE*, 24 NOVEMBER 1919, age 38

JAMES J. HOLLIS, ST *ISLE OF MAN*, 14 DECEMBER 1919, age unknown

The following list gives the names of local fishermen who were held captive as PoWs:

ST *LINDSEY*

J. Dawkins, Volunteer Inn, Skirbeck

George Everitt, 44 Archer Lane

R. Brown, Bedford Place

A. Hipkin, Freiston Road

J.E. Clarke, Alfred Street

Hy. Fryatt, 4 Ashill Row, Freiston Road

Fred Royal, 3 Pipe Office Lane

ST *WALRUS*

W. Hazell, 38 Liquorpond Street

L. Green, South Terrace

W. Steele (uncertain)

A. Maltby, Freiston Road

A. Bailey, 25 Duke Street

W. Graver, 34 Norfolk Place

J. Pratten, 21 Daisy Dale, Skirbeck

ST *FLAVIAN*

W. Woods, 4 Pulvertoft Lane
W. Cole, Victoria Inn
E. Tinkler, 21 Broadfield Terrace
A. Farmer, Liquorpond Street
T. Bird (uncertain)
F.J. Jones, Albert Terrace, Skirbeck Road
J.E. Eastick, Skirbeck
J. Bontoft, 10 King Street
W. Massingham, 23 Duke Street

ST *KESTEVEN*

J.J. Eggers, Fairfield Terrace, Skirbeck
T. Baines, 10 May Villas, White Bridges
William Fletcher, 21 Pinfold Lane
H. Lawrence, 22 Daisy Dale, Skirbeck
W. Rudd, 49 Duke Street
William Harden, Crapley's Court
J. Fletcher, James Street

ST *WIGTOFT*

W. Parker, Fishtoft Road
I. Taylor, Lawrence Square
F. Yarnold, 24 Pulvertoft Lane
Thomas Lissell, 29 Drain Bank, Skirbeck
W. Brunning, 23 Daisy Dale, Skirbeck
J. Brown, 22 Duke Street
G. Anderson, 1 Daisy Dale, Skirbeck

ST *SKIRBECK*

J.T. Baker, Hospital Lane, Skirbeck
W. Ward, c/o Mrs Jessop, Irby Place

H. Marsden, 26 Lawrence Lane
L. Braime, 1 Hamlet Terrace, Skirbeck Quarter
J. Bentoft, 6 Bedford Place, Liquorpond Street
G. Warner, 38 Duke Street
H. Bentoft, 5 Spain Lane

ST *INDIAN*

J.M. Royal, 16 Cheapside
H. Crowder, Lincoln Lane
T. Rosegreen (uncertain)
C. Reece, Mount Bridge, Skirbeck
E. Rear, Charles Street, Skirbeck
J. South, 10 Stafford Street
J. Graves, Wellington House, Skirbeck
G. Christian, Dolphin Lane
D. Rushton, 28 Caroline Street

ST *PORPOISE*

J. Smith, Yarmouth
W. Blackey, Mount Bridge, Skirbeck
J. Beavers, 1 Alpine Terrace, Skirbeck
Charles Warsop, 4a Valentine Terrace
A. Clark, 26 Daisy Dale, Skirbeck
J. Bourne, 85 Liquorpond Street
J. England, 2 Jubilee Terrace, Skirbeck

ST *MARNAY*

F. Pearce, 20 Harrington Street, Grimsby
H. Boulton, 50 James Street
F. Gale, 316 Wellington Street, Grimsby
A. Read, 27 Rosegarth Street
H. Neilson, Gleeb Terrace, Skirbeck

F. Parker, 24 Daisy Dale, Skirbeck

J. Armfield, Oxford Street

F. Driver, 29 Daisy Dale, Skirbeck

W. Maltby, Harrisons Court, Blue Street

ST *JULIAN*

W. Chaffy, 4 Mount Bridge Terrace, Skirbeck

S. Skinner, 12 Pen Street

H. Blakey, 12 Queen Street

B. Dennis, 4 Station Court, Station Street

C. Walkerley, 3 St Mark's Terrace

A. Johnson, Charles Street, Skirbeck

M. Fox (uncertain)

E. Key, Bull Inn, Skirbeck Quarter

W.M. Willcock, Charles Street, Skirbeck

There were also apprentices on board some of the trawlers; they are listed as follows:

ST *SKIRBECK*: W. Moon, C. Streeter

ST *WIGTOFT*: D.R.D. Gale, J. Cornford

ST *WALRUS*: A. Armstrong, C. Henry

ST *KESTEVEN*: H. Foster, A.S. Stearns

ST *LINDSEY*: C. Smith, T. Cornford

ST *PORPOISE*: J.D. Willmott, W. Harris, J.H. Graham

BIBLIOGRAPHY AND SOURCES

Primary Sources

Archbold, Rick and Marschall, Ken, *Hindenburg: An Illustrated History* (Weidenfeld & Nicolson, Orion Publishing Group Ltd, 1994)
Churchill, Winston, *The World Crisis* (Toronto, Macmillan & Co. of Canada, 1923)
Cornford, L. Cope, *The Merchant Seaman in the War* (New York, George H. Doran Company, 1918)
D'Enno, Douglas, *Fishermen Against the Kaiser: Shockwaves of War 1914–1915*, Vol. 1 (Pen & Sword, 2010)
Goodrum, Alistair, *No Place for Chivalry: RAF Night Fighters Defend the East of England Against the German Air Force in Two World Wars* (Grub Street, 2005)
Gurnham, Richard, *The Story of Boston* (The History Press Ltd, 2014)
Hunt, William M, M.Phil, Ph.D, *A Town Remembers*, Vol. III, Parts 1 and 2 (FOXE Graphics Limited, 2007)
Kay, Richard, *The History of Boston Project* (History of Boston series, 1975)
Langford, William and Holroyd, Jack, *The Great War Illustrated, 1915* (Pen & Sword, 2015)
Mahoney, Henry C. and Talbot, Frederick A., *Sixteen Months in Four German Prisons: Wesel, Sennelager, Klingelputz, Ruhleben* (London and Edinburgh, Sampson Low, Marston & Co. Ltd, 1917)
Meyer, Paul and Revell, John C., *Boston, Its Fishermen and the First World War* (independent publisher, date unknown)
Middlebrook, Martin, *Captain Staniland's Journey: The North Midland Territorials Go To War* (Leo Cooper, Pen & Sword Books Ltd, 2003)

Pitt, Barrie, *1918: The Last Act* (Cassell & Company Ltd, 1962)
Powell, Joseph and Gribble, Francis, *The History of Ruhleben: A Record of British Organisation in a Prison Camp in Germany* (Available free online at The National Archives website, 1919)
Rawson, Andrew, *Loos: Hohenzollern, Battleground Europe* (Leo Cooper, Pen & Sword Books Ltd, 2003)
Scheer, Admiral Reinhard, *Germany's High Seas Fleet in the World War* (London, Cassell & Company Ltd, 1920)
Simpson, C.R, *The History of the Lincoln Regiment 1914–1918* (London, The Medici Society, 1931)
Wilson, H.W., *The Great War: The Standard History of the All-Europe Conflict* (London, The Amalgamated Press Ltd, 1917)
Wood, Walter, *Fishermen in Wartime: The Struggle at Sea During the First World War* (London, Edinburgh, S. Low, Marston & Co. Ltd, 1918)

Newspapers and Other Publications

Birmingham Daily Post
Boston Guardian and Lincolnshire Independent
Boston (Massachusetts) Evening Transcript
Boston Old Times
Boston Standard
Butterwick with Benington, Freiston and Leverton Parish Magazine
Daily Mail
Derby Daily Telegraph
Grantham Journal
Grimsby Daily Telegraph
Leeds Mercury
Lincolnshire Echo
Lincolnshire Standard
Nottingham Evening Post
Sheffield Star
Yorkshire Post and Leeds Intelligencer

Online Sources

airfieldinformationexhange.org (lists Great War places of internment/PoW camps)
ancestry.co.uk

beyondthetrenches.co.uk (online resource on arts and humanities research into the First World War)
British Newspaper Archive
centenarybattlefieldtours.org
cwgc.org (Commonwealth War Graves Commission)
denkmalprojekt.org (German War Memorial website)
hulldailymail.co.uk (World War home Trawlermen BBC highlights)
fishingboatheritage.com (comprehensive resource on fishing boats)
Scarletfinders.co.uk (resource on British Military Nurses)
shipbucket.com (Archive of Naval Drawings)
southhollandlife.com (Dr Katherine Storr, First World War Archive)
thelincolnshireregiment.org (resource on The Lincolnshire Regiment)
The National Archives (TNA) website
www.iwm.org.uk (Imperial War Museum)
www.warmemorials.org (War Memorials Online)
www.redcross.org.uk

Museums, etc.

Boston Library Archives
British Library, London
IWM (Imperial War Museum), London
The National Archives, Kew (TNA)

Index

Italicised numbers refers to illustrations within the text. Street names are in Boston unless otherwise stated.

1st Somerset Light Infantry, 135, *137*
1/4th Lincolns', 116–229
1/5th Lincolns', 116–229
59th Division, 133, 187
177 Brigade, 133

Aboukir, HMS, 38–45
Achiet-le-Petit, 188
Adinfer, 190
Ainsworth, Henry, 56, *57*
Aisne Valley, 187
Albatross, 7
Aldershot, 219
Alexandria, 177–8
Allan House, 99, 112–13
Allen, Frank, 101
Alsatian (trawler), 37
Amiens, 208
Angerton (trawler), 37
Anchises, TSS, 176
Antwerp, 44–53
Arctic (trawler), 54–5
Armagh Wood, 145
Arras, 181, 187–8
Ashby, Rev P.O., 143
Assembly Rooms, 213
Auchy-les-Mines, 157

Bailey, Sgt T., 174, *176*
Bailleul, 137
Baines, Pte William, *219*
Baines, Thomas, 35, 56, *57*
Baker, John, 78
Balonwing (tender), 62
Banyer (trawler), 55
Bapaume, Battle of, 207
Barber, Pte Tom, 156, *246*
Bargate, 119, 220–1, 223
Barrell, Maj, 144, *146*
Bateson, Rev J.H., 141–2
Bavarian Regiment, 137, 143
Bavincourt, 185
Beanland, Lt J.W., *223*
Beanland, Rev J., *223*
Bedford, Bedfordshire, 76
Belloy-en-Santerre, 188
Belper, 122–3, 129
Belton Park, 132
Bennett, Flt Sub-Lt Owen Hewitt, 82
Berles, 185–6
Bienvillers, 181, 185
Biggadyke, 2nd Eng Bert, *247*
Birmingham, 73, 90
Bishop, Rev A.S., 142
Blyth, 12
Boat Inn, 40
Bosse Wood, 191
Boston (trawler), 14
Boston Borough Police Court, 133
Boston Civil Guard, 55
Boston Company of the

Territorial Artillery (Boston Battery), 116, 119–20, 126, *154*
Boston Company, C Company, 117–229
Boston Deep Sea Fishing Company, 7, 15–16, 133
Boston Deeps, 3, 56, 60
Boston Grammar School, 143, *220*
Boston Station, 101
Boston Stump, 50, 62, 67
Boston Territorials, 116–229
Boston Town Bridge, 8, 92, 119
Boston Town Guard, 67, 69, 133
Bostonian (trawler), 37
Boulogne, 78–9, 214, 238
Bourlon Wood, 202
Bourne, John, 28
Bouvigny, 193–4
Bridges, Pte F., 143
Bridlington, 117, *118,* 135
Brighton Queen, 56, *58–9*
Bristol Scout, 79, *80*
Brocklesby, Percy, 56, *57*
Broodseinde, 198, 228
Brothertoft (trawler), 101, 255
Brotherton (trawler), 14
Bruges, 52
Buck, Pte J.H., 143
Bucquoy Graben, 188
Burchnall, Cpl C.H., 146, 148, *149*
Butler, Thomas Charles, 38, 40–2
Butterwick, 78, *84*, 146

Caborn, Pte Arthur, 178
Cadbury, Maj Edgar, 76
Cambrai, Battle of, 201–202
Cambrian (trawler), 37
Cambrin, 203
Cantenwine, Leonard and George, 35–6
Carlton Road, 45, 70, 112
Carter, H.P., 92
Caudwell, George, 90
Chamberlain, Pte James, 141, *142*
Chamberlain, Samuel B., 70
Champagne, 157
Chatham, 42, 44
Chester, Alfred, 70
Church Street, *8*
Churchill, Winston, 65
Cité St Elie, 161
Cité St Pierre, 192
Clark, John, *35*
Clift, Lt A., 223
Cook, George William, 211
Cook, Rev A.M., 222
Cooke-Yarborough, Alderman A., 221
Cooper, Maj Oliver, 141, 144
Cornford, Thomas, 17
Cousens, Arthur, 38, *40–2*
Cressy, HMS, 38–45
Crick, Sgt Andrew, 152, *154*
Crucifix Corner, 210
Cuxhaven, 16, *17,* 18

Dallywater, Pte E.W., 141, *142*
Damery, 188
Dardanelles, 53
Day, L/Cpl Percy W., *254*
Deal, 46, 52
Deep Sea Fishing Co., 15
Derby, 129

Dickebusch, 173
Dickinson, CO Stanley, 219
Dixon, Frederick, 56, *57*
Dobson, Deck Hand Thomas, *248*
Dogger Bank, 7, 9
Donaldson-Hudson, John, *216*
Douchy, 190
Doullens, 179
Dover, 46, 52, 65
Dranoutre, 135–7, 144, 150
Drill Hall, Main Ridge, 117, *118,* 123, 219
Drummond, Capt J.E., 40–1
Duke Street, 16
Dunkirk, 46, 52, 82

Earl Roberts (tender), 60
East Yorkshire Cycle Corps, 117
Eastville, 104
Ecoust Ridge, 206
Egypt, 123, 175, 179, *180*
El Shalufa, 177
Elms Corner, 199
Empress Queen, SS, *136*
Ervillers, 207
Etrurian (trawler), 37
Evans, Pte W.H., 204
Excelsior Band, 117
Exeter, 212

Falklands, Battle of, 1
Fellows, Fireman Alfred, *256*
Fishtoft (trawler), 37
Five Lamps, 213, 220–1
Flamborough Head, 12
Flavian (trawler), 7, 15–16

Flesquières, 201–202
Fletcher, J., 32
Foch, Gen Ferdinand, 156
Foncquevillers, 181, 184–5, 187
Forster, Robert, 17
Foster, Pte A.F., 193
Fox, Herbert, *35*
Freiston, 79–81, 146, 150, 223
French, Sir John, 156
Frenchman (tender), 60
Fry, Dr, 122
Fuller, William, 54–5
Fydell Street, 69–70

Gallipoli, 156, 179
Ganzel, Kapitänleutnant Wilhelm, 65, *67*
Gardner, Lt Col H., 181
Gibraltar, 123
Giles, Lt, 126
Gobey, Pte Herbert, *215*
Gommecourt, 182
Gommecourt, Battle of, 183–7
Good, Fred Walter, 102
Goodacre, Pte A., *237*
Goodacre, T., 28
Gosling, Arthur, 56, *57*
Graham, John, 17
Graincourt, 202
Grand Sluice Bridge, 69
Grantham, 103–104, 132
Graves, John, 34, *35*
Great Northern Railway Station, 119
Great Yarmouth, 65
Grevillers, 188
Grimsby Chums, 115, 214
Grimsby, 9, 11, 32, 55–6, 115

Grinling, Adj E.J., 172
Grummitt, Sydney William, 53–4

Haking, Lt Gen Sir R., 173
Haldane, Sir Richard Burdon, 116
Hall, Arthur, 150
Hall, R Adml Geoffrey, 150
Hallingbury Park, 133
Hamburg, 16
Hamburg, SMS, 6
Hamilton, Gen Ian, 130
Hamp, Sgt W.E., 172
Hannover, 18
Hardy, Keir, 88
Hargicourt, 191
Harris, Lizzie, 17
Hart, Capt, 154
Hartlepool, 65
Heathcote, Lt Col C.E., 155, 170
Heligoland, 5, 7, 12
Hennes, 183
Hesbecourt, 191
Hesdigneul, 173, 175
Hibbs, Pte F., 171–2
Higgins, Arthur, 9
High Street, 36, 40, 92, 220
Hiley, Herbert, *40*
Hill 60, 146, *149*
Hill, L/Cpl B., 186
Hindenburg Line, 187, 190, 201, 210
HMS *Amethyst*, 53
HMS *Hogue*, 43
HMS *President*, 46
Hobhole Station, 42
Hocknall, Pte C.A., 172

Hohenzollern Redoubt, 157–75, 179–80
Holden House, 90, 99, 101–103
Holland, 2nd Lt G.R., *216*
Hollum, 72
Holy Trinity Church, Spilsby Road, 112, 223, *226*, 232, 245
Hooge, 144, 151–3, *155*
Hook of Holland, 41
Hoyles, Pte J.T., *238*
Hulluch Quarries, 161, *164–5*
Humber (tender), 60
Hungarian (trawler), 37

Imperial Queen, 37
Indian (trawler), 7, *8*, 15, 35
Ingamells, L/Cpl A.C., 172
Ingenohl, Adml von, 1, *3*
Irwin, Lt Col N.M.S., 203

Jackson, Cpl C.W., 171
James Street, 55
Jessop, Col, 130–3, 144, 155
Jessop, Pte F., 129
Joffre, Gen, 156
Jones, Col, 144
Julian (trawler), 7–8, 15, 35, 60
Jurassic (trawler), 54
Jutland, Battle of, 1

Kemmel village, 144
Kemp, R.W., 9
Kerby, Cmdr Harold, *81*
Kesteven (trawler), 7, 15, 35
Kiel, 3, 6
King Stephen (trawler), 72–4
King's Lynn, 65
Kirton Fen, 67

Kirton Town Hall, 101
Kirton, *125*
Kitchener, Lord, 115, 131, 156
Kitchener's New Army, 115, 211–14
Koln, 6
Kronprinz Wilhelm, 6
Kruistraat, 156

La Bassée Canal, 156
La Cauchie, 185
Ladds, Daniel Frederick, 40–2
Lady Ismay (minesweeper), 55, *57–8*
Langrick Bridge, 101
Lans, V Adml von, 1
Le Harve, 133, *136*
Le Kirlem, 135
Leadbeater, Cpl C., 170–1
Leckie, Capt Robert, 76
Leeds General Infirmary, 104
Lens 196–8
Lewis, Arthur James, *42*, 43–5
Liévin, 194, 196
Lijssenthoek Military Cemetery, 152
Lincoln, 120, 122, 129
Lincolnshire Imperial Yeomanry, *117*
Lindenhoek, 151
Lindsey (trawler), 7, 14, 15, *21*, 32, 35
Lion House, 55
Liquorpond Street, 28
Lloyd, Lt Col E.P., 203
Lobelia (trawler), 9–10, 12–13, 18, 23–4
Loewe, Kapitänleutnant Odo, 72–4

Loggerheads Hotel, 32
London Rifle Brigade, 135
Loos, Battle of, 156–75
Lowestoft (trawler), 44
Lucas, Mayor Alderman C., 213
Ludendorff Offensive, 205
Lusitania, 36
Luton, 120, 122, 127, 132–3, 210

Maass, R Adml, 6
Mace, Walter, 54–5
Mack, Thomas, 78
Madge, Capt R.E., 168–9
Maizières, 203–204
Malta, 123
Maltby, Cpl F., 178, *179*
Maple Cross, 144
Market Place, 70, 103, 119
Marks Terrace, 8
Marnay (trawler), 7–8, 15, 35
Marple (tender), 60
Marris, Geoffrey, 179, *182*
Marris, Harold, 179, *181*
Marris, Lt E.N., 220
Marseilles, 176, 179
Martin, Fred, 55
Martin, William, 72–4
McCall, Brig Gen H.B., 133
Meeds, Pte J., 177, 179
Megantic, 178
Menin Ridge, 198
Merchant, Capt John Victor, 106
Merchant, Frances, 106, *111*, 112
Messines Ridge, 144
Messrs Frank and Co., 36
Meuse, 157
Mills, Pte J.W., 218
Minnesota (boat), 52

Minnewaska, 178
Montagu-Stuart-Wortley, Maj Gen Edward James, 130–1, 144
Moore, Mr Temple, 223
Moralee, Pte Matthew Henry, *244*
Morgan, Ebenezer Hugh, 70
Mory, 205–206
Mount Temple, 46
Moyenneville, 190

National Terrace, 55
Nautilus, 7
Negara, 53
Neilson, Henry Peter, 8–9
Neuve Chapelle, 175
Norfolk, 65
Normandy, 135
North Midland Division, 116, 122, 131, 133
North Sea, 3, *4*, 6, 38, 54–5, 65, 72

Old Leake, 36, 112
Oldrid, Miss M., 222
Order of St John of Jerusalem, 95, 101, 219, *221*
Osmanieh, SS, *106*
Ostend, 52
Ouderdom, 144, 173
Oughton, Horace, 69
Oxford Street, 174

Paderborn, 18
Page, W.J., 248
Park Council School, 99
Parker, Fred, 21
Parker, William Henry, 60

Parkes, Cllr Fred, 55
Passon, Cook Harry, 256
Payne, Lt G.H., *216*
Peacock Hotel, 90
Peasgood, CSM A., 171
Pen Street, 119
Perkins, Pte A.E., 132, *133*
Pesterfield, Aaron, 55
Pesterfield, Ernest William, 54–5
Peterborough, 76
Ploegsteert, 135, *137*
Polygon Wood, 198, *200*
Pont-Remy, 179
Porcher, Edward H., 45–53
Porpoise (trawler), 7, 15
Preussen Graben, 188
Punchbowl Lane, 211
Pustkuchen, Herbert, 56

Quéant, 187

RAF Cranwell, 79, 82
Rawson, Pte G.P., 193
Rear, Pte George, 173
Red Cross, 95–114
Red Lion Bowling Club, 35
Reed, Lt L.A., 154
Rice, 2nd Lt N.D., *215*
Richardson, Deputy Mayor Cllr E., 221
River Derwent, 122
River Haven, 3, 76, 102
Robinson, Gnr W., 225
Robinson, Pte G., 237
Roisel, 191
Royal Flying Corps (RFC), 78
Royal Hotel, 90
Royal Navy Division, 45–53
Royal, Walter, 32, 34, *63*

Ruck, Nurse, 104
Rugby School, 143
Ruhleben, 16, 23–35, 56, 60
Rushton, Daniel, 8
Ryalls, John, 65

Sailly-Labourse, 203
Sanctuary Wood, 144–5, *147*
Sandall, Lt Col T.E., 168, 180, 184
Sargisson, Mabel, 106
Sawyer, H., 217
Scala, 220
Scarborough, 65
Scherwin, Count, 25
Sennelager, 14, 16, 18–24, 34
Sexton, Eric J., *254*
Sharp, Robert, 56, *57*
Sharpe, L/Cpl H.E.J., 137
Shaw, Rec Sgt, 211
Sherwood Foresters, 116, 169, 184, 202
Sills, Capt G.R., 120
Simmons, Lt J.S., *123*
Skinner, Pte W.W., 150
Skirbeck (trawler), *6*, 7, 15
Skirbeck Quarter, 8, 38, 40, 55
Sleaford, 119
Smith, Apprentice C.C., *249*
Smith, Charles, 35
Smith, Charlie, 17
Smith, Pte B., 143
Smith, Sgt Wallis, 175, *176*
Snettisham, 67
Somme, 183, 187, 190–1, 205, 207–208
Souastre, 184
Souchez, 179
Spain Lane, 103

Spanbroekmolen, 137, 143–4
Spurn Point, 15
St John's School, 117
St Amand, 187, 190
St Botolph's Church, 150, 153, 221
St James's Church, 79, 84
St Lambert's Hall, 90
St Mary's, Old Leake, 112
St Omer, 175
St Thomas Memorial, 222
St Thomas's School, 223
Staniland, Capt Meaburn, 104, 117, 122–6, 135, 143, 145, 149–53
Staniland, Geoffrey, 104, 143, 150–1
Staniland, Frances, 104, 106
Stansted, Essex, 13
Stearns, Albert, 17
Steenwerck, 135
Stephens, Sgt, 123
Stephenson, Susan Elizabeth, 112
Still Hotel, 220
Strazeele, 135
Strickland, Thomas, 55
Stringer, Alfred, 55
Staffurth, Nurse Miss A., 103
Sus-St.-Léger, 181
Sutterton, 14
Swanton, Lt Col T.H.S., 204

Talus des Zouaves, 179
Tawney Street, 70
Taylor, George, 78
Taylor, James, 54–5
Theodore Sims, Flt Sub-Lt James, 79
Thesiger, Maj Gen, 157–8, *161*

Thomas, John Stanton, 117
Threadneedle Street, 78
Tirpitz, Alfred von, 1
Todd, Edward, 55
Tower Road, 106
Treaty of Brest-Litovsk, 205
Triangle Wood, 188
Trotter, Rev J.R., *84*

U-9, 38–45
UC-5, 56
UC-34, 106
Ungar, Julius, 36

VAD (Voluntary Aid Detachment), 90, 96–114
Verdun, *189*
Vermelles, 173
Verney, Sir Harry, 88
Verquin, 175
Victory (boat), 52
Villers-au-Bois, 179
Vraucourt, 206

Wakefield, 35
Wakefield, L/Cpl W., *198*
Walkerly, Charles, *8*, 60
Walmer, 46, 52–3
Walrus (trawler), 7, 15
War Agricultural Committee, 88
Wardown Park Hospital, 132
Wardown Park, 130
Warlincourt, 182
Wash, 3, 65, 67, 74
Watkins, Lt Col H.A., 203
Watson, Pte J.E., *139*
Weddigen, Otto Kapitänleutnant, 38, *40*, 42–5
West Skirbeck House, 102

West Street, 119, 220
Weston, 90
Westphalia, 18
Whitby, 65
White Horse Lane, 38
Whitham, 74
Wigtoft (trawler), 7, 15, *21*, 35, 60
Wilhelmshaven, 1, 7, 8, 9, 12, 13, 14, 15, 18
Willmot, John, 17
Winnezeele, 191
Winnington-Ingram, Bishop Arthur, 74
Women's Land Army, *86, 89–93*
Women's National Service Department, 88
Wood, Lt Charles Sinclair, *40*
Wood, 2nd Lt Basil, 126
Woodham, Pte, 148
Woodthorpe, F.M., 62, *63*
Wrack, Chief Engineer Thomas, *250*
Wrangle, 36, 112, *125*
Wright, Lt W.R., 180
Wright, Maj S.C., 222

YMCA, 127
Yool, Lt Col G.A., 194, 203
Ypres, 142, 144, 152, 170, 212
Ypres, First Battle of, 144–75

Zeppelin, 36, 65–78, 220
Zeppelin, Count Von, 65
Zeppelin, L19, 72–4
Zeppelin, L23, 65–70
Zeppelin, L70, 76
Zevencote, 198
Zillebeke, 152, *155*